BOMBS, BULLETS, & BRIBES

The True Story of

Notorious Jewish Mobster

Alex "Shondor" Birns

RICK PORRELLO

Bombs, Bullets, and Bribes

The True Story of

Notorious Jewish Mobster

Alex "Shondor" Birns

Rick Porrello

Next Hat Press
P.O. Box 23
Novelty, OH 44072

www.rickporrello.com

Cover and interior design by JD&J Design and Rick Porrello

Library of Congress Control Number:2019909279

Publisher's Cataloging-In-Publication Data
(Prepared by The Donohue Group, Inc.)

Names: Porrello, Rick, author.
Title: Bombs, bullets, and bribes : the true story of notorious Jewish mobster Alex Shondor Birns / Rick Porrello.
Description: First edition. | Novelty, OH : Next Hat Press, [2019] | Includes bibliographical references and index.
Identifiers: ISBN 9780966250848 | ISBN 9780966250831 (ebook)
Subjects: LCSH: Birns, Alex, 1907-1975. | Gangsters--United States--Biography. | Jewish criminals--United States--Biography. | Organized crime--United States--History--20th century. | LCGFT: Biographies.
Classification: LCC HV6248.B565 P67 2019 (print) | LCC HV6248.B565 (ebook) | DDC 364.106092--dc23

First Edition

Also by Rick Porrello

To Kill the Irishman—
The War that Crippled the Mafia
(Next Hat Press, 1998)

The story of bold Irish-American racketeer Danny Greene, who took on the Mafia in a 1970s bombing war. The book was adapted for the 2011 motion picture *Kill the Irishman*, directed by Jonathan Hensleigh and costarring Ray Stevenson, Vincent D'Onofrio, Val Kilmer, and Christopher Walken.

Superthief –
A Master Burglar, the Mafia
and the Biggest Bank Heist in US History
(Next Hat Press, 2005)

A raw and candid accounting of burglar and Mafia associate Phil Christopher's life, with focus on the 1972 United California Bank heist. As the biggest in US history, the UCB burglary has been featured in documentaries on Court TV and the Discovery Channel. *Superthief* is a second-place true crime winner in *ForeWord Magazine*'s 2005 Book of the Year Awards. It is currently in development for film.

The Rise and Fall of the Cleveland Mafia—
Corn Sugar and Blood
(Barricade Books, 1995)

This is the author's first book, which was conceived out of curiosity about the Prohibition-era killings of his grandfather and three uncles, Mafia leaders who fought the powerful Lonardo family for control of corn sugar, a lucrative bootleg ingredient. Angelo "Big Ange" Lonardo avenges his father's murder and survives the ruthless battles to become a mob boss. Facing a life sentence, he causes havoc in the underworld when he agrees to testify against his associates and becomes the highest-ranking Mafia turncoat in US history.

AUTHOR'S NOTE

This is a true story. Occasionally I formulated conclusions based on facts. Quotes were usually taken from the source material. On occasion I crafted dialogue based on a documented summary. Rarely, I created a quote based on theory supported by related facts. Also on rare occasion, I edited quotes for clarity or adjusted the timelines of conversations or other events to help form a cohesive story. Endnotes provide additional information.

Rick Porrello

July 2019

I dedicate this book to law enforcement officers everywhere—
those men and women who face danger daily in their commitment
to protect and serve community or country.

Acknowledgements

After working on this project for ten years, I thank the following individuals and organizations, and those persons who wish to remain anonymous, for their contributions and assistance.

Tom Armelli; Sandy August; Bruce Ballash; Phil Barragate; William C. Barrow; Avi Bash; Mike Baumiller; Beverly Beuck; Gina Drake Busch; Chuck Cabot; the Call and Post; Bob Cermak: Judith Cetina; Cleveland Magazine; the Cleveland, Ohio Police Department; the Cleveland Plain Dealer; the Cleveland Police Museum; the Cleveland Public Library; the Cuyahoga County Archives; Kenny Davis; Russell Davis; Tom Doyle; Gary Eisner; Sr. Barbara Eppich, OSU; the Federal Bureau of Investigation; Rebecca Ferlotti; Sarah Flinn; Steve Gleydura; Jerry Gold; Marisa August Heidt; Mark Hetrick; the Kent State University; Thomas Kirk, Lisa Lewis; Dick Lillie; Jim Lynsky; John Luskin; the Mary Ferrell Foundation; Chris Mathers; Allan May; John McCaffrey; Brian Meggitt; Ryan Miday; Frank Monastra; Joe Mosbrook; The National Library of Israel, Jerusalem; Dennis Nicklas; the Northeast Ohio Broadcast Archives - John Carroll University; Mike O'Mara; Len Orcino; Richard Peery; the Perrysburg Twp., Ohio Police Department; Dave Piekarczyk; Lejune Pier; Beth Pollack; Rocco Pollutro; Danielle Randolph; Bill Riedthaler; Cherie Rohn; Harry See; Mutawaf Shaheed; Henry Stoken; John William Tuohy; the US National Archives and Records Administration; James Willis; Howard Wise

Thank you to the newspaper and magazine reporters, editors, and photographers whose coverage of Shondor Birns, from the early 1900s through the 1970s, helped make this book possible.

Forrest Allen, George J. Barmann, William C. Barnard, Bus Bergen, Powell Caesar, III, W. Joseph Campbell, Louis Clifford, Richard T. Conway, J.C. Daschbach, Van Dillard, Anthony J. DiSantis, Robert Dolgan, Christopher Evans, Joseph M. Gambatese, Pat Garling, Marvin L. Greene, Thomas H. Greer, John Griffith, John F. Hagan, Ann Hellmuth, Robert J. Holmes, Marion Hopwood, Christine J. Jindra, George E. Jordan, Clayton Knipper, Rosemary Kovacs, Ron Kuntz, Frank Kuznik, Jerry Kvet, Brent Larkin, Paul Lilley, Jim Marino, Samuel F. Marshall, Fred McGunagle, Dick McLaughlin, Roy Meyers, W.C. Miller, Fred Mollenkopf, Larry Nighswander, Bernie Noble, Doris O'Donnell, Philip Porter, Ted Princiotto, Robert Quinlan, Karl J. Rauschkolb, Marty Richardson, Michael D. Roberts, Herman Said, Terence Sheridan, Todd Simon, Robert E. Tidyman, Sanford Watzman, Edward P. Whelan, Bob Williams, Brian Williams, Mairy Jayn Woge, Glenn Zahn.

Special thanks to my editor, Laurie Viera Rigler, and my copyeditor, Kim Bookless, for their fine services and enthusiastic support.

Rick Porrello

August, 2019

It's not surprising that no one has written a biography of Shondor Birns. What's astonishing is that no one has composed an opera about this larger-than-life gangster.

—John Stark Bellamy II, author of *The Killer in the Attic*

PART 1

CHAPTER ONE

Alex Shondor Birns. Public Enemy Number One. The city's most-arrested and least-convicted criminal. He was a respected ally of powerful Jewish and Italian mobsters and a trusted partner of black gambling racketeers. Race, religion, and ethnicity were nonfactors. It was loyalty above all by which Shondor measured a man. Or a woman.

Brought here as an infant, Shondor was never naturalized. As a noncitizen, he still loved the United States. It was the only home he knew, and in his own way, he was patriotic.

Life as a powerful racketeer brought him many adversaries. The cops wanted him in prison, immigration officials wanted him deported, and IRS investigators wanted his house, nightclub, car, and cash. Some black gangsters emboldened by the civil rights movement wanted the old white man out of the numbers gambling racket. And then there were attempted coups by rogue associates like Mervin Gold. After decades of beating cases and dodging prison, Shondor's freedom would come down to the loyalty of this former friend and protégé.

It was 1963, and as an international fugitive, Mervin Gold was forced out of Israel and back to the US. But he sure as hell wasn't going down without a fight. He was an expert at manipulating paper money, such as mortgages and business loans, to create capital. He just wasn't an expert at getting away with it for long. And Mervin couldn't keep his mouth shut. He was facing lengthy prison time. And he had, unwittingly, a minor role in an international drama. Shondor didn't know all of the details, but he did know about the stolen Canadian bonds.

As he had done with many of his underlings, Shondor helped Mervin with funding for a defense attorney. But the con man demanded more. Business associates owed Mervin money, and he wanted Shondor to put pressure on them. With Shondor's generosity waning and his patience exhausted, a phone call between the two men didn't go well.

"Can you get some help for yourself on money?" Shondor asked Mervin.

"My answer is this," Mervin said. "On this case, I'll help myself. If I can't help myself, then I want you to help me, because my problems, sir, are as numerous as yours."

"Now just a minute," Shondor said. "You want me to fight your case all the way to the Supreme Court?"

"I need legal help on this particular case," Mervin said. "I expect to have help from my friends. I will do everything I should do as a man, but I want my friends to act the same way."

"OK, pal. I wish you'd acted like a man before, but you thought you were so smart. You know, Mr. Gold, you're the smartest man in the world. But I think you're the dumbest."

"The dumbest?" Mervin said. "There are a lot of deals I made that I didn't want to. Sometimes I did things to accommodate other people."

"You didn't accommodate me. Because you were told not to."

"I was? You've got a hell of a memory, my friend," Mervin said. "Now look, Merv, don't give me that fucking shit. Listen, you gonna keep talking to me like that? You think you're talking to a fool? I'll come up there and make you talk the way you're supposed to talk."

"I'm glad you said that because here's what I've done, point blank, Mr. Birns. Listen to me carefully. Every last drop is down on twenty-three sheets of paper. Notarized, signed, sealed, and delivered."

"Yeah?"

"And distributed. Just in case you get the clever idea of getting cute."

"OK, pal."

"Now don't ever threaten me again," Mervin said. "Don't you ever dare to make an implication like that again."

"Oh, well, we understand each other now."

Mervin Gold considered himself a fighter who didn't frighten easily. And he had Shondor on the ropes. But overcoming constant challenges was Shondor's theme. Survival was written in his DNA.

***

Shondor Birns was born Sándor Birn in 1906, in the kingdom of Austria-Hungary, to Hermann Birn and his wife, Illona, in the village of Lemes. (Family acquaintances believed the name may have been shortened from Birnstein.) Sándor would later add an "s" to his surname, from "Birn" to "Birns." Lemes was in the district of Presov, an area of mostly Slovak people. Hermann spoke Slovakian.

Though Jews in Austria-Hungary fared better than those in Russia, many dreamed of a better life elsewhere, especially in the

United States of America. They arrived in the US during a period when millions from southern and eastern Europe sought peace, political stability, and potential prosperity in the land of opportunity.

Hermann, Illona, and their children, Gyulias, Sari, and baby Sándor, left Austria-Hungary in 1907, departing from Germany on March 2 aboard the steamship *Chemnitz*. The perilous journey across the seemingly infinite expanse of the Atlantic Ocean took sixteen days. Like millions of other newcomers to America, the Birn family was greeted finally by the impressive Statue of Liberty and disembarked at Ellis Island in New York City. They stayed in Manhattan with the Birnbaum family for one month then headed west to Cleveland, Ohio.

A Great Lakes port city with railway access and a thriving steel industry, Cleveland was an attractive destination for immigrants who needed jobs quickly to feed and house their families. Cheap labor was needed to build goods for World War I. Southern blacks desperate for work flooded in. Poor Jewish immigrants, followed by Italian newcomers, found affordable housing along Woodland and its sister avenues of Cedar and Central.

Within a few years, the aristocrats moved. Gone were their carriages. Their grand mansions became tenements and flophouses, and there were now thousands packed into where there had lived only hundreds.

Hermann and Illona settled near Woodland Avenue and East 55th Street. They "Americanized" their given names. Hermann dropped one "n" to become Herman. Illona became known as Ellen. Gyulias was spelled Julius. Sari's name was changed to Sarah. Sándor, (a form of the name Alexander) was known as Alex, or more commonly, Shondor. In 1908, Herman and Ellen had another daughter. They named her Hermine, later spelled Hermina.

At the time, there was widespread, ingrained, almost casual discrimination against ethnic groups, including Italians and Jews.

18

Such attitudes manifested in restricted opportunities for housing, employment, and social mixing. For the newcomers, there was comfort and a sense of security in living and working among those of their own culture. It was also a time of individualism and entrepreneurialism. Many immigrants started businesses—groceries, dry cleaners, barbershops—and thus were part of a new foundation for America. This afforded employment opportunities to immigrants like Herman Birn, who got a job as a butcher. As for Ellen, she joined Deborah Lodge, one of many Jewish women's organizations that formed in the second half of the nineteenth century.

Shondor attended Outhwaite Elementary School. He spent much time at the Council Educational Alliance (CEA), a settlement house founded in 1899 and one of the forerunner components of the city's future and venerable Jewish Community Center. The settlement house movement originated in Britain to help immigrants assimilate into the mainstream labor force. In the United States, the movement grew in response to overcrowding and other social problems of the rapidly evolving environment of new immigrants.

The CEA sought to better the social, economic, and educational life of Jewish families. It offered classes in English and citizenship. There were music, theater, literary, and athletic programs. Presentations by rabbis, judges, and other community leaders addressed economic and social issues such as juvenile delinquency and the importance of education.

The Jewish Orphanage Asylum was another significant social service organization that served as a Woodland Avenue and East 55th Street anchor. It was an imposing and stately structure, behind which Shondor played baseball. As a young teen, he was tough, athletic, and competitive. But he was also a sore loser prone to temper flares, and he could be a bully. On one occasion, after his absence from a marble shooting tournament, he confronted the champion and wrestled away his medal.

"I would have won it anyway if I was here," Shondor told the boy.

A former neighbor of the Birn family recalls, "Shondor pestered my brother and me about a pair of binoculars until he just took them. After that, everything was fine. He would even give us rides on his bike."

At the CEA and Kennard Junior High School, Shondor was an in-demand teammate. And he was a scrapper. If there were trouble, and there sometimes was in connection with athletic competitions between rival settlement houses, especially of differing ethnicities, Shondor would be at the front of the pack.

"He was reliable and smart," recalled a former CEA member. "It was evident that Shondor was an extraordinary thirteen-year-old. He would protect the other boys. He was the leader."

Shondor gravitated toward the neighborhood ruffians, of which there was no shortage. Many of them went on to lives of crime. Gus Zukie, a future cop who grew up near Shondor, recalled the period.

"As kids in the summer, we would go to the railroad and steal ice," Zukie said. "We'd fill our mothers' iceboxes and the neighbors'. The neighbors would pay if they had money; otherwise, they didn't. It didn't matter. During the winter we stole coal. We got everybody in the neighborhood coal. Black, white, Jewish, Mexican, Italian—that was the melting pot of friends. We were all in it together. We were all poor."

Shondor's reputation as a tough kid with smarts landed him a job in the rough world of newspaper distribution. As millions of immigrants became citizens with the right to vote, the press became an essential tool for politicians. Some of the wealthiest bought existing newspapers. To increase sales, keep deliveries on schedule, and counter offensives by competitors, the owners appointed tough circulation managers. Those men hired young ruffians like Alfred Polizzi, Fred Angersola, and Morris "Mushy" Wexler. Occasionally fisticuffs between competing newspapers' turf guards escalated to gunplay. Arthur B. "Mickey" McBride was circulation manager for the *Cleveland News*. Shondor was a delivery boy on one of his trucks and hawked papers at Woodland Avenue and East 55th Street.

***

In 1920, the Birn family had been in Cleveland thirteen years, and the city had grown to the fifth largest in the United States. As a lakefront town only fifty miles across Lake Erie to the Canadian shore, and set midway between New York City and Chicago, it was a destination for many and a stopover for travelers—well and ill intentioned. The city had seventy-six hotels. Many housed the best restaurants and bars in town, like Hotel Hollenden with its lavish Vogue Restaurant and unique Showboat Room with a mock boat-deck stage. Most restaurants were in clusters downtown, in the adjoining Warehouse District, and in the low-lying Flats District along the bank of the Cuyahoga River, which split the city by east and west. Within downtown was Short Vincent Avenue, a one-block area jammed with taverns and nightclubs.

Playhouse Square emerged in 1921, and on the upper east side, in an area called Doan's Corners, there was another impressive cluster of theaters. In both districts, vaudeville performers attracted big crowds. Jazz came to the city from plenty of homegrown talent and through the migration of musicians, many from New Orleans. Nationally known bandleaders appeared regularly at dance halls and nightclubs. With the birth of the Museum of Art and the Cleveland Orchestra, the city was on its way to becoming a cultural hub. And it was launched as a sports town when the Cleveland Indians won the 1920 World Series. The Birn family lived in a city that was vibrant, diverse, and flourishing. And opportunities for the ambitious and industrious abounded.

With the federal ban on liquor in 1920 came an era of lawlessness and corruption that reached from the highest levels of federal and state government to the lowliest American citizens, including immigrants who sought to continue drinking certain beverages containing alcohol simply for the cultural tradition and religious importance. Some, like Ellen Birn, operated small in-home stills and resold the finished product to earn desperately needed income.

It was during this part of Shondor's adolescence that his life irrevocably changed. On a Tuesday afternoon in November 1920, his mother was boiling mash in a ten-gallon still in their E. 59th Street apartment. She was making a sweet wine known as raisin jack. Suddenly the still apparatus flared then exploded, setting Ellen's clothing afire. Scalding raisin mash spewed out. She ran outside, where her screams attracted the attention of a passing motorist. He smothered the flames then rushed her to the hospital.

When police raided the apartment, they located four barrels of mash and three gallons of finished raisin jack. They arrested Herman Birn and charged him with violating the liquor law.

What happened to Ellen Birn, though horrific, was not unusual: faulty gas line connections on stills were often the cause of explosions and fires in backyards, garages, bathrooms, and attics.

Ellen Birn survived the night. She was in critical condition, with most of her body covered by burns. The next day she died. The Birn family, friends, and members of Ellen's lodge assembled the following day at Deutsche's Funeral Parlor. Herman buried his wife and the mother of his four children. Two weeks later he appeared in court.

"You have been sufficiently punished by the death of your wife," said Judge Samuel H. Silbert. "You may go free."

For young Shondor Birn, the death of his mother ushered in a period of turmoil. He was sheltered briefly at the Jewish Orphanage while his father struggled to move forward as a widower. Shondor also spent time at Camp Wise, a weekend retreat for disadvantaged Jewish children. The camp had an athletics program that included baseball games between the campers, and the group leaders and counselors. When Shondor belted a home run and won the game for the leaders, the campers protested. Shondor wasn't a camp leader, they argued. He should have been playing on the campers' team. Nevertheless, Shondor became well liked at Camp Wise and occasionally helped as a volunteer.

Through the first months of 1922, the affections of Herman Birn lay largely with a woman fourteen years younger. They took out a marriage license in August of that year, but the couple never married, probably because Herman met a recent immigrant, who, like him, was from the Slovak region of Austria-Hungary. She was a widow named Sara Schwartz (nee Weiss), with an eleven-year-old daughter named Rose. Within months, Sara and Herman married, and Sara was called Sadie to avoid confusion with Herman's daughter.

Sadie loved her stepchildren like her own. But that love was insufficient to ease Shondor's increasing desire for independence. He had been moved from East Technical High School to Longwood High School of Commerce, but he didn't last at Longwood either. After completing the tenth grade, he dropped out of high school. He was sixteen years old. He told an enlistment officer he was eighteen and joined the US Navy.

After six months of service, Herman and Sadie filed paperwork to get Shondor released. It took about four months, then navy officials gave the boy an honorable discharge and sent him home. Shondor returned to his Woodland Avenue neighborhood with a US Navy anchor tattoo and tales of his experience for his friends.

***

For many Americans, economic prosperity followed World War I. New inventions came along—television, the radio, Henry Ford's Model T. There was a new sense of independence and freedom, bringing about a revolt against morals. Young men and women found intimate pleasure more comfortable with the shelter and seclusion of the newly closed-in automobiles. Young women bobbed their hair, donned makeup, and took jobs. These "flappers" swayed and gyrated with their boyfriends to swinging new jazz bands and danced cheek to cheek to the alluring sounds of the solo saxophone, which was replacing the violin as a favored front instrument. And when the women returned to their table or the bar, they would likely enjoy a cigarette and a cocktail.

The Roaring Twenties expanded the bootleg market splendidly. There were raw ingredients like sugar and yeast. There were bottling and labeling equipment, containers, and distribution and delivery needs. It was a simple business principle—supply and demand—and there was much money to be made. By 1923, small-time bootleg racketeers were earning reputations and accumulating wealth. These independents and others with small operations were forced out of business or murdered, as larger ones expanded and strengthened into regional syndicates.

Many of the street soldiers of the more extensive operations emerged from ethnic-based gangs of street-savvy young men. Some were the tough newspaper boys who brawled for control of high-traffic street corners. And some were independent criminals like Joe Kater, who served a prison term for robbing a speakeasy and married Shondor's sister.

Joe Kater and his brother Harvey ran with the E. 55th and Woodland Avenue gang headed by tavern operator Maxie Diamond. In the early 1920s, Diamond was a key member of a major bootlegging syndicate headed by Morris Kleinman, Moe Dalitz, Sam Tucker, and Lou Rothkopf. They had wholesale access to good Canadian whiskey, a distribution and delivery system, and a team of enforcers who ruled by bribery, intimidation, beatings, and murder.

Joe Kater and other criminals like him became influential in Shondor's life. In May 1925, nineteen-year-old Shondor was arrested for burglarizing a house. The record shows that the charge was dropped. Nevertheless, three months later, Shondor was back in court for stealing a car. He pleaded guilty and was sent to the Ohio

State Reformatory and started serving his sentence in November. The felony conviction was pivotal for Shondor's future.

Some of the counselors at Camp Wise wrote letters on Shondor's behalf, and in early 1927 he was released on parole after having served fifteen months. Soon he got a job racking balls at a pool hall and bowling alley. It was part of the Haltnorth Recreation Company on E. 55th Street at Haltnorth Court, near Woodland Avenue. But young Shondor had ambition and chutzpah. With vice rampant, he found he could make more money and make it more easily by selling bootleg booze and women.

Within a year of release from the reformatory, he used his profits to buy a pool hall and a small adjacent kitchen. During that time, Shondor was a frequent companion of Joe Kater, who divorced Sarah Birn after only two years of marriage. She and her baby son, Leonard, moved in with Herman and Sadie. Shondor continued to help his family, especially Sarah, who became addicted to diet pills. He took her to doctor's appointments and often paid the bill.

With an increasing mind-set for business, Shondor, now in his early twenties, was attracted to the success of older men like Bill Presser and John Nardi, who were involved with labor racketeering and the vending business. He befriended others from those circles who lived nearby, including Johnny Scalish and Frankie Brancato. They were among some immigrants of Italian descent who were associated with a sinister organization, the culture and methods of which were transplanted to the US in the late 1800s and early 1900s. The origin was a tradition bred centuries earlier on the largest island in the Mediterranean. It would become known as the Sicilian-American Mafia or La Cosa Nostra. Secrecy was its primary tenet for members. It was called *omerta*—the Sicilian code of silence, the violation of which was punishable by death.

On a national level, the Mafia merged with other ethnic-based groups, primarily Jewish. This crime syndicate weaved its way into the fabric of American society. It was continuously fed by tough and ambitious young men like Presser and Nardi, who wanted fast money without working too hard. Younger but of the same ilk, Shondor Birn increasingly associated with and availed himself of established members of the Jewish mob and Italian Mafia.

To become an official or "made" member of the Mafia, one had to be of Italian descent, of course, commit a murder for the outfit, then take a blood oath. A former Mafia boss recalled his induction ceremony.

"I was invited into a room at a hotel and asked if I knew what I was doing there. You naturally say, 'No.' Present were the acting boss, the underboss, a capo, and a made member. They explained to me that I had been proposed to be made a member of La Cosa Nostra and defined the rules and regulations of the organization. They told me that you cannot fool around with narcotics; you cannot own a house of prostitution or have prostitutes working for you; you cannot fool around with a woman that's married to a member of La Cosa Nostra; and that whatever illegal activity you engage in, you have to report to the boss and receive permission to engage in that activity.

"Once you accept the rules of membership, they lift a cloth off a table; underneath is a gun and a dagger. You are told that you now live and die with the dagger and the gun. You are then given a card with a picture of a saint on it. This card is placed in the palms of your hands and lit. You shake the burning card back and forth until it is burned down to ashes. They then prick your finger to draw blood, and then everyone gives you a kiss on the cheek and says, 'You are now a member.'"

By the late 1920s, Mafia crime families and their national crime syndicate partners were entrenched in two dozen major US cities. As this force matured, battles were waged for control and revenge between these groups, their crews, and other ethnic organized crime groups and independent gangsters. Most of the conflicts were related to money and power-making opportunities presented by Prohibition.

Then there were the battles over corn sugar. It was the essential ingredient for in-demand corn liquor. For a few years, two families of immigrants from Licata, Sicily, reigned supreme as corn sugar barons. They were Big Joe Lonardo and his three brothers and Big Joe Porrello and his six brothers. Small-time bootleggers were making big money too. But as they expanded, they drew the wrath of the powerful Lonardo network.

The Lonardos and Porrellos enjoyed small fortunes until a series of conflicts called the sugar war nearly wiped out both families. Young Angelo Lonardo murdered the man responsible for his father's death. He and members of his father's crew and other racketeers, including Frank Brancato and Shondor Birn, were absorbed by the Mayfield Road mob, part of a growing affiliation of mostly Italian and Jewish gangsters led largely by brothers Frank and Tony Milano and Moe Dalitz. This combination was affiliated with powerful mobsters across the country, including New York City's Charles "Lucky" Luciano and Meyer Lansky. These men followed the philosophy of older gambling racketeer Arnold Rothstein, who showed how treating crime such as gambling like a business brought more profits.

Shondor used an office above Haltnorth for bookmaking and bootlegging. Pool rooms were favored haunts for the misguided wannabes—captivated by local mobsters and their fancy clothing and expensive cars—who might even get a "Hiya, pal" from a passing foot patrolman. They were also favored targets for raids by police responding to gangland violence.

With several arrests and a prison stretch to his name, twenty-four-year-old Alex Shondor Birn was bright, capable with his fists, and already earning his own reputation for muscling into the business of selling female flesh. These were admirable traits for established gangsters looking for new blood. Consequently, Shondor fell in with Maxie Diamond and his partner, Philip Goldberg, Woodland and East 55th Street gang leaders affiliated with the Mayfield Road mob.

Most of the older mobsters had no compunction about using violence, even murder, to keep or acquire power and money or to secure their ruthless reputations. But a new breed, which included Shondor, was learning to be cautious about the attention that violence brought from the law and media. These men were business-minded visionaries. Instead of viewing ethnic, religious, and geographic lines as barriers, they worked across them to their benefit. They paid attention to emerging trends and changing laws and sought out corruptible government officials.

As the need for a retail infrastructure grew, ambitious men launched small operations. As small-time operators were forced out of business or murdered, larger ones strengthened and expanded into regional operations then merged to become affiliated with the national crime syndicate. With a tendency toward violence as needed and a desire for independence, Shondor fell somewhere in the middle. It was through this period that a "demand for respect and admiration welled deep within him," as Michael D. Roberts would write for *Cleveland Magazine*. "It was a flaw that ultimately grew into a burden. Above all Shondor wanted to be *the man* among men."

CHAPTER TWO

Gambling. Combine the recreation of playing a game with the chance—however remote—to win a prize or strike it rich, and the lure for many is irresistible. It was essentially what Shondor Birn was doing with his life. For him and others like him, there was a certain blessing to their unholy pursuits, just like lotteries had once served as an acceptable system to raise revenue to fund major public improvements such as roads and bridges and even provide startup capital for some esteemed higher institutions of learning.

A lottery is a form of gambling involving the random selection of numbers. The player wages a small amount of money for a shot to win a much larger amount or another prize. In the US, lotteries date back to colonial times. However, not everyone who wanted to play could afford a lottery ticket. As the games became more popular, ambitious men recognized the potential for easy profits. They established a side game. It was called "insuring the lottery" or "policy." For as little as a penny, the poor could take a chance on a cash windfall. Policy was popular in New York City and Chicago and with southern blacks, where it was played on plantations and in cities like Memphis, Mobile, and New Orleans.

Typically, policy was played twice daily. Seventy-eight numbered balls were used for the day drawing, and one hundred in the night drawing. The balls were placed in a bag then shaken to distribute them randomly. Twelve balls were pulled in the day drawing, and ten in the night game, and they comprised the winning numbers.

Policy games were exciting neighborhood events in which eager crowds gathered on the front lawns of policy houses.

The payout amount for winners depended on wager type. For night house games, a simple bet in which one of the player's three numbers was pulled paid 5 to 1—a dime bet paid winners fifty cents. If the gambler played "flats," she would win, at a payout of 30 to 1, if two of her selected numbers had only one other number between them on the results slip. A players could bet "sides" and get paid at 200 to 1 if two of his numbers appeared next to each other. If he played a "gig," and three of his wagered numbers appeared anywhere on the results slip, then he would win at 400 to 1.

Many policy players believed future winning numbers came to them in hunches, from significant events, or in dreams. Dream books, which associated certain subjects with certain numbers, became very popular and a lucrative component of numbers gambling. If you dream about a baby, play 2-1-1. Put some money on 7-6-9 if your dream is about death.

The police first noticed organized policy drawings around the turn of the nineteenth century. In the background were William Thier and his protégé, William Lark, running "dream shops." In 1906, police celebrated the arrest of the unassuming Lark, who was nabbed with a check for $1,000, two diamonds, and $2,750 in cash.

As policy gained popularity, reverends preached for reform, and police chiefs ordered more raids. Premature announcements of victory alternated with aggressive enforcement drives. In 1909, it was said that over $1,000 in bets came to the operators weekly from poor blacks and Italians.

By 1920, the numbers racket was firmly entrenched, particularly in the black neighborhoods on the southeast side. The big operators included Rufus Jones and Buster Matthews. Benny Mason, a mild-mannered tailor, employed two hundred writers who fanned out daily across mostly poor neighborhoods to collect penny, nickel, and dime bets.

"If it weren't for policy, my race would find conditions in this town terrible," Benny told a newspaper reporter. "I keep many people in food, pay their rent and gas bills, and give money for shoes for needy children . . ."

Though Mason touted the benefits of his B&M policy house operation, it wasn't an atmosphere in which he wanted his children. He kept a second house where he conducted drawings.

"I got no college education," Mason said. "I can't be a doctor or a lawyer, so I got to scratch where I can. I've been trying to put my kids through college. I don't want 'em to be where any business like the policy is going on."

And Mason knew the players had no chance.

"Gambling is a game for suckers," Mason said. "But the suckers keep coming. And as long as the house has cash enough to back a few bad days, it is bound to win." The folks who play the numbers game all lose in the end. But you can't stop the gambling spirit."

As the 1920s progressed, there was no shortage of suckers. So more men like Mason, ambitious and almost exclusively black, took notice of the easy income. They launched their own games. The nature of policy presented easy opportunities for some operators to avoid paying out on a heavily played number by cheating. They could rig the results of the draw by heating or freezing the selected balls or shaving them slightly concave or convex. A puller in on the fix, and with his hand concealed in the bag, would know by touch which particular balls to pull. Balls in the desired outcome could be pre-placed in a sleeve or "fingers" stitched to the inside of the bag. But Benny Mason ran a clean business.

"My people know I'm honest; that's why they got me to run this policy game."

The ease of cheating in policy led to the popularity of clearinghouse, another lottery game in which the winning number was determined from daily stock exchange figures published in the newspaper. An import from New York City, it was introduced to Cleveland around 1923 by Harry "Pony Boy" Weinzimmer.

Like policy, clearinghouse was played in stores and shops—any location where somebody in charge agreed to accept bets. Writers went house to house. Housewives would pause from their chores to greet a writer at their back door and bet a penny, nickel, or dime. Despite the improbability of winning, "playing the number," whether policy or clearinghouse, became very popular with blacks and not unpopular with whites. Ragtime singer Arthur "Blind" Blake sung of the hope and frustration of numbers gambling in his 1932 recording, "Policy Blues."

> *Numbers, numbers 'bout to drive me mad*
> *Thinkin' about the money that I should have had*
> *I dreamed last night the woman I loved was dead*
> *If I'd have played the dead row, I'd have come out ahead*
> *I acted the fool and played on 3, 6, 9*
> *Lost my money and that gal of mine*
> *I played on Clearinghouse, couldn't make the grade*
> *Lord, think of the money that I should have made . . .*
> *I'm gon' keep playin' policy 'til some good luck come.*

By the late 1920s, a partnership known as the Big Four emerged as the leaders in policy. They were three black men, Rufus Jones, now known as "the Emperor," Willie Richardson, John "Hot Stuff" Johnson, and a white man, Frank Hoge. The Big Four consolidated their power through payoffs to government officials to keep law enforcement pressure off of them and on their competitors.

Benny Mason continued as a policy gambling power. At the height of his success, in 1930, Mason's operation grossed about $1.3 million. But after expenses, he reported earning less than $15,000.

"I don't make much," Mason said. "I've got to pay income tax, you know. I'm honest about it."

Cousins Angelo Sciria and Angelo Lonardo, and George Angersola, young members of the Mayfield Road mob, took notice of the gambling profits being generated in black neighborhoods. They wanted in. An associate from Chicago helped organize a takeover. By 1929, Sciria and Lonardo were moving in and making demands. Their crew included white lieutenants Joe Artwell and Nick Satulla. Larry Gaskins and Tommy Boyce were their black street enforcers. Boyce got his start in the numbers racket as an employee of Benny Mason. He became a feared numbers enforcer known as "Bad Man." When Sciria ordered a particular policy house shut down, Boyce often barged in and accomplished the job alone.

Most of the policy operators fell in line quickly to the threats. When Willie Richardson was shot at, it wasn't long before he went to work as a front man for Sciria. Some of the gamblers, including young Bill Seawright, and Jacob Collins, were not intimidated. Sciria gave Collins an ultimatum: shut down or give up 40 percent of his weekly profits.

"I wouldn't give you forty percent of my business if you could make the Statue of Liberty walk here to Cleveland," Collins said. A few nights later, Sciria and Lonardo led a crew armed with guns and clubs. They raided the stubborn policy man's house, but Collins started shooting down a hallway, sending them fleeing.

Other defiant gambling operators, black and white, were not so fortunate. They included James McCauliffe and Fred Capillo, both killed in the early 1930s. When Clarence Murphy tried to rally fellow black numbers men to oppose Sciria and Lonardo in 1933, he too was murdered.

Godfrey "Mac" McDonald and his wife, Eva, were operators of the Independent Clearing House Lottery, headquartered at their home. Eva was stopped in her car at a Central Avenue corner collecting bets. In her passenger seat was a young employee named Joe Allen. Suddenly another car quickly swerved up, screeched to a halt, and blocked her in. The driver was Mayfield Road mob lieutenant Nick Satulla.

"He wouldn't let me pull out," Eva recalled. "He came up to the car. I had envelopes with bets slips and money in my hand. He said, 'Give me what you got.' I said no and put the slips down my bra. He reached in, ripped my blouse, grabbed the envelopes, and threatened to kill Joe."

A few months later, in the fall of 1933, Eva was at a hospital picking up bets. An elevator operator handed her a stack of slips, and just then Nick Satulla and Joe Artwell rushed up. They grabbed the slips and ripped them up. The next year, members of Angelo Sciria's crew caught up with Godfrey McDonald. He was found in his car on a lonely road in rural Moreland Hills, having been shot five times in the head. The following day, Artwell warned Joe Allen.

"You better start making payments or get out of clearinghouse, or you'll get what McDonald got last night," Artwell said.

As a member of the Mayfield Road mob, Shondor Birn joined Sciria and his crew in extorting numbers operators. Birn also muscled pay-offs from slot machine owners. For the Mafia, gambling would remain a major source of revenue for decades to come. But Shondor was looking for a racket to call his own.

***

As the roaring twenties closed, Shondor Birn was paying attention. Booze was going legit. It could have spelled doom for mobsters. Not so. As most citizens suffered through the economic plight of the Great Depression, organized crime flourished with ready supplies of cash. As the various factions of the Mafia and national crime syndicate grew in power, leaders planned for the coming end of the dry era. There would still be profits to be made in the manufacture of booze, especially by dodging federal taxes.

Meyer Lansky, his Cleveland partners, and a network of other powerful racketeers established a company called Molaska. Its objective was to manufacture dehydrated molasses, a less costly substitute for sugar, for distillation into alcohol. Lansky obtained his molasses from Cuba, and his relationship with dictator Fulgencio Batista served him well in years to come.

Much of Lansky's success was due to his collaboration across regional and cultural lines. Shondor noticed. A ready supply of cash and willingness to diversify his partnerships would become key strategies.

With the rise of powerful and organized racketeers, mainly as a result of Prohibition and the Great Depression, most major cities fell under the influence of organized crime. Business owners threatened by bankruptcy turned to mob loan sharks for cash. If they couldn't keep up with payments or other terms, they took on new partners who took advantage of the business in any way they could.

Powerful labor unions, many with mobbed-up leaders, were under Mafia control. Labor racketeers waxed profitable and powerful through embezzlement of union funds and extorting employers through work stoppages. They paid favored associates for no-show jobs or cut them regular checks as ghost employees. Union leaders steered their members to vote for friendly politicians.

Shondor's education through the 1920s and 1930s also included corrupt public officials as a necessary component of mob rule. One of the highest ranking Cleveland cops "on the pad," or in the secret bribe payoff ledgers of local racketeers, was Captain Louis Cadek. Except for cigars and occasional fine dining, Cadek lived modestly. For steering law enforcement efforts away from particular policy operators, he slowly amassed a small fortune. But the criminal conviction came fast, and he was sent to prison.

***

Shondor Birn was not averse to cursing for verbal punctuation or settling conflicts violently. If he wasn't formally charged with assault by a right cross, knife, or bullet, he was being questioned. Despite his emerging influence in Maxie Diamond's crew, Shondor managed to go three years without trouble from the law. Then, in the summer of 1929, he was arrested for stabbing a man in the stomach. When the man died, the charge was raised to manslaughter. In the end, the case was dropped without explanation. Shondor went free.

By winter, Birn was back in court—this time as a witness to a minor gangland murder that occurred in his pool hall at the Haltnorth Recreation Center. It wouldn't be the first time that Shondor rushed a seriously wounded cohort to the hospital. When questioned by police, he insisted he knew nothing.

In early 1931, former Cleveland Councilman William E. Potter was found shot to death. Maxie Diamond and several members of his crew were arrested for being suspicious persons. They were released when the charges were dropped. Shondor's buddy "Pittsburgh Hymie" Martin was tried for the murder, convicted, and sentenced to life in prison. He won a retrial and was acquitted. Potter was killed, it was believed, to prevent him from implicating others in several crooked deals.

One night in the summer of 1931, Shondor was in a speakeasy. Though only a beat cop's whistle call from the central police station, the joint operated openly. Shondor made a rude comment toward a girl, and her companion took offense. There was a struggle, a shot rang out, and the man fell to the floor. Customers rushed out the door. The wound was severe but not fatal. Birn was charged with shooting to kill. He was tried and acquitted.

In fall 1931, Birn robbed a candy store. With him was Joe Harris, another suspect from the murder of William Potter. Birn was arrested for assaulting and robbing the female shop owner of $1,480 in cash. Shondor was tried and acquitted. A month later, Harris was killed in a shootout with police following a failed payroll robbery.

Meanwhile, the rest of the Birn family was attempting to move up in the world in a more modest and peaceful manner. They had moved out to East 149th Street and were members of Heights

Orthodox Jewish Congregation and the Kinsman Jewish Center. Herman had been promoted to foreman at the Ohio Provision Company, a west side meat packer and renderer.

***

Shondor Birn's penchant for violence continued unabated. He was an impatient driver, and on one occasion when a cab driver in front of him took too long to make a turn, Shondor jumped out of his car and started a fight. Despite the presence of witnesses in the stopped traffic, Shondor punched the cabbie in the face several times and broke his nose and jaw. He was convicted of assault. When the sentencing hearing began, Birn produced a fall guy who claimed it was he, not Shondor, who broke the cabbie's jaw. The victim said he had never before seen the would-be defendant.

"Shondor Birn is the type of man who should be eliminated from society," argued a youthful assistant police prosecutor. "It is time the courts put away this man whose reputation is one of rampant criminality."

Nevertheless, Shondor's power to influence key decision makers behind the scenes was growing through payoffs to local officials and his association with established racketeers. He was sentenced to thirty days in jail and fined. The judge deferred sentencing, pending a motion for a new trial that never occurred. The case faded. Shondor went free.

In the early 1930s, Shondor and his pals spent much of their summer leisure time at a formerly exclusive lakeshore cottage colony. It was in the suburb of Euclid, bordering Cleveland's northeast side. On a Saturday night in the summer, the beer was flowing swiftly at a party. Those present included Shon's ex-brother-in-law Joe Kater, Johnny Scalish, and Artie Miller, all reputed stick-up men. Miller wound up with a bullet in his neck. When it was discovered that Shondor drove Miller to Lakeside Hospital, he was questioned by police.

"I don't know what happened to him," Birn said. "I was driving on Lake Shore when I saw him staggering along. I thought he was drunk. I'm no guy to go back on a pal, so I picked him up. When I got him into the car I saw he was shot, so I took him to the hospital."

Miller was paralyzed from the shoulders down. He died a few weeks later, having never revealed details of the shooting.

During the same period, three men burst into a Carnegie Avenue card game and robbed gamblers of their cash and jewelry. They escaped in a car belonging to Rufus "the Emperor" Jones, the big policy gambling boss. Police later located the car outside the same Euclid cottage where Artie Miller was shot. The cops hauled in Birn, Vincent Dolinsky, and Abe Zeid. Zeid was singled out of a lineup by witnesses who remembered his thick lips and his furrowed forehead made permanent by habitual squinting or frowning.

For Shondor's circle of pals, robberies were not uncommon. Those inclined to stickups included Meyer Harris Cohen, a New York City native who spent a brief time in Cleveland as a teen while trying to launch a boxing career. He eventually settled in Los Angeles and emerged as top hoodlum Mickey Cohen. Johnny Scalish, another future outfit luminary, was convicted of robbing a bottling company and served a prison term.

Shondor was busy on the streets but also spent time at home, where his father was sick. Herman Birn was diagnosed with diabetes and was losing weight and getting weaker. The increasingly public criminal exploits of his son did not help. Shondor's name appeared in small articles as Alex Birns. During these troubled times, some say Shondor purposely amended his surname to distance his mother and father from his damning press coverage. He would be forever known as Alex Shondor Birns.

And the coverage wasn't just occurring in Cleveland. In Pittsburgh, Birns was the suspect in another robbery. By the time an arrest warrant was issued, Shondor was back in Cleveland. He wasn't extradited, because Ohio's governor, George White, would not sign the papers. Clearly Shondor was acquiring influential friends. The case was eventually discharged.

Shondor took notice of how successful racketeers operated discreetly. By decreasing out-in-the-open violence, they reduced attention from the law. And by treating their operations like businesses, they increased efficiency, thus boosting profits. Starting in the early 1930s, Birns was making his way off street corners, away from beer parties, and out of saloons. He sold the Haltnorth Recreation Center, where young hoods were stymied by attention from the law.

"I had a nice little pool room and restaurant," Birns once said, "but the cops used to come in and shake down—I mean search—my patrons. They drove me out of business."

Shondor became a frequent companion of Maxie Diamond, who was active in labor racketeering and operated nightclubs. Diamond managed the Willowick Country Club in Lake County just outside Cleveland. Birns partnered with him in another joint downtown, the Parisian Village Cafe, but found a niche of his own, one that afforded him the trappings of the gangster elite—costly suits, overcoats, hats, sharp pointed shoes, an expensive car, and quality cigars. That niche was the sale of flesh.

"He had prostitution houses all over Cleveland," said Belle Herman, a longtime madam. "He didn't bother much with actually running them; he just took them over—shook down the owners for regular payments. It's the same thing he done in policy and slot machines. I have never known Shondor Birns to have made an honest penny. And you won't get anything on him because he always pays off the police."

Steady payoffs to cops netted Birns influential and lasting friendships within the Cleveland Police Department. That protection meant that men could patronize Shondor's brothels without fear of being caught up in a raid. Some of those clients eventually became government officials who, over the years, looked with favor upon Birns.

Besides growing his influence and accumulating favors owed, Shondor enjoyed other benefits within the sex trade. One of his prostitutes, Joan Johnson, was seventeen when she left home in Hot Springs, Arkansas, in 1934. She remembered meeting Shon at one of the brothels.

"When I got to a hotel in Cleveland, I was dropped off at a house at East 55th and Woodland Avenue. It was a big house with an empty store on each side. There was an arbor over the front door and a driveway that went to a garage in back. A big fat woman greeted me. Her name was Ophelia. She put me to work right away and sent men in to see me. I thought Ophelia was the madam. There were six other girls, and some were talking about someone named Shondor. So then I figured she must be the madam."

One of the other girls gave Joan advice.

"If any of these punks want to take you out for a drink, Joan, just tell them you can't go because you have a tough pimp."

On the third night Joan was at the house, Ophelia called out and told her to go upstairs to meet someone. When Joan got to her room, a man was sitting on her bed. He was in his mid-twenties and his hair was reddish blonde. He motioned toward Joan's dresser, where she noticed he had placed a five dollar bill.

"I like your dress," he said. "What are you doing when you close up?"

"I can't be bothered 'cause I have a tough pimp," Joan said.

The man chuckled then muttered to himself, "Cut it out, Shondor."

"What did you say?" Joan asked.

"I was just talking to myself. I said, 'Cut it out, Shondor.'"

"You're Shondor?"

40

"Yes. Why?"

"You're the madam?"

Shondor laughed. "You're a crazy kid. Would you like to go and have a sandwich?"

"I can't."

"It's all right. I'll ask Ophelia if you can go."

"I know I can't. I have to go home."

Shondor went downstairs. A moment later, Ophelia called out.

"It's okay if you go, Joan."

"Shondor took me to a place called the Torch Club," Joan said. "There were women performing. Shondor told me they were men. I didn't believe him. He had one of them come over to the table and then I could tell it was a man.

"The next day the other girls wouldn't talk to me. They were jealous 'cause I went out with Shondor. He took me out a few other nights. One time he was with a guy named Sammy Salupo. And once he took a bag of money to the back of the police station. He said it was a payoff."

Many foolish girls were enamored by the ways of the racketeer. Runaway Clementina Damiano, thirteen, was a fan of *Little Caesar*, *Public Enemy*, and other mob movies. In the summer of 1933, she left New York City on a train bound for Chicago to fulfill her dream of becoming a gangster's sweetheart. During a stopover in Cleveland, she was picked up by police. A probation officer was tasked with getting her back home.

With no such funding in the probation department budget, the officer solicited his fellow city employees for donations for train fare but

41

came up empty. He had an idea. If the girl was a fan of cinematic gangsters, maybe she would elicit sympathy from real gangsters. He headed up to the Willowick Country Club, a known mob hangout. Indeed, he found Tony Milano, Maxie Diamond, and his young associate Shondor Birns. When the men were told of the girl's plight, they didn't hesitate and reached deep. A few hours later, the wannabe moll was riding a train back to New York City.

The next day, the *Cleveland Plain Dealer* ran an article entitled "Racket Boys Raise Fare to Send 13-year-old Gang Gal Home." Occasional acts of charity by hard gangsters tempered their reputations and bought them respect from some in the square world.

***

Shondor Birns was building his reputation as a stone-cold and ambitious gangster who could be trusted. Simultaneous to his takeover of brothels, he was working with the Mayfield Road mob as they moved in on the policy racket. Birns accompanied Mayfield soldier Angelo Sciria and his cousin Angelo Lonardo when they raided the home of Oscar Williams, a headstrong policy man, to make sure he wasn't operating without their approval.

In September 1933, Shondor was arrested along with Yale Cohen and two other members of his crew. They were charged with the drive-by shootings of two minor policy figures. Birns was acquitted but was convicted of bribing a juror. He was sentenced to sixty days in jail. While not always effective, thumbing the scales of justice by paying off corrupt cops, judges, and jurors became one of Shondor's signature strategies.

While in jail, Shondor granted his first newspaper interview. He told the reporter that he was doing his time happily and enjoying the hard work. In years to come, he befriended many of the city's reporters. From time to time, he could be found chatting with one over a cocktail. His escapades made good ink, and he always paid the tab. Shondor was Cleveland's hood. And Cleveland was Shondor's town. Michael Roberts, writing for *Cleveland Magazine*, said

Shondor's "flamboyance and desire for prominence along with his mercurial temper made him an undesirable executive for what was to become the corporate organization of crime."

That organization, Moe Dalitz and the rest of the Jewish boys, was largely focused on expanding outside of Cleveland, building casinos, acquiring wealth, and investing in legitimate businesses.

"Shon was too much of a freelancer," Roberts wrote. "He was too spirited and reckless for the low-profile constraints of the mob. But if his 'business' did not infringe upon theirs, he had their blessings, for there was one thing certain about the man: He would never talk. His word was his honor and his silence was that of the Sphinx. It was his social security, too . . ."

***

One of many defining moments in the life of Shondor Birns came at age twenty-seven when he and some pals were getting liquored up at a downtown spot called the Keystone Club. Shondor went to the coatroom to fetch cigars from his overcoat. Because he could not produce his check, the attendant refused him access. He ignored her.

"Hey, you can't come in here!" the girl insisted. She blocked Shondor's path.

He responded with a quick slap across her face. "Get out of the way," he warned while shoving her aside. She ran from the coatroom.

"I guess I can get my cigars from my coat if I want to," Shondor said.

Shondor retrieved his cigars and returned to his table. He had two more drinks and smoked one cigar.

"C'mon, let's get outta here," he told his friends. The men arose and went to get their coats.

This time the coatroom girl was ready. She had summoned Rudy Duncan, the bouncer who also happened to be her live-in boyfriend. Duncan, a thirty-six-year-old ex-boxer and ex-con, had had previous run-ins with Birns. When the girl refused to let him pass, Birns shoved her aside and reached for his coat. Duncan came up behind him.

"What are you doing in here?" Duncan said.

Birns muttered something, and the two lunged at each other.

"So you're trying to get tough, are you, Rudy?"

Birns held Duncan back with one hand. He pulled a revolver from his waistband with the other. He raised it to hit Duncan in the head, but four drinks had slowed him. They struggled and one of Birns's pals moved in to help. Two shots popped off. Birns was hit in the shoulder. His friend was shot in the leg. Duncan ordered Birns and crew out of the bar at gunpoint.

When the police arrived, they found Shondor sitting in his car, holding a bloody handkerchief to his shoulder. They searched his car and confiscated the revolver which he had placed in the glove box. He denied ownership of the gun and would not tell who shot him. The police drove him to the hospital.

After two days, Shondor checked himself out of the hospital. He lost several pounds but was well on his way to a full recovery. As a result of the Keystone Club shooting, police arrested Birns and charged him with carrying a concealed weapon. During the trial, Shondor refused to name his assailant.

"Well, it was a small room, wasn't it?" the assistant prosecutor asked. "Can't you tell us who that man was?"

"No, I was shot and hit over the nose and in the head," Birns said. "You know how it is when you're in a fight. Blood was coming down over my eyes and I couldn't see."

He denied knowing Duncan. Duncan claimed lapse of memory. He wasn't even called as a witness. Shondor was acquitted of the gun-toting charge.

A few weeks after the trial, two well-dressed men loitered outside the Uptown Theater at E. 105th Street and St. Clair Avenue. It was evening. They were wearing white cotton gloves. Watching from a car were two more men. Inside the theater, Rudy Duncan and his eleven-year-old son were watching the end of a movie. After the show, Duncan took the boy to a store next to the theater and bought him candy. Then they headed for the car.

Duncan exited the lot and headed west on St. Clair as he and his son chatted about the film. Moments later Rudy noticed two cars coming up fast, one from behind and one on his left. The car on the left held a man standing on the running board. He had a handkerchief tied about his face. Duncan slammed on his brakes and pushed the boy out of the car.

"Run! Run!" he yelled. The boy dashed onto the sidewalk.

Duncan stepped on the gas. Too late. The two cars were right on him. The men had pistols and let loose a barrage. As they sped off, Duncan's car drifted aimlessly to the right, bounced off the curb, then rolled to a stop. Duncan's son came running to his father's aid.

"Daddy! Daddy!" the boy screamed.

He peered into the car. Duncan was taking his last labored breaths. His murder went officially unsolved, but Birns remained a prime suspect.

Not quite an eye for an eye, but nobody pushed around Shondor Birns.

CHAPTER THREE

For Alex Shondor Birns, the bold daylight killing of a nightclub bouncer, a crime for which he was never charged, ushered in a new era of notoriety. Shondor had challenged Rudy Duncan in that coatroom brawl and lost. It demanded swift and severe retribution. Birns, or at least those loyal to him, delivered.

Many such murders occurred in the 1920s and early 1930s in American gangland. When crime overran the efforts of local law enforcement, determined police chiefs ordered drives to arrest known racketeers on sight. Often the value was in police characters—thieves, pimps, fences, safe men, stickup men, and other criminals—being paraded before young detectives to familiarize them with their foe. Birns was often a target.

Shondor developed a knack for beating criminal charges. He gloated in his courtroom victories and delighted in the newspaper coverage. The often suspected, occasionally charged, but rarely convicted antihero's exploits brought serial entertainment to unprincipled citizens, crime romantics, and just plain curious Jacks and Jills.

The newspaper accounts belied his life at home—that of concern for his sick father. Herman Birn had worked in the butchering department of the Ohio Provision Company for eighteen years before he was forced to retire in 1934. A few months later, Shondor was arrested in connection with the murders of two prominent rackets figures from Akron, Cleveland's sister city fifty miles to the south.

He was questioned and charged with being a suspicious person. He was fined, but the additional court costs were suspended.

The suspicious person law was eventually ruled unconstitutional, in 1971, due to its vagueness.

***

Through his involvement in prostitution, bookmaking, and the Maxie Diamond/Lou Rothkopf bootlegging empire, Shondor was pocketing enough cash to travel by airplane to see the big prizefights. He had become Diamond's protégé. Like Maxie, Shondor spent winters in Florida, trading sleet and snow for sand and sun.

In January 1937, Shondor was walking out of a Miami Beach motel. Two detectives approached. They carried a police mug shot of Birns and a copy of his rap sheet. They patted Shondor down and handcuffed him. The charge? Failing to register as a felon. It was a pet ordinance for Miami Beach officials and an annoyance for many visiting ex-convicts.

When Shondor addressed the judge, he hinted that his visit might be good for the local economy.

"Your Honor, I came to Miami to mind my own business and spend money. That's what I'm doing. That's all."

The judge wasn't impressed. "Costs and ninety days suspended if you get out of town in twenty-four hours."

"I got," Shondor later said.

Back home, Birns found hospitality still lacking. With Maxie Diamond going legit in the restaurant business, newspapers identified Shondor as the new leader of the East 55th and Woodland mob. Increased attention from reporters fed Shon's desire to be somebody. But it invited even more attention from the police.

Following the coverage of his booting from Miami Beach, Shon knew the Cleveland cops would be looking to haul him in for the slightest reason. Or for no reason. He avoided several of his regular haunts, but on one occasion when he sat down for a bite to eat, a passing patrol officer noticed him through the restaurant window. A few minutes later, Shondor was on his way to Central Police Station.

A supervising officer paraded him in front of fifty-five detectives. "This is Shondor Birns. He is twenty-nine and lives on East 149th Street. He is five feet eight inches tall and weighs 165 pounds. He is known as a plain racketeer."

The officer pointed to Shon's sharp-toed English walkers. "He is wearing racket shoes."

Attorney Henry Galen filed a writ to compel Birns's release. A few hours later, the lawyer accompanied a smirking Shondor from Central Police Station. It would become a familiar occurrence—arrest, detention, release secured by an attorney, no charges, interview with a reporter.

Like his mentor, Maxie Diamond, but unlike most mobsters, Shondor Birns did not shy away from inquisitive newspapermen. He shared his opinion confidently and often complained about police harassment.

"Phooey! What a business," Shondor said. "Thrown in the can the minute I hit town! I'll tell you the cops themselves won't let you go straight. I come into Cleveland Sunday. I've got to drive around with my clothes still in my car. I sit down in a restaurant to eat something. A cop looks through the window—and whoops—just like that, they throw me in the can! What a business, what a business."

The reporter asked Shondor about his trip south.

"Was I bothering anybody down in Miami? I was not. I spent my time swimming and going to shows and the races. Oh, I did some booking, but nobody bothers you on that."

Another reporter interviewed Shondor. "Where's the sun tan, Shon?"

Birns chuckled. "Sun tan? You can't get any sun tan when you have to run around hiding behind palm trees all day to keep the police away from you."

Shondor continued his rant against Miami and Cleveland police action.

"Them cops. Funny thing, ain't it? I was associating down there with some of the best business people from Cleveland. They thought my company was OK. Funny, ain't it? The fact is it's the cops themselves that won't let you go straight. All I gotta say is it's a pretty rotten setup. Why can't they leave a guy alone? I can't go anywhere without being picked up. They don't give you any break. Oh well, it was getting cold in Florida, anyway."

Shondor also took a jab at Miami Beach.

"The motels were only half full, and the amusement stops were poorly attended," he said. "And prices were high. That didn't bother me, though. I did pretty well at the track the first two weeks."

The *Cleveland Press* responded with an editorial.

Well may Shondor Birns be boastful. Well may he be pleased to be back where the gold of the Woodland-E. 55th district prostitution racket is mined, where the worst that happens is the annoyance of sporadic arrests "for investigation." Shondor, back and boastful, is a challenge to every policeman, rookie to Chief Matowitz.

Shondor is a symbol of all that is wrong with police, with our flexible laws, with our too tolerant attitude to these mites we make mighty. Harassing him by sporadic detention isn't enough. The challenge is to get Birns for his past crimes, to go back over the killings, the sluggings, the robberies, to make one case stick . . .

***

By 1936, celebrated crime fighter Eliot Ness was settled in as safety director and beginning a campaign against police corruption. Like he had done in Chicago with Al Capone, Ness assembled an A-team of supposedly incorruptible or "untouchable" investigators. He also started an investigation into complaints of extortion, violence, and murder against policy operators by a "muscle mob" affiliated with Little Italy gangsters.

During the same period, the Federal Alcohol Tax Unit was investigating a sizeable bootleg ring operated by Lou Rothkopf and Maxie Diamond. Most of the evidence was coming from physical surveillance and wiretaps. Technicians connected into telephone lines at Rothkopf's apartment, allowing investigators to listen in on what they called "supervised phone calls."

As a result of the wiretap evidence, Diamond, Philip Goldberg, Lou Rothkopf, Birns's former brother-in-law Joe Kater, and seventeen members of their bootleg syndicate were indicted for defrauding the federal government out of $150,000 in taxes.

By May 1937, the trial was underway. During a recess, Diamond and Goldberg wandered over to their gambling headquarters inside a building just a short walk from the Federal District Courthouse. The timing of their audacity could not have been worse. They walked right into a raid being led by one of Ness's right-hand men, Cleveland Police Lt. Ernest Molnar. Diamond and Goldberg were arrested on the spot.

Molnar's squad located records implicating Diamond, Goldberg, and Shondor Birns in the gambling ring. Diamond denied any connection to the operation. In fact, he tried to use the arrests to his advantage. In a creative legal maneuver, Diamond refused to post bond. He hoped that his forced absence from the trial would create a rift for Ness in federal court. But Ness simply released Diamond without bond and had detectives escort him back to federal court.

"It never rains but it pours," Maxie muttered while riding the elevator back up to the courtroom.

Diamond suggested that Ness had timed the raid to prejudice the federal jury. A motion for a mistrial was overruled.

Later, Diamond telephoned a reporter and attacked Ness's record.

"Crime is more rampant under Eliot Ness than any other time."

Ness was amused.

"The fact that Maxie is sore indicates perhaps that the records we seized are more accurate than his passing observations."

The trial concluded and went to the jury. They returned guilty verdicts against Rothkopf, Diamond, Goldberg, Kater, and numerous henchmen for conspiracy to violate federal tax laws and running wholesale liquor operations without paying proper taxes. Ten others were convicted for their roles.

By June, Rothkopf, Diamond, Goldberg, and several others were off to the federal penitentiary in Lewisburg, Pennsylvania, to serve their time. To the casual observer, Diamond and Goldberg could have been taking in the air on a fine summer's day instead of having their last taste of freedom. Clad in wide-lapel suits and their fedoras at a jaunty angle, Goldberg smiled as if he hadn't a care in the world. Maxie Diamond's air was equally confident as he strode beside his partner in crime, a cigar in his mouth and a small paper-wrapped package balanced on his hip. The fact that the pair were cuffed to each other and escorted by a US marshal appeared to be of no consequence. It was almost as if they knew that their conviction and sentencing was to be a short-lived victory for federal officials. An appeals judge would later rule that the wiretap evidence was illegal because there was no search warrant.

As for Shondor, he had not been arrested, let alone indicted, as a result of the evidence gathered in the raid on Diamond and Goldberg's gambling headquarters. At least not yet.

By this time, Shondor had turned thirty. At home he looked after his nephew, Leonard, stressed the importance of education, and even gave the boy an allowance every Friday. Meanwhile, Herman Birn's health deteriorated to the point that Shondor had to carry him from room to room.

Shondor continued to have easy cash coming in from muscling brothels. In February 1937, police raided a Carnegie Avenue whorehouse. Officers searched the premises and heard a man sneeze. It came from the backyard woodshed. Inside, hiding under an overcoat, they found Birns and three young lovelies. Shondor was arrested and held overnight.

With an inability to convict Birns and lock him up, police officials were frustrated. A standing order to pick him up on sight was issued. It was not much more than a pattern of harassment, Birns's attorney filing for his release, and perhaps Shondor paying a fine. During one arrest, he was with his crony Abe "Hoot Gibson" Katz. Shondor was held for participation in several lineups.

"Someday you guys will be in lineups too," he told detectives.

In the spring of 1937, cops picked up Birns at a Euclid Avenue gambling spot. It was his fifth bust since he was booted from Miami. While one participant escaped through a window, Shondor and Katz were nabbed and charged with being suspicious persons. The charges were dropped for lack of evidence.

In the meantime, Safety Director Eliot Ness was overseeing various organized crime investigations, including labor racketeering violence, especially in the window cleaning business. During this time, Shondor's pal Sammy Salupo and Salupo's girlfriend were killed in a car bombing. Bill Presser, the future national Teamsters president, was shot at. As often happened when mob-related police investigations were ongoing, crime figures who had too much to gain by testifying ended up dead.

Ness and some of his investigators, including Lt. Ernest Molnar, completed a lengthy investigation into the numbers racket. Grand jury testimony from more than seventy policy and clearinghouse operators revealed there were dozens of men connected with the group of Mayfield Road mob extortionists headed by Angelo Sciria. The group dominated gambling, having first muscled in on the numbers racket in 1931. They were involved in labor racketeering and had infiltrated Cleveland city government.

Indictments were issued against Angelo Sciria, Angelo Lonardo, Frank Hoge, and twenty others, including Shondor Birns. Some of those charged fled town before police could make arrests after the grand jury action was leaked to the *Cleveland Press*.

"This investigation was undertaken because we felt that this gang of racketeers was encroaching on legitimate enterprises," Ness said. "As long as Cleveland has an underground empire, with tremendous revenues and headed by unscrupulous racketeers, it hangs as a threat over every decent citizen and every decent business."

Several copies of the statements and affidavits made by witnesses were placed in different locations to protect against theft. The case would be heard in four separate trials that would take two years.

By the time of his indictment for extorting policy operators, Shondor Birns's criminal history filled three pages in the record books of the Bertillon system, a method of criminal identification using physical measurements and eventually replaced with photographs and fingerprints.

In the fall of 1938, two patrolmen were assigned to pick up Birns and bring him to Central Station. The officers located him at a downtown nightclub. When they grabbed him, Shondor reportedly resisted and hit one of them. He was charged with assault.

"I'll be surprised if they don't find me guilty," he told his attorney. "The judge just as much told them I was."

Shondor would have lost the bet. It took only twenty minutes. The jury returned a verdict of not guilty. Shondor was being called the "most-arrested and least-convicted racketeer."

Slugging a cop put Shondor bright on the radar of Cleveland police, and they had a long memory. In November 1941, he was eating at a Carnegie Avenue barbecue when Captain Mike Blackwell was passing by; the captain rousted him from his table and escorted him outside. Shondor protested.

"What is this, Germany or something where a man can't even walk down the street?" Birns said.

"What do you do for a living?" asked Blackwell.

"I'm an honest man just trying to get along. I bother no one, and I don't want anyone to bother me. I would tell you what I do for a living, but you would not believe me."

"Tell us, Shondor," Blackwell said in mock sympathy. "What do you do?"

"I'm a towel salesman."

"What are you doing here?"

"I'm looking after a sick friend," he said, motioning toward his brand new chrome-plated Cadillac.

Blackwell peered inside and observed a gorgeous twenty-something blonde passed out in her fur coat. "Well," he said to Birns, "get someone to look after your car and your friend, and let's get going."

"You're inhuman. Making me leave my sick friend. What did I do now? Why can't you guys let a man alone?"

Blackwell made a habit of arresting Birns on general principle whenever he saw him. He explained why in a report.

"When a racketeer of his kind is arrested, he should be held for a while. He should be placed in a lineup where the younger members of the force can become better acquainted with him."

***

It was earlier that same year, on June 21, 1941, that Herman Birn died after battling complications of diabetes and pneumonia. This was one day before Germany invaded the Soviet Union. Sadie Birn went to work as a Red Cross volunteer to support the war effort. Shondor, too, fancied himself a patriot. In 1942, he filed papers to enlist in the United States Naval Reserve. While awaiting approval, he eagerly displayed to friends his official letter confirming his application.

Being shipped to fight the Nazis would be good timing, since his policy extortion trial was approaching. It wasn't to be. When he was classified as "4F," or unsuitable because of his felony convictions, Birns protested. He emphasized his navy service as a teenager and asked the draft board to reconsider. They did. Reclassified as eligible for service in any branch, Shondor applied for enlistment in the navy. The process neared completion. Then, citing Birns's unsavory reputation as evidenced in numerous newspapers, a commanding officer turned him down. Shondor pressed on and wrote to officials in Washington.

While Shondor waited for a response, his name hit the newspapers again. But it wasn't the typical coverage that was building his unsavory reputation. This story was of a Friday night date gone bad—a skirmish with two girlfriends, one blonde and one brunette. While Shondor was out with the blonde, they argued. He abandoned her downtown and headed back to his apartment. On the way, he picked up a replacement date—a brunette.

The ditched blonde wasn't happy. When she dialed Shondor's number and the brunette answered, the blonde taxied forthwith to the apartment. Shon had split. While the brunette cowered, the blonde broke windows and took the place apart. When police arrived, they found the blonde "panting from her exertions after wreaking $200 worth of havoc on the furnishings, windows and woodwork." A reporter joked that Shondor wanted in the army to get far away from "the battling blonde."

A few weeks later, Birns received a telegram from the Navy Department's Bureau of Navigation. Officials there recommended that he enlist in Detroit. He drove to Detroit but was again turned down because of the prison time he had served seventeen years ago. Back in Cleveland, he tried to join the army.

"Despite Shondor's highly regarded abilities as a marksman in the underworld," a *Cleveland Press* reporter wrote, "the Army said flatly and emphatically, 'No.'"

***

As Shondor's trial in the numbers extortion case approached, he was suffering from a hernia. He had surgery to have it repaired. Because he was recovering in the hospital, Shondor was given a separate trial. The timing was either fateful or a brilliant strategy by attorney Henry Galen.

During the trial, Galen grilled victim Oscar Williams about never mentioning Shondor in the previous trials. Williams said he didn't focus on Birns then because he wasn't at the defendant's table. The attorney got Williams to admit that he was confused by dates and places. Galen then took advantage of Williams's lack of recall. On one day, Galen and Birns wore identical suits. In the afternoon, they switched positions at the defense table. Birns and his lawyer were somewhat similar in physical appearance. The ploy worked. When Williams was instructed to identify Birns, he pointed at Galen. Shondor was acquitted.

"I've been carrying that charge over my head for more than three years," Shondor told a reporter. "It sure feels good to be able to forget about it now."

By the end of 1942, most of his fellow defendants in the policy extortion cases were convicted, fined, and imprisoned for up to ninety days.

CHAPTER FOUR

World War II and a trip to Canada: together they produced a long-lasting legal hurdle for Shondor Birns, with a potential for dire consequences. It had to do with the Alien Registration Act of 1940, which the US Congress passed after Germany invaded Poland and World War II expanded to Europe. Noncitizens had to register as "aliens" or they would be fined $1,000 and get six months in jail. The law was one of numerous homeland security measures. It affected Shondor because he was never naturalized.

A federal investigator, reviewing reentry files as a result of the 1940 law, discovered a two-week vacation that Birns had taken in 1938 to Canada. Shondor had failed to get permission to leave and reenter the US. Because of his prior convictions of car theft and bribery of a juror and his involvement in prostitution, he was restricted from reentering the country due to the Immigrant Act of 1917. As a result, he had to join sixty-five thousand noncitizens in Cuyahoga County and five million across the US who visited their local post office or Immigration and Naturalization field office to be fingerprinted and fill out questionnaires about their birthplace, family history, political allegiance, and criminal background.

The influence that Shondor enjoyed with many local officials did not extend much into the federal arena. Local authorities could not seem to put him in prison for long. Now federal officials had legal standing for deportation.Immigration and Naturalization agents arrested Shondor and booked him into county jail. He was charged with being a criminal enemy alien who had entered the US illegally. Henry Galen filed a writ of habeas corpus to have Shondor released. The US attorney opposed the motion vigorously.

The deportation process moved quickly through the next week. No doubt many law enforcement officials were celebrating. Their delight, however, was short-lived. Birns could not be deported, at least not to Hungary, which did not recognize its nationals who had been gone more than ten years. Holding Birns in jail would be useless. The deportation order would stand, but there was no place as yet to deport him. Birns was ordered released but not before his bond was increased from $500 to $3,000 because of his reputation. He walked out of jail, but it was a temporary reprieve.

***

When Japan bombed Pearl Harbor in 1941, the US declared war. President Franklin Roosevelt signed a law ordering the lockup of potentially dangerous enemy aliens. They were arrested by the FBI on the authority of presidential warrants, rushed through closed hearings, and imprisoned or "interned" in detention camps. In Cleveland, the US attorney ordered an investigation to determine whether Birns was engaged in subversive activities or otherwise a national security danger. The FBI interviewed several associates of Birns, including the manager of the Union Linen and Towel Company where Shondor started working in 1941.

"I've known Shondor since he was a young boy," the manager said. "His word is always good. I've had him to my home on many occasions, and he has always been a gentleman. I know he's been involved in bookmaking, but I believe he is patriotic."

The man described Shondor's influence as a labor troubleshooter.

"Shon is able to settle labor difficulties on short notice and without any trouble at all," he said. "And he contacts potential clients as a salesman. He's tried to get other jobs, but the police caused him so much embarrassment that he could not hold any job."

A neighbor of Birns told the agents that the members of Shondor's family, including his sister and her son, dressed nicely but had nothing to do with anyone in the neighborhood. She said Birns did not stay at the house regularly but often came home on weekends and drove different cars. The neighbor knew Birns had been in trouble and noted that the police frequently paid him visits. She knew of no unpatriotic activity on Shondor's part and said she even heard that he might be joining the military.

Another neighbor said that he purposely kept his distance from Birns and only knew him to offer a quick hello. "I would not want to know persons with his reputation," he said.

At the Sidney Hill Health Club, the manager said Shondor had been a regular patron since 1933. He said Birns exercised and took Turkish baths three times weekly but lately had time for only two appointments a month. He mentioned that Shon was so disappointed at being rejected by the army and navy to fight in World War II, that he actually cried.

Investigators found no evidence of subversive or un-American activities. Nevertheless, Don C. Miller, US attorney for the Northern District of Ohio, was determined to lock up Birns. He requested a presidential warrant. When it was denied, Miller sent another request to higher-ups in Washington.

Miller wrote: "In view of the fact that the proclamation of the President of July 17, 1942, provides that any Hungarian national who is violating or is about to violate any criminal law of any of the States or territories, shall be subject to summary arrest as an enemy alien and to confinement in a place of detention, we request the issuance of a presidential warrant."

This time, US Attorney General Francis Biddle granted the request and sent a presidential warrant to Cleveland authorities. The warrant deemed Birns to be "dangerous to the public peace and safety of the United States." It ordered him detained until further order.

Newspaper reporters in Washington, DC, tipped off their associates in Cleveland, who called the FBI and inquired about Birns. In the meantime, someone tipped off Birns. He checked into a room at the Carter Hotel after registering under the alias of "Al Sands."

A police lieutenant tracked Shondor down and reported his location to the FBI. Three agents apprehended Birns in his room and turned him over to the Immigration and Naturalization Service. While Shondor was held in a city jail, Cleveland reporters, notified again by DC counterparts, started calling the FBI and inquiring about Birns's whereabouts.

On December 9, 1942, Birns appeared before the Northern District of Ohio's Alien Enemy Hearing Board. It consisted of a stockbroker, a lawyer, and an architecture professor. The proceedings were overseen by a young agent of the FBI. Enemy aliens were not permitted legal representation but were allowed one witness who could speak for them. Shondor chose attorney Gerard Pilliod, a former US attorney. In earlier years, Pilliod was a chief police prosecutor known for quashing criminal charges that were not levied fairly or properly. He was a man whose integrity Birns considered "above reproach."

The board heard from several police officers who testified to their personal knowledge about Birns's past, especially his connections to houses of prostitution. Then Birns was given fifteen minutes to plead his case.

"I came up from the gutter," Shondor said. "As a boy, my bed was a pile of newspapers in a downtown alley."

Birns admitted to selling bootleg booze to help his family and later booking horse race and baseball bets. He denied any connection to prostitution and argued that he should be classified not as an enemy alien but merely an alien. He was armed with affidavits of friends and relatives who knew the history of his birthplace. It was a town swallowed by the new border of Czechoslovakia after Austria-Hungary was dissolved. Pilliod suggested that Birns would have excelled in the navy had his parents not intervened.

"Alex gave every promise of an honorable and successful career in his country's service," Pilliod argued. "But after six months of service, his parents applied to the government for his release, and due to his minority age, it was granted. This proved to be most unfortunate."

The attorney said Birns returned to Cleveland and because of his age and "impulsive temperament," he succumbed to the "dangerous temptation" of crime.

In spite of that argument, Pilliod also pointed out the absence of any recent criminal convictions.

"While I was chief prosecutor from 1938 to 1941, no charge of illegal conduct had been proven against Mr. Birns. His numerous arrests with no subsequent convictions are probably the result of either personal malice or animosity or a misguided police policy, only too familiar to experienced prosecutors, of arresting a given suspect for questioning whenever a certain type of offense occurred."

When the Alien Enemy Hearing Board members voted, it was unanimous. They were unmoved by Pilliod's argument and Birns's testimony. They ordered Shondor interned for the duration of World War II, pending the definite establishment of Birns's Hungarian nationality.

Before Birns was taken from Cleveland, he complained to a friend about the hasty hearing.

"There was not one mention of subversive activities," he said. "Just my past record, acquittals, and reputation. I produced five affidavits in reference to my birthplace. It became Czechoslovakia. The US attorney mentioned the fact that I was born in Austria but never once mentioned the affidavits about my birthplace. I didn't have a chance to fight back. If some of the people that put me in this trouble did one-half the work that my family does with the Red Cross in regards to this war effort, I think I would call them honest-to-goodness patriots. My mother is a sewing instructress, has donated blood four times, has taken the first aid course, and now she is trying to find a job in a defense plant. If you visit her house, you'll see an American flag in the front, and 'V for Victory' sign on the door."

Sadie Birn was distraught.

"How could this be?" she said to a friend. "My son is a good Jewish boy. They call him an enemy alien. How could he want Hitler to win the war?"

Shondor's pals threw him a two-night going away party at a Carnegie Avenue barbecue joint. Cash gifts totaled $1,500. Then on January 14, 1943, federal officials shipped Birns out of Cleveland. He was destined for the McAlester Internment Camp in Oklahoma. Military planners established alien enemy and prisoner of war camps in states with mild climates. Construction and heating costs would be low. The designs were the same—with separate barracks for prisoners and guards, a canteen, and a fire department—like small towns. McAlester camp had a capacity of forty-eight hundred and held mostly Italian enemy aliens.

When Shondor arrived at McAlester on February 4, officers questioned him about his history and collected his property. He had $743.66 in his pocket and $3,500 in a checking account. He said he owned a $1,400 Cadillac.

Back home, Louis Clifford, city editor for the *Cleveland Press*, criticized the federal government's alien enemy hearing process in a scathing editorial entitled "Dangerous to Liberty." It read, in part:

The delivery of Shondor Birns, a Cleveland racketeer, to a concentration camp without any public hearing of the charges against him calls attention to the fact that there now exists in this country a procedure contrary to all American ideas of justice and dangerous to liberty . . . It may have been imagined that proceedings against enemy aliens need to be secret, lest information of value to the enemy be made public, concerning our attempts to combat subversive activity. In the Birns case, however, there is not the slightest reason to sup-

pose that he has been purposely working for Hitler, whom he, as a Jew, professes to hate intensely.

Clifford sent Shondor a copy of the editorial. Birns wrote him back.

"I'm glad to hear from you, and I received the editorial," Shondor wrote. "I would appreciate if you could send me about three copies. I never thought that the Press would put in an editorial like that especially where it concerns me. But most important is that I understand it is not a personal affair. I can see they did not pull any punches. The only thing they missed, as far as the government is concerned, was I enlisted in the Navy here more recently and received the internment camp for my efforts. But, a person could not even dream or realize the way the editorial made me feel. It made me a new man, and it gave me a new lease on life. Instead of a lot of animosity, I'm going to keep on fighting. I never will give up until the day I am vindicated from being branded an enemy alien to the country. Well anyway, I hope everything will come out in the wash one of these days."

Birns settled into the camp and was put in charge of a tree planting crew. He was described as a cheerful and hard worker.

Gerard Pilliod continued to work on Shondor's case. He researched Shondor's birthplace, a community known as Litinye in the Carpathian Alps, and filed a brief. It laid out the history of complicated border realignments that had occurred in Central Europe, starting with the dissolution of the Empire of Austria-Hungary by the 1919 Treaty of Versailles, one of several peace accords at the end of World War I. Litinye, later known as Lucina or Lutina, became part of Czechoslovakia.

A friend of Birns offered her own help in the form of a written plea directly to President Franklin Roosevelt:

Our beloved President! For 20 years I am a close friend of the Birns family. I am turning to you for help. Alex is a victim of a terrible newspaper publicity. Mr. President, you know too, a newspa-

per could kill a man. They had nothing on him. Headline publicity was the reason.

With a few words I will describe this boy's character. What kind of a "gangster" he is. Years ago his sister anything but killed herself with her dieting. Her husband divorced her. She lost her house. This boy took her to doctors for 5 years. Many hundreds of dollars he spent on her. Today she is happily remarried and a mother. His father 8 years ago became an invalid; the family did not know of want. He made his father's home and final years the most comfortable. Ever since his father died he supported his step mother.

Our beloved President! You are and you were my idol, a living symbol of—justice, and Democracy! I am begging you, please order a speedy investigation, why this boy was taken to an enemy alien camp, he does not belong there. This case is exactly what we are fighting against to the whole world. Mr. President, again I am begging you, please help him. I do not give up hope, that, I will hear an encouraging answer from you. God bless you our Beloved President.

With my greatest respect.

—Signed, Mrs. J. Kovacs.

On March 12, 1943, two months after Shondor was interned, US Attorney General Biddle ordered him to be paroled.

"It was a complete surprise to me," said Assistant US Attorney Don Miller in Cleveland.

Shondor was released. He took with him a letter of commendation from the commander for his excellent attitude and conduct. Birns's parole was conditioned on him being placed in the custody of a reputable US citizen to whom he would report twice weekly. So it was that Cuyahoga County Sheriff Joseph Sweeney agreed to sponsor Birns and was approved forthwith by the Alien Enemy Hearing

Board in Cleveland and by officials of the Immigration and Naturalization Service.

After Shondor arrived home, *Cleveland Press* city editor Louis Clifford wrote him again.

Alex: I am glad to hear that you hope soon to be relieved of your status of being on parole as an "enemy alien" charge. It was personal feeling at the time this charge was first brought that there was no foundation in fact for it and that sentence was based solely on your past reputation. It seems to me that your past record of having twice sought to join the armed forces and your conduct since leaving the Detention Camp justifies complete lifting of the "enemy alien" stigma.

"It was not always easy to trace Birns' influential contacts," wrote Michael Roberts. "Years later Shondor would brag that a *Cleveland Press* newspaper editor helped secure his release."

Shondor spent the following months complying diligently with his rules of parole. With concern over his enemy alien classification and travel restriction, he wrote a letter, with editorial guidance no doubt, to a US Department of Justice official.

Dear Sir:

By virtue of your gracious and kind heart and by the inherent justice that prevails in America, a little better than a year ago I was released from the McAlester Alien Enemy Camp.

Now sir, I am of the Jewish faith and came here with my parents when I was an infant. I have lived all my life in Cleveland, Ohio and as a result thereof I don't know any other country but the United States of America. At the time of my release I received some identification papers, these papers indicate and brand me with the worst stigma a person can be identified (Alien Enemy).

I am not an enemy of America, never was, and never will be. Ameri-

ca is my country, a country that I learned to love, respect and willing to defend. I am interested in an American victory and besides have offered myself to the Army, Navy and any other division of the government's armed forces. Meanwhile I have solicited and procured subscriptions for war bonds and also promoted additional funds for this wonderful of all institutions the Red Cross.

I feel very confident that I can surmount the stigma of the past by leading a life devoted to my work and doing everything to achieve the goal of a good American. Therefore, in the name of God and in the name of Justice grant me this plea, please remove this stigma of being an Alien Enemy, release my parole and restore to me my freedom. You can rest assured that you will never have to regret it.

Hoping that this plea of mine will be received with some hope of realization, with obedience, I am.

Respectfully yours, Alex S. Birns

***

By late 1943, Shondor was being paid $300 monthly for handling restaurant sales accounts for napkins and tablecloths and managing labor conflicts for the Union Linen Supply.

With legitimate income and after a year of complying with the restrictions, Birns was released from parole. He was still under an order of deportation, but he was cleared of the alien enemy status he detested. It was a new beginning for him.

Birns told reporters he was trying to go straight. And it was going to be in the restaurant business, long an interest from when Shondor had his first taste of the food industry with the Haltnorth Recreation Center grill and later when his mentor, Maxie Diamond, ran clubs.

Shondor became a partner and manager with Morris "Mushy" Wexler at the Theatrical Grill, a onetime brewery turned into a popular restaurant by Wexler and his brother-in-law. Wexler had previously run the racing newswire system that provided bookies and gamblers with instant horse racing results.

Shondor concealed his financial interest in the Theatrical through Rose Scheiner, his now-married stepsister. Though the Theatrical would remain a favorite hangout for life, Shondor's partnership was short-lived. Mushy decided to bring in his new son-in-law as a co-owner. In 1946, Wexler wrote a check to Rose Scheiner for $25,000 and bought Shondor out.

In a plan to have his own joint, Birns engineered a deal to operate the Ten-Eleven Club at 1011 Chester Avenue. The manager, no doubt at Shondor's convincing, assured skeptical city officials that Birns would serve only as a bouncer. But it was only four months later that Birns and his pal Chuck Amata were identified as the restaurant managers when they were cited for serving alcohol past midnight. The curfew was a recent federal restriction on places of entertainment to help conserve coal for heating and electricity for the war effort. The violation was the least of Birns's worries, as his deportation case continued with hearings in Cleveland and the central immigration office in Philadelphia.

With Shondor as host, the Ten-Eleven Club was favored by local and out-of-town big shots. Newspaper reporters and cops ate and drank on the house. And when the East Ohio Gas explosion killed 134 persons and left thousands homeless in 1944, Birns kept the Ten-Eleven Club open twenty-four hours a day, feeding policemen, firemen, and rescue workers for free.

While Birns built his reputation as a restaurateur, policy operators were vying for control of the Goldfield Policy House after the death of Oscar Williams. Buster Matthews inherited the operation, but Frank and Willie Hoge and Arthur "Little Brother" Drake called on the influence of their associate, a corrupt Cleveland police lieutenant.

"If we have to get tough, we will get tough," said the cop. "I'm in the driver's seat."

The next day, Drake and several of his men, armed with pistols, visited Buster Matthews. The day after that, the Goldfield reopened with Hoge and Drake as new partners. The corrupt cop? He was one of Eliot Ness's own. Ernest Molnar was clearly touchable.

Molnar knew that policy and clearinghouse were not just penny games but rather a big-scale racket worth millions. He knew that the business could not flourish without cooperation from local law enforcement. For several years, racketeers had passed him envelopes of cash. In exchange, Molnar ignored certain gambling operations. And he supplied the Mayfield Road mob with confidential information on their competitors.

A grand jury investigated. They indicted Molnar and released a special statement.

"It is our impression that the Cleveland Police Department is composed of honest, brave, and able officers," the grand jury wrote. "However certain members of the department have been corrupted to protect the policy racket by Frank and Willie Hoge. Corruption cannot be eliminated from the police department until the Hoge brothers are eliminated from their position of power over law enforcement and position of freedom from imprisonment."

County Prosecutor Frank Cullitan said that Molnar had virtually controlled the policy racket for several years. On a salary averaging less than three thousand dollars a year, Molnar's bribe income brought him four cars, real estate investments, and tuition for a private school for his son. One of Cullitan's assistants called Molnar's clan the "cashingest family" he had ever seen. In the end, the disgraced cop went to prison.

Alvin Sutton, a former FBI agent who succeeded Eliot Ness as safety director, set his sights on the Hoge brothers and Arthur Drake. Willie Hoge started providing Sutton information about Hoge's competitors. When a Hoge associate complained about the strategy, Shondor stepped in to settle the matter.

"Stop fighting, get down to business, and make some money," Birns warned the man. "I'm connected with people coast to coast and can stop you anytime I want. I know what kind of car you drive and where you live."

***

With the end of World War II in 1945, national sentiment was focused on a new beginning. As a professed patriot, Shondor Birns shared in the sense of renewal. For him, too, the future looked bright—as bright as the neon lights of Uptown, the bustling entertainment district around East 105th and Euclid Avenue. Known also as Doan's Corners, it was the neighborhood of English immigrant Leslie Townes Hope, who became comedian Bob Hope. Uptown was home to five movie theaters and countless shops, restaurants, bars, and nightclubs. The Alhambra Building, with a bowling alley, a poolroom, taverns, offices, and apartments, sat across from the Fifth District police station and anchored this area, which some referred to as Cleveland's "second downtown."

The Alhambra Building was part of a $4 million family of corporations. The owners were expanding and wanted to add a restaurant. Shondor sold his share of the Ten-Eleven Club and invested in the Alhambra Grill Company. His rent was based on a percentage of the restaurant's monthly sales of alcohol. Always wary of his deportation order and tax issues, Shondor listed his stepsister, Rose, as the primary shareholder.

The state liquor enforcement chief offered no objection to Shondor's application for a liquor license. This was despite being informed by local police officials of Birns's criminal history. When higher-ups confronted the chief about slot machines placed in taverns he visited, he resigned.

Wanting more income, Shondor engineered a deal with George Harvey, partner in Doan Realty, the Alhambra's umbrella corporation. Shondor would serve as the company's public relations man, and Harvey would pay him $150 weekly. Birns would use his association with prominent sports figures and other big spenders to promote the Alhambra, solicit banquets, and lure local celebrities.

Birns employed Chuck Amata, who had worked for him at the Ten-Eleven Club as a manager, and gave Amata's fiancée a job as a bookkeeper. Shondor scheduled the Alhambra's grand opening for March 17, 1947—St. Patrick's Day. Advertisements boasted the "finest food, wines and liquors," as well as a new parking convenience. "We will park your car and deliver it to you when you need it. No charge."

The restaurant was on the lower level of the Alhambra Building. Once patrons descended the stairs off East 103rd Street, they might be greeted by Shondor Birns. A *Cleveland Press* reporter called Birns the Alhambra's "major domo" and described him as "prone to being whimsical, with a penchant for flashy clothes, bizarre entertainment, high-powered cars, and lovely lady companions." One of those companions was Joan "Vickie" Kanesic, an eighteen-year-old blonde waitress, gorgeous but marred by bad teeth.

With excellent food, top entertainment, and a gregarious host with a spicy reputation, the Alhambra was a quick success. It was busy during weekdays and packed on weekends. Shondor soon expanded the dining room to concentrate less on liquor and more on food.

"The Alhambra was a great place with terrific food," said Birns's friend Hymie Mintz. "Shon was a hell of a restaurant man."

The Alhambra sat about seventy people, including thirty at the bar. The dining room had a pleasant and upscale ambiance—white tablecloths, walls with murals, mirrors and large candelabras, dim lighting, and bartenders in tuxedos. The band played on a red-carpeted stage with a red-draped backdrop. With an intriguing mix of saints and sinners, the Alhambra became Uptown's version of downtown's Theatrical.

Cleveland Indians owner Bill Veeck frequented the Alhambra and called Shondor Birns friend. He often ordered full dinners and had them delivered to his apartment via taxi. The cab driver, along with the waiter who accompanied the food and then returned for the dishes, were assured of generous tips.

For Shondor Birns, owning a successful nightclub was a dream. But it didn't preclude his other proclivities. He wouldn't be the charismatic star of Cleveland's underworld without the whole package. Whether in the dining room, kitchen, office, or out in the parking lot, Shondor never forsook his street affairs for the Alhambra. He possessed a network of trusted acquaintances, including twenty-year-old Joe Cannata, to act as messengers and couriers.

A few months after he opened the Alhambra, Shondor was sitting in the nightclub's kitchen at a table with three chairs. It was lunchtime, and an older Hungarian woman was cooking. Cannata walked into the kitchen, greeted Shondor, handed him an envelope from a well-known bookie, and turned to leave.

"Get over here, Cannata."

Joe turned back to face Birns. Shondor motioned toward the woman cooking.

"Are you hungry?"

"Yes," Joe said.

Shondor had the woman bring over a roast beef sandwich with gravy. Joe ate while he and Shon made small talk. Joe never asked about the contents of the envelope, which Shondor had not yet opened.

"You know how to mind your own business," Shondor said.

"Well, your business is not my business," Joe said.

"That's what I like about you."

Joe finished his sandwich. "How much do I owe?" he asked.

"Don't ever ask," Shondor said.

Likewise, Shondor appreciated the discretion of his bookkeeper, whom he instructed to set aside a few hundred dollars weekly for Shondor's personal use.

Whether in the dining room or at the bar, Shondor's circle of underworld associates expanded. He often kept the band playing until four o'clock in the morning while entertaining out-of-town racketeers and shady businessmen, some traveling between Chicago and New York City. And he got to know many of the region's best burglars. Always the enterpriser, Shon found he could make commissions by connecting holders of stolen property with buyers. He was now Shondor Birns, the fence.

Shondor ruled the Alhambra lounge like a fiefdom. It was his turf, and he expected all employees to take took good care of his customers. When an employee helped himself to some wine then took a customer's car for a joyride, Shondor fired him. The young man said he wasn't leaving without his final paycheck. Shondor told him he could return the next day to be paid. It was a chilly night, and the man insisted that either he be paid or he was going back into the warmth of the restaurant. Shondor made it clear that the man was neither being paid that evening nor going back inside. Suddenly the man lunged at Shondor. Birns felled him with one punch. Shondor turned to go back inside the Alhambra. Brandishing a small knife, the man came up behind Birns and stabbed him in the back then ran. Birns, barely fazed by the injury, was treated at a hospital and released. The next time the ex-employee was seen in public, he was missing several of his teeth.

Shondor's various pursuits, legit and not, kept him busy. He did a lot of driving—usually at the wheel of a new Cadillac—with a stogie clamped in his teeth and the accelerator straining under his foot. It's how he met Carl Delau. Blue-eyed and handsome, Delau had served five years in the US Army during World War II. He was with the Third Calvary under General George Patton and helped liberate a concentration camp in France. When he was discharged, Delau looked for a job with action. He was twenty-seven when he joined the Cleveland Police Department. His first assignment was traffic accident prevention.

It was the summer of 1948 when the rookie cop was patrolling for speeders on a thirty-five-miles-per-hour stretch of the Shoreway. He observed a Cadillac racing past the new Cleveland Burke Lakefront Airport at seventy-five miles per hour. He pulled it over.

The driver handed Delau his license and asked, "Do you know who I am?"

Delau looked at the name: Alex S. Birns. "Yes, I've heard tell of you," Delau said. "And you're under arrest."

Shondor's flagrant violation precluded issuance of a summons. Delau instructed Birns to follow him to the police station. Birns was cooperative. He wasn't one to give a hard time to a cop doing his job. He paid a fifty-dollar fine and was released. However, an alternate version of the story appeared and persisted through the years in newspaper coverage about Shondor. This particular account had Birns offering Delau a bribe.

"You're under arrest," the exchange reportedly began.

"Don't be silly. Let's make a deal."

"Put that billfold back," Delau said. "With your reputation, you're the last guy in the world I'd take anything from even if I was on the take, which I'm not."

"Listen," Shondor said, "I'm one guy you can take it from and trust I wouldn't jam you up."

Delau denied the tale of the bribe offer. Birns did too.

"Sure I took out my billfold," Shondor reported. "How else could I show him my driver's license? But if I tried to bribe him, why didn't he arrest me for that?"

***

Being stabbed by a fired employee wasn't Shondor's only scrape at the Alhambra. In the fall of 1948, an argument broke out in the parking lot between several men, including Merrill Cowan, a principal in the restaurant's umbrella corporation. Someone summoned Shondor who, in one version, sucker punched the man he believed was threatening Cowan. The fight would have likely ended there, since it was Shondor Birns, but the man he slugged was Edward Kirk, an off-duty cop.

"You don't want to do that, Shon," Kirk said. "You know I'm a policeman. You're under arrest."

"Don't be a damned fool," Birns shot back. "I know you're a copper, but you're not taking me across the street."

Kirk grabbed Shondor, but he pulled away. They started brawling. Two other off-duty cops who were eating and drinking came running out. Then two on-duty policemen arrived and pulled Birns away, handcuffed him, and walked him over to the district police station. Birns had a scrape on his nose. Kirk had cuts to his face and mouth.

Birns was booked on charges of assault and resisting arrest. He posted a bond of one hundred dollars cash and walked out. Two reporters were waiting outside and asked him for a comment.

"I've got nothing to say to anybody," Birns said.

Al Sutton was furious when informed that Shondor Birns had slugged one of his cops. He met with Chief George Matowitz.

"Chief, from now on these hoodlums will be plenty roughed up," the safety director said. "Tell your men to crack their skulls. Any of these characters who have the gall to attack our men will not get away with it scot-free. It'll be an eye for an eye. I want you to take whatever steps you need, but be sure the blue comes out on top from now on."

At the trial, two Alhambra barmaids testified for Shondor. They said they had served Kirk five or six beers. Merrill Cowan stressed that Birns was trying to protect him from a drunk cop. The witnesses were unconvincing. Shondor was convicted of assaulting a police officer and resisting arrest. The judge sentenced him to seven months in jail.

"Some say that it was this incident that ultimately led to a chain of events that would turn Shondor's fortunes downward for the rest of his life," Michael Roberts wrote.

In June 1949, Shondor was booked into the Workhouse. It was the City of Cleveland's nationally recognized penal institution, housed on a two-thousand-acre tract containing the city infirmary, a halfway house, and a tuberculosis sanatorium called Sunny Acres. Within a few days, Birns met a tall and husky thirty-one-year-old black guard named William Billingslea. Shondor spoke to him about getting on the Workhouse baseball team. The men became friendly. Billingslea brought Birns newspapers and liquor and got him special access to the kitchen.

When Birns complained that he had everything except a girlfriend, Billingslea arranged for a house call from a prostitute. He let them use a matron's office while he waited outside, listening to the Sam Spade radio show. When the visit was complete, Shondor gave the guard twenty-five dollars for the girl, ten dollars for the matron, and five dollars for the girl's cab ride home.

While an inmate, Birns reportedly attended a clambake at the home of the Workhouse kitchen director. Also in attendance was John Fleming, a Cleveland police captain and pal of Shondor's who did not discourage the forty-three-year-old racketeer's affections for his eighteen-year-old daughter.

Meanwhile, Shondor followed newspaper accounts of the trial of Arthur Drake and Willie Hoge, a sequel to the case against dirty cop Ernest Molnar. They were indicted for menacing and muscling their way into the policy operation of Buster Matthews. The state's robust case was quickly burying a weak defense. When the case concluded, Hoge and Drake were convicted and given prison terms.

With the two men incarcerated, independent gambling operator Joe Allen emerged as the biggest numbers baron in town. He spoke of plans to build a grand home, and his success did not go unnoticed. As a result, Birns used Billingslea to deliver a warning to Allen to pay 25 percent of his profits. Allen refused.

Shondor felt that serving time in jail should not preclude him from getting a paycheck. Several days after learning that George Harvey had taken him off the payroll of Doan Realty, the Alhambra's umbrella corporation, an explosion rocked a neighborhood in well-heeled rural Gates Mills. Harvey's front door was blown off its hinges.

An hour later, someone stalked up to Joe Allen's East 100th Street home. The prowler placed two sticks of dynamite underneath Allen's green fishtail Cadillac. The ensuing blast ripped the car apart, leaving a pretzel of mangled steel. Dozens of windows on Allen's house and that of his neighbors were shattered.

Deputy Inspector James McArthur and eight detectives followed leads and charged that Birns engineered the bombing from the Workhouse. They arrested Birns, Angelo Lonardo, Joe Artwell, and Chuck Amata. Safety Director Al Sutton praised McArthur's work.

McArthur questioned William Billingslea, who was hired at a time before extensive background checks were conducted on corrections officers. He was associated with numerous policy racketeers, worked as an armed guard for Buster Matthews, and even tried running his own policy game.

Billingslea made a twenty-seven-page confession and agreed to testify against Birns and the others. The indictments alleged bombing, malicious destruction, and blackmail. The biggest names in northeast Ohio criminal defense represented the mobsters, including Neil McGill for Birns. Billingslea testified that Birns sent him to E. 105th Street and Cedar Avenue to meet with Lonardo, Satulla, and Amata just before the bombing.

"They were in a car with Amata at the wheel," Billingslea said. "I walked down to Allen's house and passed it to see if there were any police were around. I rang their doorbell and checked on the position of Joe's Cadillac then reported back to the others. I told them the coast was clear."

The trial saw fireworks between prosecution and defense.

"Birns is one of the slickers, one of the smart guys," said county prosecutor Frank Cullitan. "He is in consultation with the board of directors. He has his plug-uglies and gunmen out on the firing line. He is not risking his hide, but he is in there to get his cut out of the profits. In the old days, witnesses saw him with a gun."

"No more gunplay and the loudmouth threat is passé," wrote *Plain Dealer* reporter Todd Simon. "The muscle or shakedown has become velvety, deceptively smooth. And the old roughnecks live in high style."

After a victim submitted to protection payments for his gambling operation, Birns told him, "Now you can go out and see a movie with your wife."

Cullitan tried to hint that Birns had made his money from Doan Realty and the towel company by selling insurance against his own henchmen causing damage or labor problems. Defense attorneys threw objection after objection. The trial ended with a hung jury.

Within a few days, evidence of tampering emerged. Chuck Amata was charged. Apparently Birns was not in on the fix, and he was hot at his pal Chuck.

"I don't want to tell you how to run your jail," he told the chief deputy sheriff. "But don't put that dumb dago in here with me. You'll have some trouble if you do."

Amata was tried and convicted of jury tampering.

In January 1950, Birns was released on bond for the retrial on the bombing of Joe Allen's car. In the second trial, an alert Al Sutton knew something was amiss. He observed an attractive young blonde swish into the courtroom. She was the type that turns heads. But some heads didn't turn. Namely those belonging to Birns, Amata, Artwell, Lonardo, and Satulla.

After court adjourned, Sutton brought the mysterious blonde girl in for questioning. It was Shondor's tender companion Vickie Kanesic. And it didn't take long. Threats of imprisonment brought near hysterics and talk of suicide. She agreed to testify against Birns.

Wearing a green silk blouse and accented with a brown-and-green print scarf, the teen described how her relationship with Birns had begun.

"I would spend time with Shondor in the Alhambra office," Vickie recalled from the witness chair.

She spoke of how Birns took her out to other nightclubs, including black and tans where whites and blacks mixed openly, and on a weekend getaway to Chicago.

Influential contacts, she indicated, were a key part of Shondor's business.

"One patrolman, who often made passes at me, drank with Shondor in the office night after night," Kanesic said. "And the drinks were always free. Shondor would call a certain police lieutenant when he needed a favor. And he knew plenty of social figures who he could call and say 'get going' to help."

Al Sutton's suspicions were correct. Vickie Kanesic had been used in a plot to influence the outcome of the jury. She explained how, in a bait-with-sex scheme, she telephoned a forty-seven-year-old single male and offered to meet him at a tavern for a date. He declined Kanesic's repeated invitations, so Birns's friends dropped the bait deeper. They drove her in Shondor's car to the juror's home and dropped her off at the front door. Already rattled by the phone calls, the juror was panic-stricken as the cream-colored Cadillac slowly circled the block. He hid in a back room while family members spoke with Vickie and ultimately convinced her to depart.

Vickie, too, was unnerved as her testimony ended and the trial concluded. With witness testimony from the first trial and the addition of Kanesic, the state's case appeared solid. When the bailiff read the verdict, the courtroom erupted in shouts and cheers. Not guilty. Judge Joseph H. Silbert was stone-faced as he rapped for order. He thanked and dismissed the jury.

Birns and the others and their attorneys were elated. Decked with smiles, they filed out and posed for photographers. Newspaper reporters scrambled for comments. Well-wishers congratulated Birns.

Attorney Galen shook hands with a female juror. "If you ever come to Los Angeles, I'll show you the town," he told her.

The verdict vexed Safety Director Sutton and Deputy Inspector McArthur.

"If they think this means a green light, watch us turn that light red," declared Sutton. "We've only lost a battle, not the war."

"Go ahead, give them the keys to the city," McArthur told reporters. "They've got carte blanche. That's the way twelve good citizens of the community want it."

Reporters sought out the former defendants, but only Birns would speak to them.

"I'm happy," he said. "I'm going to keep my nose clean too."

Silbert ordered a contempt of court summons served on Birns for trying to influence a juror. He had already left the court building, so Sheriff Sweeney started looking for him.

Meanwhile, eighteen-year-old Vickie's disloyalty to Shondor weighed on her. She was in near hysterics as police officers escorted her out of the courtroom. To hide her from news cameras, they covered her with a men's camel hair coat and drove her home.

The next day, Sheriff Sweeney still had not located Birns. The following day, his telephone rang. It was Birns. He told Sweeney that he heard he was looking for him. Shondor said he was broke and had gone to Chicago to borrow money and rest. The sheriff informed him of Silbert's summons. Birns telephoned the judge at home.

"Judge Silbert, this is Shondor. I'm in Chicago."

Birns told the judge that his new attorney said he had to appear in court the following week to answer the charge. Silbert explained that Birns had to be served with the summons in person.

"I'll come back whenever you want me to," Birns said.

The judge instructed him to return the following day.

"I'm satisfied it was an honest misunderstanding," Silbert later told a reporter.

Several days later, at the contempt hearing, Judge Silbert rebuked Birns. This was even as evidence was developing that Birns may have tried to influence a second juror.

"Your attempt to sway a juror using that young woman was a brazen and corrupt act," he said.

Silbert found Birns guilty of contempt of court and smacked Shondor with a $1,000 fine and six months in jail. Lawyer Frank Azzarello asked for bail and postponement of sentencing.

"Go to the Court of Appeals," Silbert told the attorney.

Deputies escorted Birns up to the jail floor where he had served the final four months of his sentence for slugging a cop.

Six months was a record long sentence for contempt of court. Birns wasn't happy. He proposed a deal to the judge. In exchange for his immediate freedom, Shondor offered to move out of Ohio for ten years and return only occasionally to visit his mother. When Silbert refused the offer, Birns penned an angry letter. He wrote that the sentence was illegal and he would continue to appeal. He suggested that an appeal victory would make the judge "lower in reputation."

There was no appeal victory for Shondor Birns. The higher courts ruled that Silbert had a right to protect his administration of justice and that the six-month sentence was not unreasonable. Shondor spent the summer and fall of 1950 in jail socializing, playing cards, receiving visitors, and contemplating his next move.

CHAPTER FIVE

Naturally they would want to question the man dubbed Public Enemy Number One. So it was that in January 1951, the US Senate's newly formed Special Committee on Organized Crime in Interstate Commerce subpoenaed Alex Shondor Birns. Chaired by Senator Estes Kefauver from Tennessee, the committee traveled to numerous big cities, seeking testimony and business records of powerful mob figures active in gambling, extortion, and labor racketeering. The Kefauver hearings were a sensation on television, which was rapidly gaining popularity in American homes. The inquiry served as the basis for the Senate hearing scene in *The Godfather Part II* film.

In Cleveland, officials like Al Sutton were called to testify to the history of organized crime in northeast Ohio, and regional connections to the national crime syndicate. For their investigation, the Kefauver Committee subpoenaed Birns, Moe Dalitz, Morrie Kleinman, Frank Brancato, Tony Milano, and numerous others. Shondor had no intention of being grilled in a televised setting. Like most of the others called, he failed to appear. Birns, however, reluctantly complied with a records request and provided a few files from the Alhambra. It was the documents he left out that piqued the curiosity of the senators. As a result of questions they raised, state liquor officials and the US Internal Revenue Service began an investigation into Shondor's role at the Alhambra.

Doan Realty officials denied in their testimony that Birns was in charge at the Alhambra. On the contrary, they claimed, he was simply an indispensable public relations expert who brought in customers for banquets. Several police officers countered that Birns was indeed boss man at the restaurant, and as a result, state officials yanked the Alhambra's liquor license. In a subsequent legal shuffling of corporate structure, the Alhambra's name was altered, and Birns was hired by the new entity. When the bar section went bankrupt, an attorney purchased it, renamed it, and testified that Birns had no affiliation with the lounge.

Shondor's future at the restaurant, however, was not his problem. It was his past. For the federal order of deportation that had so far been unsuccessful in removing the career criminal from the country gained a new twist when Cleveland Mayor Anthony Celebrezze issued his own edict against Birns. Known as "the little deportation order," the mayor's directive ordered police to arrest Birns anytime he entered the city limits. Suddenly it was a good time for Shondor to take a vacation. He got travel permission and flew to Florida, where he toyed with the idea of partnering in a Miami barbecue restaurant.

By the fall of 1951, Birns was back home. He was regularly seen in the company of a gorgeous model named Jane Collins. She was twenty-two—twenty-three years his junior. The couple was often seen cruising about town in Shondor's new $4,600 cream-colored Cadillac. Questioned by a reporter about the young beauty, Shondor confirmed his engagement to Jane.

"This will make a new man of me. I'm going to work for a living," Shondor said.

Jane's parents objected. In 1952 he took Jane to Florida, and they married secretly.

When they returned home, IRS officials seized Shondor's Cadillac. The confiscation and auctioning of cars was part of an effort aimed at gamblers and racketeers who owed federal taxes. Shondor showed up at the auction with a lawyer who started bidding on the Cadillac. When some of the other buyers saw what Shondor was trying to do, they shouted, "Let him have his car back." The crowd acquiesced. His attorney purchased the car for fifty dollars. But if Shondor thought he'd pulled one over on the revenuers, his gloating wouldn't last long. As he enjoyed his reclaimed machine, the IRS had tasked a very capable investigator with digging into Birns's finances.

In 1953, Shondor became a father when Jane gave birth to a red-haired boy that they named Michael. Shondor's income tax headaches were born that same year when a federal grand jury indicted him for fraud. The charge was the scourge of many a racketeer who failed to declare their income and pay federal taxes. It brought down Chicago's Al Capone and New York's Frank Costello. The true bill alleged that between 1947 and 1950, Shondor earned $105,400 but reported only $24,400. Additionally, he was accused of taking $45,000 in skim—cash stolen or "skimmed off the top" of the Alhambra's receipts—before they were tallied as taxable income. He was arrested. After posting his bond and getting released, Birns took his wife and son to Florida. He considered relocating there but decided to continue calling Cleveland home. He returned to plenty of heat.

Police Deputy Inspector Richard Wagner had reports that Shondor established himself as a "peacemaker" in the East 105th Street and Euclid Avenue area. He was offering "protection" services to business owners whose places were being vandalized. After the Play Bar and Towne Casino were bombed, Wagner warned Birns that he would be arrested every time he was seen in his district.

"It's my feeling that you can't and won't make a legitimate living," Wagner told Birns. "And I'll have you make no other kind of living in this district. Only one of us can be in charge of this area and it won't be you."

Mayor Celebrezze had had enough.

"I want you to use every legal means to drive that man out of the city," he told Chief Frank Story. "His arrogance, his utter contempt of the rights of others and his flouting of the laws of this community will not be tolerated by this administration."

Police Chief Frank Story called Shondor into his office and banished him from the city.

"If you want to come into Cleveland to see your attorney, you will not be arrested," Story told Birns. "However you must clear the trip with me or Deputy Inspector Wagner."

A reporter asked Birns for a comment.

"I could go to work tomorrow if the police would quit harassing me and the people who might hire me," Shondor said. "I've been arrested and released without charges already six times this year. If they see me, they'll pinch me."

Birns said two restaurant equipment companies offered him employment.

"The police run in and want to check me out. It's been an embarrassment and I can't accept any of the offers."

Meanwhile, IRS Agent Leo Baumgartner completed his audit of the Alhambra's books and Shondor's own records. A methodical man who rolled his own cigarettes, Baumgartner had spent three years painstakingly reviewing and reconciling canceled checks, ledgers, and statements—all of Shondor's business and personal finances. When the 1954 trial got underway, the daughter of the former police captain testified for Birns regarding $2,500.

"Shondor gave it to me in 1949 after we were engaged," Patricia Fleming O'Neill testified. "It was supposed to be a sort of nest egg for when we got married. But by 1951, we had called it quits."

US Attorney Sumner Canary tried to connect the money with the cash Birns skimmed weekly from the Alhambra. Birns's bookkeeper testified that she put money aside for Birns. Canary reviewed withdrawals recorded in the ledger.

"What did you do with the money?" Canary asked the bookkeeper.

"I put it in an envelope and put it in the safe for Mr. Birns," she answered.

The bookkeeper maintained that the cash was used for repayment of loans and business expenses. During the trial, it was also learned that Shondor was receiving weekly checks from an El Paso, Texas-based horse racing wire.

Birns was found guilty of evading taxes in 1948, 1949, and 1950. He was sentenced to three years in prison. It was one of the few times that Shondor was not only convicted of a crime but was also forthrightly shipped off to start his sentence.

In the federal penitentiary in Atlanta, Birns got a job in the records office. Later he worked in the prison library and the check room where clothing is issued to new prisoners. As usual, Shondor consistently earned credit for good behavior.

Meanwhile, a new era emerged in the gambling racket. It followed the 1954 death of old policy king Benny Mason and the tax evasion conviction and imprisonment of Joe Allen. Mason died in a car crash. Bets on the death number were high in the days following the news. When the number came out, many small operators took a big hit. Those who could not pay all winners in full lost their most valuable business asset—their reputation.

On the law enforcement side, Carl Delau was promoted to sergeant. He was assigned to the office of Safety Director Alvin Sutton, who tasked him with aggressively investigating gambling.

Other headaches festered from the inside. Most were related to the failure of all operators and workers to consistently follow certain standards, like payoff odds. Pickup men diverted bets to other operations that paid them a higher percentage. In some cases, they retained small bets themselves and passed along the bigger, riskier bets to their operators. And operators were increasingly having difficulty paying off on "bad" numbers (winning numbers that were heavily bet) without ready access to big cash loans.

As a result of increasing instability, conflicts raged. In the fall of 1955, the target was Arthur "Little Brother" Drake, recently released from the relative safety of prison. Someone wired a dynamite bomb to the ignition of his new Cadillac. But the next one to use the car was Drake's girlfriend. She was killed instantly in the explosion. Her passenger, the wife of Drake lieutenant Robert "Geech" Bell, was seriously injured.

Police hauled in dozens of racketeers for questioning but reached a dead end. They theorized that the attempt on Little Brother's life was by independent policy operators who had taken over while he was imprisoned.

While Shondor was imprisoned, he earned a credit of forty-seven days for good behavior. He was fifty when released in the fall of 1956.

Jane flew to Atlanta to greet him at the prison gate. A reporter was there, too, and Shondor, in typical fashion, was more than happy to be in the spotlight once again and get his picture in the papers. He was also undaunted by Jane's cool refusal to look at the press photographer as she walked on ahead, her back to the camera.

The reporter asked Shondor how he felt to be out, and offered him a Perfecto.

"It's like being born again," Shondor said while waving off the cigar. "No, thanks. I haven't smoked in eight months. I don't want to get into the habit."

Technically, Shondor was not free. He was under a deportation order to Czechoslovakia, within the borders of which his birth village was now located. The communist country, however, refused to accept him. A Washington, DC, newspaper wrote of Shondor's plight in an article titled "MAN WITHOUT A COUNTRY."

Birns's pal Frank Brancato was also under the threat of deportation. As with Shondor, it originated in the 1930s. When Brancato returned from a trip to Italy, it was determined that a 1932 perjury conviction forfeited his citizenship. Orders of deportation would be a lifelong legal battle for Brancato and Birns.

***

Shondor received friends at a party in honor of his release from prison—a tradition in the underworld. After buying a new wardrobe of expensive suits, blazers, double-knit pants, checkered dress shirts, and an alpine hat, he got back on the payroll of Union Towel Supply Company.

In 1956, Shondor moved Jane and three-year-old Michael from Lakeshore Boulevard in the suburb of Euclid to Judson Avenue on Cleveland's southeast side. Shondor purchased the newer brick three-bedroom ranch through a sister.

For protection while he was out, Shon bought a Doberman pinscher, a German military and police dog, and named it Fury. He had it professionally trained. This first dog led to Shondor's enjoyment of breeding Dobermans. Out of prison, with a new house and new car, all was good. And on the business side, a new opportunity was about to come his way.

Gambling racketeers were feeling the pressure from Sergeant Delau's mandate from Safety Director Sutton, and Birns associate and clearinghouse operator Edward Keeling recognized that something had to change. Keeling called a meeting with four other clearinghouse operators. The group was known as the "Big Five" and included Willie "Buckeye" Jackson and Donald "the Kid" King, who ran his numbers business and sports gambling book out of his record shop. They met at the home of attorney Charles Mosely.

The meeting opened with the men complaining about mutual problems, like access to cash to recover from bad numbers and increased heat from Sgt. Delau.

"We need to move out of Cleveland to get away from Delau and his crew," said Keeling. "We should set up in Geauga County."

"That's a good idea," said Buckeye Jackson.

The men grumbled about pickup men quitting while owing them money.

"We didn't put up with that in the old days," Buckeye said. "By the way, do you know Birns is out? He's operating again. We should get him on our side so he won't take business away from us. He'll keep the boys organized and in line."

The others liked Buckeye Jackson's idea. Shondor had a good reputation and was trusted in the black community, where many pronounced his name Shando. Mosely went into the dining room, telephoned Birns, and discussed the proposal. Shondor was amenable. He said he would make sure the other operators paid the same odds and the pickup men brought in their slips and money, and he would handle any disputes. He would also provide access to cash loans in case one of the operators got hit hard with winning bets.

After the phone call, Mosely returned. "Birns wants two hundred dollars a week each."

The men agreed. All clearinghouse operators would have to pay Birns a monthly fee. His services would provide stability, cash supply, and decreased heat from law enforcement. And that would increase profits.

The Big Five decided to consolidate their headquarters at a place called Locust Farm. Mosely was to make the arrangements. Locust Farm was a motel and resort used by black community and religious organizations for banquets and picnics. More importantly, it was in Geauga County, putting it outside the jurisdiction of the Cleveland PD.

The Big Five met again.

"Let's get up the two hundred dollars each so Shondor can start to work," Keeling said. "Let's tell all the others they've got to join. We'll make up a list of the others who don't go along. We'll give it to Shondor, and he will take care of them."

When Shondor's fees started coming in, he established a formidable team of "torpedoes," headed by Tommy Boyce. Boyce had a long history as an enforcer, though he had the ambition to go further. The others included Samson Powell, Elijah Abercrombie, Frank Cook, Fred Stitmon, and Billy Cox.

The Big Five reconvened. Attorney Mosely said he got the lease for Locust Farm. The discussion turned to several smaller clearinghouse operators who did not want to be part of the consolidation.

"We will break the arms, legs, and heads of everyone on the list who refused to go along," Buckeye Jackson said.

The list was sent to Birns. His henchmen attacked and beat two holdouts. Fred Stitmon fired several shots into another holdout's house.

The gambling combine quickly established the secluded headquarters, taking up six of the motel's twelve units and moving in their clerks and equipment. Locust Farm was a $40,000-a-day operation. It went as fast as it had come.

On an afternoon in October 1956, the electric adding machines were clacking away. Police officers from several jurisdictions burst in. They surprised fifteen clerks who were recording and tabulating thousands of bets. Geauga County sheriff's deputies were present, but leading the raid was Carl Delau. Technically the sergeant and his detectives were only observers, since they were out of their jurisdiction. They had located the gambling office by following a known pickup man.

A dozen cops searched the premises. They located hundreds of receipts and tally tapes and thousands of bet slips. The paper evidence and adding machines were seized by Geauga County Sheriff's Office deputies. Edward Keeling and eighteen office workers, runners, and pickup men were charged with gambling and eventually convicted and fined.

Not long after the Locust Farm convictions, Donald King cut his payment to Birns down to one hundred dollars per month. Then he quit paying altogether. Birns telephoned him several times then sent Tommy Boyce. King still didn't make a payment.

Birns threatened King by phone from Florida.

"I'm going to pay it," King said.

"I know you're going to pay me. I'm not worrying about you. I got ways of getting my money from people who owe me. I never worry about people paying me. I want some of that money by Friday."

King made a $200 payment, which was picked up by Elijah Abercrombie. The next month he refused to pay anything.

"I want my money," Birns told King. "If I don't get it, I'll send the boys out to get you."

Elijah Abercrombie warned King, "We'll break your arms. We'll break your legs. Then if you don't go along, we'll kill you."

Meanwhile, Tommy Boyce had been thinking about his role in the organization. He believed he was capable of more and made a bid to take over. He informed Donald King of his plans.

"You were supposed to be killed," Boyce told King. "Shando ordered it. I was watching you two nights ago. You were whistling.

But I'm taking over now. If the boys come around, send them to see me."

About a week later, Boyce was seated in his living room chair having an evening smoke. He was wearing fancy pajamas, and his feet rested on a hassock. He had a visitor. The assassin fired a single bullet into Bad Man's head. When police arrived, the cigarette Boyce had been smoking was dangling from his lips.

Donald King had reason to worry. He owed Shondor Birns money. About three weeks after Boyce was murdered, Donald and his neighbors awoke with a start. It sounded like a surprise clap of thunder. King's front porch and part of his living room were heavily damaged from the dynamite blast. More angry than fearful, he quickly telephoned Sgt. Delau at home.

"They were sore because I wouldn't go along and bring my odds down," King told Delau. "But I told them I wasn't operating no more."

When Chief Frank Story learned of Donald the Kid's call to Sgt. Delau, he was hopeful.

"For the first time we have someone who will cooperate in a bombing," he said. "Now maybe we can get somewhere."

As a result of Donald King's statement, Shondor Birns was arrested, as were Ed Keeling, Willie Jackson, Samson Powell, and Elijah Abercrombie.

Birns denied any connection to the numbers racket.

"I know nothing about them people," Birns said. "I don't want to talk about them. I don't want to think about them. I'm a linen salesman. I sell linens to hotels and restaurants. I went to bed early last night with a sore throat and a cold, and they haul me down here at 6:00 a.m."

Donald "the Kid" King agreed to testify. As a result, Birns started scaling down his operations to avoid detection. King was costing him money.

Four months after the bombing, a man waited for "the Kid" to leave his house. The man held a shotgun at the ready. King emerged and headed to his car. But he didn't back out of the garage. He retrieved some theater tickets from the vehicle and started walking back to his house. The gunman was impatient. He didn't want to wait for another opportunity. King was some fifty feet from him and walking away.

The boom of the single blast reverberated through the neighborhood. Donald King went down with numerous tiny pellets in his neck and the back of his head.

Apparently the gunman assumed he would get a closer shot. Had that been the case, the birdshot loaded in his gun would have caused a fatal wound. Instead, the distance from which King was shot saved his life. He survived to testify.

Donald King wasn't necessarily a nervous man, but his rate of speech on the witness stand approached full automatic. A newspaper reporter dubbed him "the Talker." The judge often instructed King to repeat his answers.

In the end, the jury hung.

The reporter asked Shondor if he was going to celebrate.

"What's there to celebrate? This stuff was different when I was single. Now that I've got a wife and son, I only care about them. I'm going home to my family. Where else is there to go?"

Ultimately, there was no retrial. Like many of Shondor's criminal cases, the charges were eventually dismissed.

But more heat was coming for Alex Shondor Birns and his ilk.

During the same year as the attempted murder of Donald King, dozens of powerful mobsters from across the US convened in Apalachin, New York, to discuss business. It was twenty-nine years after the 1928 Sicilian Mafia summit in Cleveland, and, as in 1928, cops crashed the party. Cleveland Mafia godfather John Scalish was arrested with underboss John DeMarco and almost sixty other crime bosses at the failed gathering.

As a result, J. Edgar Hoover developed the Top Hoodlum Program, in which FBI field offices were tasked with developing informants and other sources to penetrate the upper echelon of national organized crime leadership. A few years later, New York City mob soldier Joseph Valachi would testify for the US Senate. In that testimony, Valachi outed the secret organization, and the name *Mafia* became a household word. Federal efforts to learn about nationally organized crime gained traction. With that increased public attention and heat from the law, Scalish would limit his exposure to strong-arm tactics. He also halted the induction of official members into his relatively small organization.

In the meantime, the Internal Revenue Service continued to dog tax-dodging racketeers. Public enemy Shondor Birns was a prized target. After years of legal wrangling, Birns finally negotiated a settlement in 1958 in which he agreed "to owe" the US 75 percent of its $105,000 claim, or $78,750. He continued to shield property like his house and yet another new car, a 1958 black Cadillac Fleetwood, in the names of trusted friends and relatives.

Shondor wasted no time getting a clearinghouse operation back up and running. Meanwhile, the Drake bombing investigation faded. No additional attempts were made on Little Brother's life, but it mattered not. He died of natural causes. His lieutenant, Edward Keeling, inherited the operation, along with Drake's son, Richard.

Carl Delau was paying attention. On a summer day in 1958, he was surveilling Shondor's house. Ed Keeling visited then left. When Birns left his home, Delau and his partner followed him.

When Shondor noticed them, he started speeding around his neighborhood. When speeds reached fifty miles per hour, Delau pulled over Birns.

"I was just having some fun with you," Shondor said to Delau.

Delau wasn't amused. He arrested Birns and charged the fifty-year-old racketeer with speeding and running a stop sign.

Keeling had been seen at Shondor's house on other occasions.

"They'll bear plenty of watching," said Lt. Martin Cooney.

Shondor spent late 1958 and early 1959 in Los Angeles, perhaps to get away from all the watching. There he was in contact with old buddy Mickey Cohen. Shon's connections and knack for getting on the payroll of legit and not-so-legit companies extended even to California. Surveillance by the Los Angeles Police Department showed Birns as an employee of the Lee Shoe Store and of the 5-11 Club at 511 West Whittier in Montebello. By March, Shon was back in Cleveland. Perhaps he should have stayed in LA.

* * *

It was March 20, 1959. Shondor pulled into his driveway and parked outside the garage. He had just exited his car when through the afternoon quiet echoed a CRACK. Birns was momentarily stunned. The bullet struck the garage at the level of Birns's chest. Another few inches and Birns would be taking his last breaths.

A boy approached on his bicycle.

"What did you do, blow out your tire?" he asked Birns.

"No. I know a tire blowout when I hear it."

Shondor didn't call the police. Instead he left for Florida. He often left town when the streets got hot. But he always returned to take care of business.

And on the streets of Cleveland's eastside black neighborhoods, one ex-con was bragging that he squeezed one off at Shando. He was thirty-five-year-old Clarence V. "Sonny" Coleman. Coleman was reputed to be "bad," even "terrible," with a rifle.

Police theorized Coleman was challenging Birns for control of the numbers racket and Birns had cut Coleman off his payroll as an enforcer. Coleman, who served two terms for drug trafficking, was occasionally used as a numbers rackets enforcer. He was an associate of Fred Stitmon, one of Shondor's longtime soldiers.

Word of the near assassination of the city's number-one racketeer quickly reached Carl Delau. He was anxious to question Shon. Along with two detectives, Delau met with Birns as soon as he returned from Florida. Shondor said he was sure it was a rifle because of the sound.

"I don't want to make a report," Birns told Delau. "And I won't press charges if you find out who it was."

Shondor had his own plans for Coleman. Three weeks after the shooting, Birns was sipping a drink at the Mirror Show Bar. He saw Sonny Coleman walk in, make a phone call, then leave. Coleman walked a block to a friend's house. The friend wasn't home, so he walked back toward the Mirror. He noticed a two-tone Chevy parked in a dark section on the opposite side of the street. A tall black man, around thirty years old, exited the passenger side and walked diagonally across the street toward him. When the man reached Coleman, he pulled out a gun. He aimed at his chest and fired.

"I jumped high," Coleman later said. "If I hadn't, the first shot would have hit my chest. It hit my leg instead."

Coleman fell. He rolled quickly toward the corner of a building as the gunman took aim and fired again. Coleman struggled to his feet. He dove through the window of a nearby building to escape more bullets. Making himself a moving target helped. Out of five shots fired at him, Coleman was hit only twice. The gunman turned to flee.

Coleman looked, and now the Chevy was on his side of the street under a streetlight. He thought he noticed Shondor in the driver's seat. When his attacker opened the passenger door, the dome light fully illuminated Birns's face.

Police arrived on the scene.

"Go check Shondor Birns and ask what his alibi is this time," Coleman said. "I'm surprised he drove away without making sure his victim was dead."

Shondor was arrested and questioned. He claimed he was home watching the Jack Paar show when Coleman was shot. He did admit that he'd stopped at the Mirror Show Bar for a drink after the show. The police held him overnight.

When he was released in the morning, news photographers gathered as he emerged from an elevator in Central Police Station. Shon hid his face with a handkerchief.

"You guys got nine thousand of these already," he told the cameramen. "Why take a picture when a guy's been in jail all night?"

Police theorized that Birns had brought in an out-of-towner who was unfamiliar with Sonny Coleman, and therefore Shondor had to identify him. Later, in a surprise about-face, Coleman refused to identify Birns. It was another acquittal and another example of Shondor Birns's experience in using various strategies, in this case intimidation and threats, to improve his odds in court.

Carl Delau was bitter at the failed prosecution.

"It's entirely possible that one of these days he'll push his luck too far with some of the people he runs with. There is as much chance of someone shooting him as there is Sonny Coleman getting hurt again. Shondor Birns was never the top dog out there. Most policy men consider him a crumbum who never was the top dog out there."

Delau liked to piss off Birns. He would say it got him talking faster than he could think. And Shondor usually took the bait. The next time their paths crossed, Birns faced off with his nemesis.

"You got it wrong, Carl. It's you who's pushing his luck."

"Are you threatening me, Shon?" Delau said. "I'll give you my address if you want it. But if you ever come prowling around my home and I catch you, they'll carry your body back across the river in a hearse."

Near the close of that same year, in December 1959, Shondor was in Miami again, perhaps to stay out of Delau's way. Instead, he found another sort of trouble. It came in the form of portly Dominick Edward Bartone.

Known to the FBI as an international dealer of weapons, much of Bartone's income came from combining his reputation as a gun-toting associate of the Mafia, a bully, and a con man. Utilizing shell corporations, Bartone obtained business loans for his personal use. He traveled frequently and muscled his way into businesses before draining them. He rarely paid debts from loans, credit cards, and hotel bills. Most of his ventures went bankrupt.

Bartone's associates included Tampa mob boss Santo Trafficante Jr. and Jack Ruby, killer of Lee Harvey Oswald, who was arrested for assassinating President John F. Kennedy. In Cleveland, Bartone was also close with Babe Triscaro, the president of Teamsters Local 436, Mafia associate, and lieutenant of national Teamster boss Jimmy Hoffa.

Bartone and Birns were involved in a plot to sell military airplanes and weapons to the Dominican Republic for ultimate destination to Cuba. They weren't the only underworld figures looking for a piece of that pie. Various schemes to sell arms to Cuba occurred in the late 1950s when Fidel Castro was progressing in his attempts to overthrow Fulgencio Batista. Under Batista, Meyer Lansky, Santo Trafficante Jr., and other powerful US organized crime figures and Cuban officials enjoyed a lucrative casino partnership. Regardless of who ruled in Cuba, Mafia bosses and their associates wanted that arrangement to remain intact.

Dominick Bartone's connection in Cuba was William Alexander Morgan. Originally from Toledo, Ohio, Morgan became a high-ranking freedom fighter for Cuba under Castro. Bartone used several companies as vehicles for the sales of arms to Cuba. They included Akros Dynamics in Cleveland. Akros was founded in 1957 to purchase eleven surplus Globemaster C-74 heavy cargo airplanes from the United States Air Force then rehabilitate them for resale for use in the Cuban revolution. The frontman for Akros was Alvin Naiman, who would become Birns's partner in the Ontario Stone Company. Shondor was also invested in Akros. And he stood to make a bundle.

In December 1959, while in Miami, Birns was with Cuban partners and decided to take a drive to see two of the aircraft. They stopped for cocktails. As they finished their drinks, it started raining heavily, so they decided against the trip. The decision was fortuitous. US Customs officers had two of the planes under surveillance. When another group, including Bartone, showed up at the airport, they were arrested. Customs officers seized the aircraft and loads of firearms, including seventeen machine guns.

Birns later told a friend, "By the grace of God, I didn't go, or I would have been arrested too. I'm staying out of Miami until the heat is off."

Back in Cleveland, Birns's connection to the Miami arrests was disclosed in newspapers. A Cleveland police officer stopped him on the street and asked if he was concerned about Bartone's case.

"We're not worried a bit," Shondor said.

Bartone and two others were eventually convicted, fined, and sentenced to probation for attempting to bribe the Customs officers to allow the plane and its cargo to depart for anti-Castro forces in the Dominican Republic.

Alex Birns in his first Cleveland Police mug shot.
(Photo credit: Cleveland Police)

Maxie Diamond, notorious Prohibition-era Jewish mobster, head of the Woodland Avenue and East 55th Street gang, and mentor to young Shondor Birns.

(Photo credit: Cleveland Public Library Photo Collection)

Rufus Jones and Buster Matthews, two of Cleveland's earliest and most notable policy operators.

(Photo credit: Cleveland Police & Bill Riedthaler)

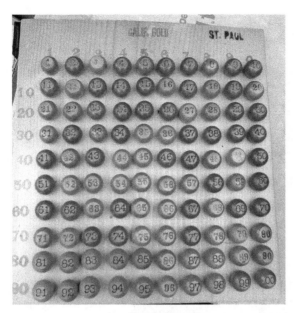

A policy ball set.
(Photo credit: Bill Riedthaler)

THE GREAT DIVINE DREAM BOOK

Animals—To dream of animals is a sign of good fortune—105.

Apples—To dream of apples indicates success and food fortune—297.

Ark—To see an ark in your dreams is a good omen, foretells all your hopes and ambitions will be fulfilled—001.

Arm-chair—To dream of sitting in an arm-chair indicates, contentment and riches for you—769.
To dream your husband or lover is with you in an arm chair indicates smooth flattery and deceit—328.

Army—To dream of an army indicates trouble with your friends—898.

Attic Room—To dream you are in the attic is a sign of trouble regarding money matters—050.

Automobile—To dream of riding in one indicates you are not contented with conditions—405.

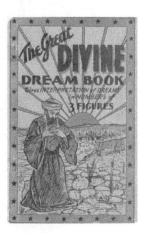

Many gamblers believed winning numbers came to them in dreams or visions. Dream books associated subjects, for example babies, death or flying, with numbers.

(Photo credit: Author's collection)

Benny Mason, Cleveland's first major policy operator.

(Photo credit: Cleveland Press photo)

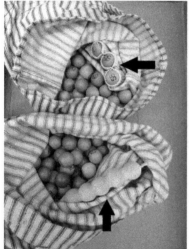

Policy drawing cheat bags. The top bag has concealed "fingers" and the bottom one has a hidden sleeve. Balls could be pre-placed in a desired outcome inside the fingers or sleeve and pulled in front of unsuspecting observers.

(Photo credit: Bill Riedthaler)

Alex Shondor Birns in an early Pittsburgh Police mug shot. (Photo credit: Cleveland State University Press Collection).

Young Frank Brancato, Mafia triggerman, sugar war survivor, and pal of Shondor Birns.

(Photo credit: Cleveland Police)

Angelo Sciria, Mayfield Road mob member who, with his cousin Angelo Lonardo, extorted a percentage of profits from policy gambling operators.

(Photo credit: Cleveland Police Museum)

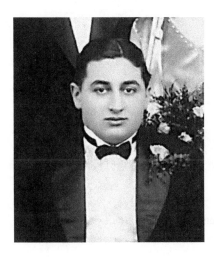

Angelo A. Lonardo was only 18 when he avenged his father's murder in 1929 and joined the Mayfield Road mob. Eventually he would became a key member of the Cleveland Mafia.

(Photo credit: Author's collection)

Gang leader Maxie Diamond, (right), his lieutenant, Phil Gold-berg, and crew members are led off to prison in 1937.

(Photo credit: Cleveland Public Library Photo Collection)

Shondor's enemy alien internment fingerprint card during WWII.

(Photo credit: U.S. National Archives and Records Administration)

Frank Hoge, key figure in a Mafia-backed operation that extorted a percentage of profits from numbers racketeers, is flanked by associates. Left to right: Charles Lardomita, Dominic Sciria, Hoge, Neal Palatrone, and Fred T. LaRocco.

(Photo credit: Cleveland Police)

Safety Director Al Sutton, (left), questions Willie Hoge, lieutenant to his brother Frank Hoge.

(Photo credit: Cleveland Police Museum)

Cleveland Safety Director Alvin Sutton testifying at the Kefauver Committee senate hearings.

(Photo credit: Cleveland Police Museum)

Shondor in jail in 1950, with no pants, and no privacy—which doesn't appear to bother him.

(Photo credit: Cleveland State University Press Collection).

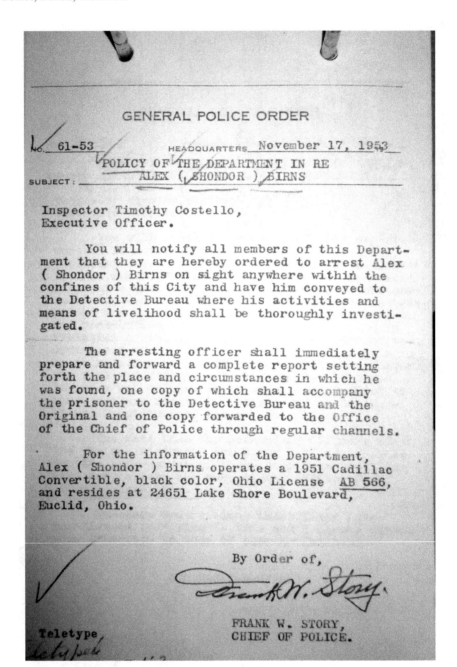

The "little deportation order" banning Shondor from Cleveland.
(Photo credit: Bill Riedthaler)

Shondor leaves Chief Frank Story's office after being banished from the City of Cleveland in 1953.

(Photo credit: Cleveland State University Press Collection)

Smiling Shondor tries to keep in lockstep behind a uniformed officer in order to hide from photographers.

(Photo credit: Author's collection)

Numbers boss Arthur "Little Brother" Drake, a close associate of Shondor Birns.

(Photo credit: Alvin Sutton Collection)

Robert "Geech" Bell, lieutenant to Arthur Drake.

(Photo credit: Cleveland Police)

Richard Drake, son of numbers boss Arthur Drake, who grew close to Shondor Birns in later years.

(Photo credit: Gina Drake-Busch)

Alex Shondor Birns in 1942.

(Photo credit: Cleveland State University Press Collection)

Leaving prison in 1956, Shondor answers a reporter's questions as Jane Birns turns from the photographer.

(Photo credit: Author's collection)

Birns enforcer Elijah Abercrombie.
(Photo credit: Cleveland Police Dep)

Cleveland police officer Carl Delau interviews numbers racketeer Donald "the Kid" King after a bomb exploded on King's front porch.
(Photo credit: Cleveland Public Library Collection)

Shondor points to a hole in his garage. It was made by a bullet that narrowly missed him.
(Photo credit: Cleveland State University Press Collection)

DELTA	NEW. D&M	ORIGINAL GOLD-BOND
640	942	240
3	14	43
30	59	65
2	71	35
55	11	15
68	51	34
70	58	77
53	47	69
42	27	72
14	43	67
21	73	6
66	13	4
18	36	32

Policy drawing result slips.
(Photo credit: Bill Riedthaler)

Clarence "Sonny" Coleman, believed to have fired a rifle at Birns.
(Photo credit: Cleveland Police Dept)

Joe Allen, a major umbers operator.
(Photo credit: Cleveland Police / Bill Riedthaler)

Three of the ranking lawmen who put heat on Shondor Birns and other racketeers during the 1940s and 1950s: Michael Blackwell, Alvin Sutton and Frank Story.
(Photo credit: Cleveland Police Museum)

Numbers boss Willie "Buckeye" Jackson.
(Photo credit: Alvin Sutton Collection)

Shondor and former co-defendants are elated as they pose with their lawyers immediately after their 1950 acquittal in the bombing of Joe Allen's house and car, and the alleged attempt to extort a percentage of his numbers business. Left to right: Attorney Henry Galen, Angelo A. Lonardo, Shondor Birns, Attorney J. Frank Azzarello, Joe Artwell, Attorney Fred Garmone, Nick Satulla, Attorney Edward G. Stanton, Charles B. Amata.
(Photo credit: Author's collection)

PART 2

Bombs, Bullets, and Bribes

CHAPTER SIX

Paying his defense attorneys in the King and Coleman cases cost Shon a great deal of his business. He was able to collect what he was owed, then he temporarily shut down his numbers operation in 1960. While on one of his many trips to South Florida, he visited with his friend George Gordon.

"Born George C. Burslem, Gordon worked in the syndicate's first gambling joints," wrote author Hank Messick. "Gordon was a front man for Moe Dalitz, Morrie Kleinman, Lou Rothkopf, and Sam Tucker."

Birns discussed his situation in Cleveland with Gordon.

"I can go back in anytime, Georgie," Shondor said. "Just last week when 7-6-9 fell, I started getting calls. They were looking for cash to stay in business. 'Please come back up here,' they told me. I can't make no money with what I was bringing in. With the ice for the coppers, the Rams—you know how much I can lose playing them— and my Pinschers, I couldn't keep it up. The coppers from headquarters came for their money every weekend."

"You might as well stay out of the business, Shon," Gordon said. "They're gonna raise hell with you."

"If I'm not there, they come to my house at one and two o'clock in the morning and rap on my fucking door wanting money. Then the district cops start coming out. They're not even doing anything to help me! But they rap on my door."

"Stay out of it, Shon. They're gonna shake you down. You ain't gonna overcome everything."

Shondor stayed in it and hustled for multiple streams of income. Still on the payroll of Union Towel and Supply as a salesman, he also had a percentage of a gambling operation in Havana. And he was always hustling for a good time. He still liked his paramours youthful and had been seen recently in the company of a twenty-year-old who was apparently bored with her husband. Shon also liked black women. His lawyer, James Willis, a well-known black defense attorney, knew firsthand.

"I was going with my girl to see the Kentucky Derby in my hometown of Louisville," recalled Willis. "Shon was involved with a black girl. He asked if I would let her come along with us, and of course I said yes. He gave her money so she could have her own room and bet the horses. He didn't want the kind of fanfare to take her himself. He was married and wouldn't gamble with having their photo in the newspaper. He just asked me to let her tag along, take her to the race and maybe some parties, and show her a good time."

Shondor spent much of his afternoons and evenings socializing and conducting quick business meetings. He enjoyed playing the horses at Thistledown Racetrack. And he could often be found at the Theatrical on storied Short Vincent Avenue, which was the hub of downtown's entertainment district.

"In its heyday, Short Vincent Avenue was Cleveland's Rush Street, Bourbon Street, and Broadway rolled into one," said Theatrical maître d' Morrie Fisher.

Birns's fellow Mayfield Road mob member, Big Ange Lonardo, operated the Tastee Barbecue and Frolics Bar on Vincent. But the anchor on the block was the venerable Theatrical Bar and Grille, its name emblazoned in gigantic letters on a looming block-like facade that was impossible to ignore. There, Mushy Wexler served fine meals to well-to-do tourists, suburbanites, sports celebrities, and colorfully monikered bookies, loan sharks, and gamblers like Charles "Fuzzy" Lakis, Abraham "Honest Yockim" Rabinovitz, and James "Jimmy Z" Zimmerman.

"And there was a higher echelon of crime . . . that mingled with judges, prosecutors and police," wrote *Plain Dealer* reporter Brian Albrecht. "There was an almost unwritten agreement that affairs of the street did not apply in the Theatrical, as long as you behaved yourself."

That higher echelon of crime included Shondor Birns and of course, old pal Frank Brancato. The Theatrical's second string racketeers included Birns/Brancato apprentice and gutsy Irishman Danny Greene, and Mervin Gold, the con artist and admirer of Shondor.

Shondor's favorite table was a lone two-top next to the cigar counter, just inside the front entrance. Fifty-one stools made the Theatrical's oval-shaped bar the town's longest. Above the bar was the stage, anchored by a grand piano. When the club was hopping on weekend evenings—and it usually was—it could take up to five bartenders to keep the cocktails flowing for the crowd, the men in suits and ties and the women in dinner dresses. The air was a mélange of cologne and cigarette smoke, and the buzz of conversation and the clink of cutlery ran beneath the music of such nationally known jazz musicians as Jonah Jones, Gene Krupa, and Oscar Peterson.

There were tables along each long side of the Theatrical's bar. Near both short ends were sets of three steps leading to the elevated dining area. Employees referred to it as the terrace. Mushy's perch was at a back table, from which he could see most of the room. Danny Greene, when he stopped in, sat in the back corner for the same reason.

As Shon grew older, he needed younger blood. Danny John Patrick Greene looked up to the legendary racketeer and quickly became a notable figure in Birns's far-flung network of not-so-savory characters.

Danny's mother had died shortly after giving birth to him, and he was largely a product of the streets. He served as a US Marine then became a longshoreman. As a proud Irish-American, Danny fancied the color green and stories about Celtic warriors. As a dockworker and member of Local 1317 of the International Longshoreman's Union, he was charismatic and a convincing, if not disingenuous, speaker. His skills eventually won him the local's presidency.

The 1960s were the glory years for the Port of Cleveland. The Saint Lawrence Seaway opened in 1959 and brought immensely profitable overseas commerce to Ohio, seven other states, and two Canadian provinces. Cleveland spent $10 million to ready the waterfront.

As a control tactic, Danny utilized the controversial hiring hall method of doling out choice work assignments to the most loyal members. And with a crew of enforcers to quell dissent, he routed illegal payroll deductions to his own pocket.

Another one of Shondor's protégés had a different way of stealing money. It was 1960 when Birns met Mervin Gold. Shon was fifty-five. Merv was thirty, and he was interested in buying two nightclubs. He suggested the two become partners. Birns declined. In the weeks that followed, Gold asked him for advice about other investments.

"Nobody knows the bar and restaurant business like Shondor," Gold told an associate. "I would take his advice over anybody."

Shondor was likewise impressed with Mervin's financial smarts. He could be useful. The two became friends.

In the months that followed, Shondor and Mervin were frequently seen at Kornman's Restaurant on Short Vincent. They were members of the same health club and would play gin rummy for hours. Shondor made several loans from Gold totaling $20,000. During this time, Shondor introduced Mervin to Dominick Bartone. Like Birns, Bartone befriended Gold and used him for loans.

Shondor also introduced Mervin to Jerry Gold (no relation), a well-known criminal defense attorney with whom he had become friendly. Jerry asked Mervin what business he was in.

"I do what Shon does but with a pen," he replied.

Mervin was headquartered out of an office on the eighth floor of the Hippodrome building in downtown and employed a secretary. He moved his wife and two children to the affluent suburb of Pepper Pike, where their spacious home, with its immaculate façade and manicured shrubbery, was a picture of respectability on impressive Gates Mills Boulevard. The Golds enjoyed the services of a maid, and Mervin was able to take his family on a European vacation.

Mervin Gold was a fast-talking mix of connivance, arrogance, and chutzpah. His face had a boyish sort of charm and a puckish grin that won over many a potential mark. Success had come to him swiftly, but it was as phony as his handshake.

Mervin's career began when he left Ohio University after only a few classes to work at the National Credit Bureau. He lost his job due to "sloppy work and his antagonistic attitude." In 1951, he joined the US Navy and served almost two years. He returned to Cleveland and took a job as a taxi driver. Unable to afford an apartment, he moved into a local YMCA. When a former friend and high school classmate found out, he offered Gold a room in his home. Gold accepted the offer and stayed with his friend until he got a job as a salesman at a fire alarm system company owned by a Cleveland councilman.

Before Gold moved out, he borrowed $5,500 from his friend. He repaid the loan with a check. When it bounced, Gold would not make good, and the friendship quickly deteriorated. The man hired an attorney.

"My lawyer and I went to Mervin's office," the friend said. "He had invited us to come out to discuss the matter. Things became tense. Suddenly Mervin jumped up. He spit in my face and took a swing at me. We have not been friends since."

Gold was arrested and later pled guilty to assault. The man filed suit and recovered most of the money. The arrest wasn't Gold's first. Seven years earlier he had been charged with issuing a bad check for a car lease payment. And the civil suit was not his last.

On a blind date, Mervin met Leah Lipsyc, a compact woman with jet-black hair and sky-blue eyes. Born in Belgium, Leah had known great misfortune. When the Germans overran the country in 1940, they took her father away. Leah, her mother, and her brother moved numerous times to stay one step ahead of the Nazis. Despite the turmoil and interruptions to her schooling, Leah learned French, English, German, Yiddish, and Hebrew. She was also sheltered by a Catholic family.

"The Catholics were good to the Jews in Belgium," she said. "A priest renamed me Lily because he said Leah sounded too Jewish. To deceive the spies that were everywhere, he even pretended to give me communion. I used to go to sleep and not know who to pray to. It was a real dilemma. I settled by praying, 'God help me—and Jesus help me too.'"

After the war, Lily, the former Leah, was reunited with her mother and brother. They never again heard from the father. The three came to the US in 1950. Five years later, Lily met Mervin Lee Gold.

Lily saw good in Mervin. "Mervin had no money, no money at all," she recalled. "He had no overcoat. I remember because people ribbed him about that. But he gave me a charm for our first date. I was flabbergasted. And when we got home, he didn't even try to kiss me. When I married as far Mervin, I was queen every day. It was perfect and everything I could ask of a marriage."

Mervin Gold worked for a life insurance company then left to start his own business. It failed. But he took his knowledge of the credit, loan, and insurance industries and developed a knack for creating money on paper. It was a perpetual game of whack-a-mole. He often started by paying off a small loan from a victim, thus gaining his confidence. He borrowed money then used it as collateral for a loan from another source. He started small companies like Mervin L. Gold and Associates, a mortgage concern. He secretly gained control of their funds and then converted them to his personal use. A drugstore was among the businesses. And all along he was failing to declare his full income to the Internal Revenue Service.

A person familiar with the specifics of Gold's methods described them to a *Cleveland Press* reporter.

"If there were ten steps to a deal, you were only in on two. Mervin was eight steps ahead of you. He would send an employee to the bank to make a deposit. Then that person would have to call him back to find out what to do next. Gold might deposit $6,000 in a savings account and then use it as collateral to borrow $5,000. He would make a large deposit into a checking account then draw heavily on it. He kept several bank accounts—one in his name and several in the names of businesses."

On the surface, Gold was an insurance and securities broker. In reality, he was a financial manipulator—a swindler—a high finance shyster whose veneer of success lay in a maze of dealings in bonds, mortgages, loans, and other paper investments. He enjoyed playing the big shot and creating a cloud of mystery about his most significant "investments," especially those involving restaurants and other real estate.

***

Shondor Birns frequented the Castle Arms Restaurant, located near his house. The building looked like a castle, complete with turret.

There, Shondor met a twenty-one-year-old waitress with a fresh face and toothy smile. It was the summer of 1960, and Allene Grace "Ellie" Leonards, a second-grade schoolteacher, was moonlighting during the school vacation. And she was charmed by the affable, big-tipping older man named Shondor.

Ellie was tall, with dark brown hair and brown eyes. She wore little makeup. Her father had recently died at age fifty-nine, and she lived with her mother in a suburban bungalow. A recent graduate of Ohio's Kent State University, Ellie had won trophies for bowling and softball. She was a member of Gamma Phi Beta, a sorority that helped underprivileged children. Ellie also was a member of Kent's Student Education Association, which conducted tours for prospective students and hosted lectures to improve education for young children and those with special needs.

Ellie's extracurricular activities suggest that educating children was something that interested her; it even may have been a calling. But if her choosing teaching as a profession was simply due to the limited career opportunities for women at that time, then it's a fair bet that she was unfulfilled. The attention of an older, generous and charismatic man would be an escape from boredom. Whatever the case, Allene Leonards was the last woman that one would imagine in a relationship with Shondor Birns.

The beginning of Shondor's relationship with Ellie coincided with his foray into the limestone supply business. Shondor partnered with businessman Al Naiman in the Ontario Stone Company, whose clients included the City of Cleveland. Naiman was also a sports promoter and operator of the swank Zephyr Lounge on the east side.

When Naiman had trouble finding space for gravel storage, Birns arranged a solution through Mickey McBride, who owed dock space on Whiskey Island, at the mouth of Lake Erie. McBride, a former gambling wire service owner and founder of the Cleveland Browns, had been a circulation manager when young Shon delivered newspapers. For brokering the deal, Shondor arranged for himself a monthly fee.

During this time, Shondor frequently took winter jaunts to Miami Beach. FBI agents occasionally saw him there with prominent mob figures, perhaps fishing or playing the horses at Gulfstream Park in Hallandale. IRS agents, focusing on Shondor's outstanding tax bill, watched him leave restaurants and stores then documented how much he spent.

Back in Cleveland, Ontario Stone Company fell into financial trouble. Babe Triscaro suggested that Al Naiman take on Dominick Bartone as a partner. Bartone purported to know the sand and gravel business. He said he could invest $150,000 immediately then obtain loans of $500,000 more. Desperate to make his payroll and settle outstanding vendor bills, Naiman agreed. It was a costly mistake.

His former bookkeeper summed up the situation.

"Shortly after Mr. Bartone came into the business, he assumed complete control. Within a matter of weeks, he somehow managed to make himself the only person authorized to draw any checks or drafts. Mr. Naiman was kept largely in the dark. I realize now that Dominick Bartone was a con man who happened to come along at a time when Alvin desperately needed financial help."

Bartone was loud, abrasive, and intimidating. On one occasion, Naiman had enough of his threats and forced him out of his office at gunpoint. Bartone continued to make enemies from Havana to Cleveland as he reneged on financial obligations.

"Many persons Bartone dealt with in Cuba wished he would return," said Bartone's erstwhile freedom fighter associate, William Morgan. "He would not get a pleasant welcome."

A few months after Shondor met Ellie, he separated from Jane. She moved to a home in Cleveland Heights with five-year-old Michael. Shondor continued to live in the house on Judson, where he utilized a cutting-edge electronic device that would answer incoming phone calls at his house when he was out and record the callers' messages.

During this time, Birns visited Gold's office almost daily, and the two would go out to lunch. Shon occasionally brought Mervin with him to Woodhill Builders, where for a short time, Shondor was on the payroll. Birns regularly stopped at a car wash near Woodhill. By now he was sporting a new pearl-gray Cadillac convertible. The young attendants looked forward to a big tip from Mr. Birns. They made sure to thoroughly scrub off the spatters of dried cigar spittle on the Caddy's bottom dashboard.

***

Mervin Gold's next venture was going to be a big one and provide an ongoing source of cash. The corporation would provide financing and advisory services to small businesses. Mervin would take advantage of federal funding provided through the recently established US Small Business Investment Company, overseen by the US Small Business Administration, and which would give loans to private companies, who in turn provided venture capital for investors.

Gold convinced six men to participate. They included his brother-in-law Nathan Lipsyc, a pharmacist.

"Mervin asked me to become a stockholder in a small business company," Lipsyc said. "He said I would be holding the stock for him. He claimed he was doing this because he wanted someone in the corporation he could trust. Mervin also stated that this company would be in a position to loan me funding for a drugstore I wanted to purchase. When I hesitated, he convinced my family that I was causing him trouble for no reason. They talked me into agreeing to enter the corporation."

Lawyer William H. Kahan recalled, "Mervin asked me if I would invest $25,000 in this company. I told him I did not have the money. He said he would loan it to me. He said if I wrote him a check, he would put the money in my account to cover it. I accepted and wrote him a check for $25,000. I knew he would have to deposit the money to my account or it would not clear."

Another investor expressed concern about not having experience with financial matters.

"You don't need experience because I'll be there to guide you," Mervin told him.

With $150,000 in checks in place, Gold started Cosmo—the Cosmopolitan Small Business Investment Company. Kahan was named vice president.

Mervin was to deposit the investors' checks on behalf of Cosmo. Instead, he visited acquaintance Bernie Schulist, president at Continental Bank, whom he had met through Kahan. With Schulist's help, Mervin opened two accounts in the name of "Mervin Gold, Trustee." He told Schulist to hold the checks but asked for a written confirmation of deposit. One of the Cosmo investors remembered Gold being "very pleased" when he received the confirmation letter.

Gold asked Schulist to notify him before putting each check through for payment. Gold also convinced Cosmo's treasurer to sign a batch of blank checks. Not long after, the partner expressed concern and wanted his name removed.

"Everything will be all right," Gold told him. "Don't worry."

Gold presented the investors with various forms, prodding them to affix their signatures. They signed a Small Business Administration (SBA) application, attesting that they had $150,000 in startup capital. Based on that amount, the SBA granted Cosmo a matching loan of $150,000, and the corporation was licensed. Gold cashed the SBA check. He took the money to Bernie Schulist and opened two more accounts in his own name.

From the outside, it looked as if Mervin Gold was a rising star in financial and commercial real estate circles. But his shady deals were already toppling. The IRS ran out of patience on $236,000 in unpaid taxes and penalties. They placed a lien on his house.

Gold needed cash. He called in the $20,000 he had loaned Birns. Shondor asked him to forgive the loans. Gold refused. Birns offered him a large number of government bearer bonds. Bearer bonds are unregistered securities with a stated rate of interest and date of maturity. Whoever held the now mostly outlawed investments collected interest by tearing off perforated coupons and submitting them for payment. The bonds Shondor offered Mervin were from Canada, and there was almost $1 million worth. The interest coupons were still attached, and they were past due.

Mervin accepted the bonds. He agreed that they would serve as security for the $20,000 that Shondor owed and for additional loans he would make. But Gold still needed cash. He visited a lawyer acquaintance and offered to sell him a bulging satchel of the bonds. The attorney sensed trouble and declined.

Mervin visited Bernie Schulist and applied for a loan of $20,000. As collateral, he provided a sheaf of the Canadian bearer bonds. The banker was pleased to have Gold's earlier deposit of $150,000. He was quick to approve the application, and Gold got his $20,000.

Gold's business with Continental Bank went well for a short time. Then he wrote several checks for more than he had in his account. After a $15,000 overdraft, Schulist called him in.

"We argued and Mervin became nasty," Schulist said. "I closed out the account."

Schulist continued to hold Gold's $20,000 loan that was secured by the Canadian bonds. It came due in June 1961. Gold failed to repay by the deadline. He offered $3,000. Schulist wanted payment in full. Gold said he had been sick and pleaded for more time.

Mervin Gold's financial situation continued to deteriorate. He was confident in his ability to stay one step ahead of everyone. First, he reported to the US State Department that he had accidentally thrown out his passport during housecleaning. They issued him a replacement. Then he put his house in his attorney's name. In early 1961, Mervin felt it important to document recent events. He started to type an affidavit.

"THE AFFIANT, being first duly sworn according to law deposes and says that his name is MERVIN L. GOLD; that on various occasions between November 1, 1960, and January 5, 1961, the affiant personally delivered or ordered the delivery of certain sums of cash in the aggregate of . . ."

Mervin completed the affidavit. He had his signature notarized. He made several copies, put them in envelopes, and gave one to Lily.

"If I ever don't return home, give this to the US district attorney," he told her.

"What is it?"

"You will be better off not to know."

***

May 1961 was not a good month for Shondor Birns. When he returned from a business trip to Pittsburgh, two Cleveland police detectives were waiting for him at the airport. They searched him and located $7,500, mostly in money orders. The funds were turned over to the Internal Revenue Service. They applied it toward Shon's tax lien balance.

Three days later, Birns was looking in on his numbers office. He sat in a comfortable chair and chatted with Ed Keeling. Four women were totaling bets. Suddenly the door burst open and three men rushed in. Birns rose quickly. He recognized the intruders—Carl Delau and two of his detectives. Delau and his men arrested the whole bunch, confiscated adding machines, typewriters, a phone amplifier, tabulating boards, and several hundred dollars in cash. It was an embarrassing moment for Shondor.

"Birns made a cardinal error," said Lt. Martin Cooney. "Never go near the tabulating headquarters. He is the last person in the world I thought my men would find there."

Birns was charged with a felony under Ohio's new and stricter state gambling law. But Cooney's celebration was short-lived. The search of the apartment was illegal, ruled Judge John V. Corrigan, because detectives had no search warrant. As with so many of his arrests, Birns walked. He was still Cleveland's own "most-arrested and least-convicted" racketeer.

***

Bernie Schulist had been unconcerned about Mervin Gold's outstanding $20,000 loan. After all, he had the bonds for collateral. But as the weeks went by, the bank president became suspicious that they were forgeries. He wrote to the Canadian bank of origin. Meanwhile, Mervin was working another angle.

The Gold residence was situated in a neighborhood of powerful men associated with the Cleveland Mafia. They included John DeMarco, N. Louis "Babe" Triscaro, Angelo Lonardo, Frank Embrescia, and mob boss John Scalish. And it was next to the home of Frank Visconti, the mobbed-up owner of Captain Frank's, a fabled downtown seafood eatery perched at the foot of the East 9th Street pier. Gold approached Visconti about partnering in a Miami Beach restaurant.

"Mervin met me in Miami," Visconti said. "We looked over the place—Sherie's on the 79th Street Causeway. We liked it. He told me to give him $5,000 in cash, and he'd put in $15,000 worth of bonds. Mervin occasionally talked about holding a large amount of bonds. When I asked him why he didn't want cash instead, he just smiled nervously. That man was always too nervous around me. I stalled for more time to consider the deal."

In the meantime, Lily became pregnant. And Mervin had a heart attack. He was hospitalized. Tests revealed that he suffered from heart disease. After three weeks, he was discharged. He telephoned Frank

Visconti and pressured him for money, ostensibly for the purchase of the Miami restaurant.

"Mervin wanted me to have my daughter draw $5,000 from the bank," Visconti said. "That's when I smelled a rat."

About the same time, Bernie Schulist received a reply regarding the bonds that Gold had posted as collateral. They had been stolen a few years earlier, when several bank burglaries in Ontario and Quebec resulted in the theft of approximately $2.25 million worth of bearer bonds. The hot bonds had filtered out of Canada through various underground networks, destined for organized crime figures in Chicago, Miami, Pittsburgh, and Cleveland to be converted to cash.

The collaborative efforts of the Royal Canadian Mounted Police and the FBI resulted in the indictments of several Mafia members. They included Norman "Roughhouse" Rothman, a mob figure and Cuban casino operator, and Sam Mannarino. Mannarino was a mob power in New Kensington, Pennsylvania, near Pittsburgh, and a business associate of Shondor Birns. Insurer Lloyds of London eventually paid off the owners then investigated to locate the remainder of the bonds. Some were found as far as Lebanon and Switzerland. Birns's involvement in the crime remained hidden. For now.

Bernie Schulist telephoned Gold. "Mr. Gold, your liberty is in jeopardy."

"What do you mean?"

"Those Canadian bonds are stolen," Schulist said.

"I got them the same way you did," Gold said. "I took them on a loan."

"Well, what are you going to do about it?"

"I need a little time to find the man I got them from," Gold said.

"This has got to be settled today."

"All right, I will settle it."

Around 2:30 p.m., Gold instructed his secretary to phone Schulist and tell him he would be at the bank at 4:30. Then he drove Lily and the children to Cleveland Hopkins International Airport. He wanted four one-way tickets for the next flight to New York City. Only three seats were available. Mervin sent Lily and the children ahead. He chartered a small private plane and met them in New York. From there they flew to Lisbon, Portugal, then to Italy. Mervin checked his family into the Hotel Excelsior in Naples.

A few days later, US Consulate officials summoned Gold to their office. They wanted him to voluntarily return to the US to talk to the FBI about the stolen bonds. Gold argued belligerently but finally agreed to return to the US. The consulate officers weren't convinced. They stamped Gold's passport "Valid for Return to U.S. Only." Gold predicted the move. Using the original passport that he had reported lost, he flew his family to Israel. He checked them into the Sheraton Hotel in Tel Aviv.

Gold was granted an entry visa. It was valid for six months. Then he applied for permanent citizenship under the Israeli "Law of Return," which gives any person of Jewish ancestry the right to settle in Israel. In his application, Gold wrote that he wanted to forget what had happened in the United States.

Back in the US, nobody forgot him. The FBI sought him for questioning about the stolen Canadian bonds. And his business associates brooded over the extent of their involvement in the whole Mervin Gold mess.

While Gold waited for a decision from the Israeli government, reporters pursued him for interviews. He dodged them when he could. When they accosted him, he was hostile. He moved his family from the Sheraton to a Tel Aviv apartment. When a newspaperman appeared at their door and displayed his identification, Mervin snatched it and slammed the door. The reporter called the police. They tried to talk Gold into returning the card, but he was defiant. The officers took him to police headquarters, where he finally relented.

Mervin Gold's situation continued to deteriorate. In Cleveland, a woman sued him for $450,000. She had turned over $300,000 in savings for Gold to invest. He'd assured her that he purchased stocks and real estate but instead converted the money to his personal use. The Internal Revenue Service seized his home toward recovery of $353,000 in back taxes. Cosmo officers filed a claim of $237,000 against Mervin. They alleged that he had taken all the assets of the Cosmopolitan Small Business Investment Company with him when he fled to Israel. Gold called the claim ridiculous.

"How much did I leave with? You can assume I left with some funds but just a reasonable amount," he told a reporter.

Federal agents believed Gold took with him as much as $800,000 worth of stolen bonds.

Under the weight of his battle for Israeli citizenship, dogged reporters, a US federal investigation into stolen Canadian bonds, lawsuits and liens back home, and a wife seven months pregnant, Gold suffered another heart attack. He was admitted to Tel Aviv's Assuta Hospital. When word reached Cleveland reporters, they tried contacting him. Hospital operators refused to put the calls through or even acknowledge that Gold was a patient.

The reporters persisted. A week later, one of them reached Lily. He asked why they had left the US. She said her husband had a heart attack and they wanted to take a vacation. When asked about his business affairs, Lily insisted she knew nothing. Meanwhile Mervin was treated for "coronary heart insufficiency" and prescribed an anticoagulant.

Israeli reporters pressed Minister of Internal Affairs Haim-Moshe Shapira for an official statement. Ironically, he happened to be in Canada.

"I am opposed to granting citizenship to persons of questionable character," Shapira said. "I will review Gold's case when I return to Jerusalem."

Two weeks later, a federal grand jury in the northern district of Ohio indicted Mervin for possessing and disposing of stolen bonds. US officials issued an arrest warrant and requested that Israeli authorities send Gold home. At the time, there was no extradition treaty between the two countries.

Amidst the turmoil, there was a period of joy for the Gold family. In early 1962, Lily Gold gave birth to a boy. Bad news followed. Haim-Moshe Shapira made his decision. He rejected Mervin Gold's application for citizenship. Mervin was given six weeks to leave Israel or face expulsion.

Back in the US, a federal grand jury probed Gold's activities in connection with Cosmo and the US Small Business Administration. Mervin retained an attorney and made his first press appearance in Tel Aviv. He denied any "formal knowledge" of the criminal charges against him in the US. "I want to stay in Israel because it is the land of my forefathers," he told reporters.

"And of your son," his attorney added.

Gold appealed Shapira's ruling. While awaiting a decision, he sent a letter back home to Judge Samuel Silbert of the Cuyahoga County Common Pleas Court. Writing that his case was misunderstood, Gold said he had left Cleveland because his wife was ill. Silbert expressed surprise at hearing from Gold, because he had no connection to or familiarity with the facts of the case. With no sympathy for the international fugitive, Judge Silbert sent a reply.

"If the facts are as you claim them to be, Mr. Gold, it seems to me you made a serious mistake in leaving the country so precipitously in seeking citizenship elsewhere," Silbert wrote. "Flight from the state where a crime has allegedly been committed is generally regarded as incriminating evidence since it tends to show a consciousness of guilt."

In April 1962, Haim-Moshe Shapira denied Gold's citizenship application because he was under indictment in the US. Gold hired a different attorney and filed another appeal. Based on information provided by Israeli police, the minister of the interior reaffirmed the decision. Apparently convinced he held a strong hand, Gold took his case to the Israeli High Court. He was either gambling to stay in Israel permanently or at least postponing his return to Cleveland.

***

In April 1962, a federal grand jury was assigned to investigate Cosmopolitan Small Business Investment Company and the loan obtained from the US Small Business Administration. Attorney William Kahan was a key witness. Kahan also happened to have grown up near Shondor Birns and was vice president of Executive Caterers, which was adjacent to the Executive Club where Shondor worked out.

When news of the grand jury investigation reached Mervin Gold in Israel, he fired off a letter to Kahan.

I have been advised of a rumor mingling our names with regard to your involvement in a matter which has recently come before the United States Grand Jury in and for the Northern District of Ohio. I know of no reason why the undersigned should be embroiled in any such allegations.

Very truly yours,

Signed Mervin L. Gold

In the spring of 1962, a federal grand jury issued indictments against Mervin Gold and six associates, including Gold's brother-in-law Nathan Lipsyc, attorney George Zimmerman, and businessman Leonard Luxenberg, for conspiracy to fraudulently obtain a federal loan. Kahan was listed as an unindicted co-conspirator in the complex case.

When Mervin Gold learned of the indictments, he telephoned Kahan and accused him of getting him in trouble. The attorney was furious when he realized he was paying for the international call and hung up on Gold. Amidst all of his problems, Mervin could still pull a fast one.

Mervin wrote to a Cleveland reporter, calling the allegations against him baseless. He said a group of his former business partners "got caught with their pants down." To describe his situation and send a message, he composed a humorous, albeit mysterious, allegory.

The sharks told the goldfish be nice, don't talk, do not sing, do not dance, and we will have our people release you from your contract to perform down at the Federal Courthouse this autumn. The sharks had a lot of muscle because they had a cousin who was a great big whale. Inasmuch as we are planning to stage a one-man spectacular, providing we can get the star out of God's country, if not we will just cancel the show.

Meanwhile, this writer decided to do a remote from the Promised Land, which infuriated the whale, who slapped the sharks, who tried eating the goldfish, however they camped on the whale's tail. Now the whale might have to eat the sharks. If I stay in the Promised Land, the goldfish will stop riding the whale and they will live happily ever after with the sharks and the whale. But if I return to Egypt, there are going to be a hell of a lot of dead fish and one damned sick whale!!!! Please be advised that I can authenticate the association of the goldfish and the epigamic attentions of Moby Dick toward our sometimes friends, the sharks. ("Epigamic" means attracting the opposite sex.) I shall await your reply with baited breath.

The pontificating swindler as the goldfish was apparent. The identity of the sharks and the whale, not so much. With Gold having become a convenient source of quick cash for Shondor Birns and Dominick Bartone, and then a liability for them, no doubt they figured in his cryptic message.

CHAPTER SEVEN

Mervin Gold remained confident that he would win his legal battle to become a citizen of Israel. In the meantime, he explored a business opportunity to rehabilitate a cotton spinning mill in the Southern District city of Kiryat Gat. The corporation started with American investors putting up $500,000 and obtaining a loan of $1 million from the Israeli Ministry of Trade. Due to poor management, the company lost money, and the Ministry of Trade threatened to foreclose. Gold proposed a deal to purchase the mill from the bank.

Rumors about Gold's offer reached Jewish businessmen in the US who had already invested large sums in the spinning mill. They protested vigorously and made inquiries demanding to know the details of Gold's offer. Some in that circle said that the failure of Israel to promptly extradite Gold was damaging relations with the US. Ultimately, Israeli bankers rejected Mervin's offer due to his unreasonable conditions.

In September 1962, Gold's efforts to flee his troubles fizzled. The Israeli Supreme Court denied his appeal for citizenship. (Ten years later, Jewish mob boss Meyer Lansky would also fail in his attempt to establish Israeli citizenship.) Ultimately, the case of Mervin L. Gold served as impetus for successful extradition treaty negotiations between the US and Israel.

In the meantime, Gold continued looking for a favorable angle from an illusory position of strength. He told American embassy officials that he would voluntarily appear at US Federal District Court in Cleveland provided he was not arrested upon arrival in New York City. The US attorney in Cleveland rejected the proposition, citing Gold's escape to Israel.

In October, Mervin Gold left Tel Aviv on TWA flight 801, bound for New York City's Idlewild Airport (later renamed JFK). There were stops in Athens and Rome then across the Atlantic. Passengers reported that Mervin was demanding of flight attendants. Lily was quiet as she tended to their restless children.

"When we arrive in New York," Mervin told her, "stay back, be the last one off. This way if I'm handcuffed, the girls won't see."

As the flight approached the US coast, dense fog caused its diversion north to Montreal where it landed. It was ironic. For two hours, Mervin Gold was beyond the legal reach of the United States while he sat on Canadian soil, from where the bearer bonds, at the root of his trouble, had been stolen.

When Mervin Gold finally arrived in New York City and stepped off the plane, three FBI agents placed him under arrest. News photographers fired away. Mervin, with manacled wrists, hid his face with a blue-black felt hat as he descended the Jetway. The US marshal who steered the former international fugitive down the steps, however, gazed directly at the press with a proud sort of half grin on his face. Lily, carrying her nine-month-old son and flanked by her daughters, trailed behind.

Mervin was booked into New York City's Federal House of Detention. The next day, he was arraigned on the bench warrants issued out of Cleveland. Mervin pleaded not guilty. The bond commissioner asked the attorney if Gold was going to waive a formal extradition hearing. Mervin started to speak in his typical rapid delivery.

Familiar with news coverage about Gold, the commissioner interrupted. "Don't you talk, Mr. Gold. You've done enough talking already. There is someone here to speak for you who can do better."

The commissioner set bond at a hefty $200,000. Gold's attorney objected. He argued that his client left the US before he was indicted and then returned voluntarily. That was after Gold had fought efforts to have him extradited from Israel, noted the US attorney. Gold's attorney said there was no basis for the high bond. He said his client would need medical treatment and drugs for his heart condition. The bond commissioner said Gold would receive proper medical attention at the Federal House of Detention. Gold was arraigned and waived an extradition hearing.

"This will blow up ten times as big once he is brought back to Cleveland," said someone familiar with Gold.

Back in Cleveland, Gold denied that he sought Israeli citizenship. "Israel has a law that any foreigner who stays more than three months must apply for temporary or permanent residence. I never intended to renounce my United States citizenship. I came back voluntarily when I learned the indictments had been returned against me. I had talked to officials of the American Embassy in Tel Aviv, and they would tell me nothing about the details of the charges. In fact, they had no official notice of what they contained."

Attorney Fred Garmone successfully argued for a 50 percent reduction in Gold's bond. Mervin was released and was then admitted to a hospital for additional treatment for his heart disorder. Shondor visited him several times, and they played gin rummy. When Mervin was discharged from the hospital, he granted a series of exclusive interviews to *Cleveland Press* reporter Forrest Allen. Mervin told Allen that he had returned from Israel on his own to see that justice was done.

"I wanted to come back and settle up," Gold said. "It's the only thing I could do. The persons really guilty of these charges will be exposed with the aid of federal authorities."

Gold would not reveal the names of those he thought were guilty.

Though his house was in foreclosure, Mervin was able to return to the home with his family. Most of the furnishings had been seized and sold off to settle legal actions brought against him by his business partners.

"I found my home gutted by my former friends and associates," he complained to Allen.

Gold went to work defending himself against various legal claims. He was defiant when contacting lawyers. "I am going to file a lawsuit charging conspiracy," he told one. "Tell your client he has a tiger by the tail."

Gold called bankers with whom he did business. He pressured them for the information they provided to investigators. One said the US Securities Exchange Commission had inquired about his accounts. Another said the Internal Revenue Service had made inquiries about Gold's holdings. Gold interrogated one bank official so long on the phone that the man cut him off.

"You are wasting my time, Mr. Gold."

"Let's have an understanding about time," Gold said. "My time is more valuable than yours, sir."

Forrest Allen said, "Gold would open a phone conversation all honey sweet. He would appear to be shocked at the first sign of non-cooperation. Then he would work up to a rage and a flowering of threats and bluffs."

After a court-appointed receiver sold his Cadillac, Gold spent hours trying to get copies of the paperwork.

"He had no sense of proportion," Allen said. "Mervin seemed to feel as strongly about losing his car as he did going to jail for many years over stolen bonds. He left little doubt in my mind that his close association with Shondor Birns involved the bonds. But he would never say to me that the bonds came to him from Birns. He kept insisting that several persons were involved."

**

While Mervin Gold was fending off allegations about his involvement in the stolen Canadian bonds, Shondor was fending off rumors about his income from the number rackets. In January 1963, he was back in Miami and visiting with George Gordon and Hymie Martin.

Portly Hymie Martin, called "Pittsburgh Hymie" in his early days, was known now as "Fat Hymie." Martin was under FBI surveillance as a major operator in the Miami bolita racket. Bolita, Spanish for "little balls," was the Cuban version of policy. According to author Hank Messick, Hymie was the operating director of the numbers racket in South Florida. He was bankrolled by Moe Dalitz, Morrie Kleinman and Sam Tucker.

Shondor, Hymie, and George had been friends since their early days. The three men were kibitzing when a hidden microphone caught Gordon asking Birns about a report from Cleveland mob members.

"They said you and Panz are getting a weekly fee from numbers operators," Gordon said.

"What kind of bullshit stories are you getting?" Shondor asked.

"Who's the talker?" Gordon asked Birns.

"Christ, now listen, George. That's Donald King, the colored guy I shot at that testified against me, goddamnit. Do I have to hear from that—let those guys move in. I'm getting tired of hearing that bullshit."

"I don't know him," Gordon said.

"They call him Donald the Kid. He's the guy that took the stand on me. Now listen—I don't want to hear about him."

"I'm not worrying about the colored guy," Gordon said. "I'm just telling you what the guy wanted me to go in there to straighten out. I said as long as you can do it with Shondor, you can't . . ."

Shondor continued his tirade and belittled his associates in the Cleveland Mafia, who were more concerned about his business than hustling for their own money.

"There is nobody there to straighten out," Birns said. "I had to shoot the guy to beat my case. Now you're going to tell me—where did you hear this bullshit?"

"This was quite a while ago," Gordon said. "Now don't go getting . . ."

"Who is sticking their nose—I get knocked and these guys worry what Shondor is doing. When Shondor is in trouble, they don't come to Shondor. Shondor helps himself."

"Listen to this guy, Hymie," Gordon said. "I can't even talk to him."

"I'm hot," Birns said. "I don't like to hear this fucking bullshit. They haven't got nothing around that goddamned town. Johnny and his top guys got the skim—easy money. The rest sit back, throw some cards, and ask, 'What's this guy doing, what's that guy doing?' In the meantime, I'm hustling nonstop. Next thing you know, they'll want to count my money. You tell them I got plenty of fucking money, George."

Shondor was referring to John Scalish in his comment about "Johnny and his top guys." The mob boss and his closest lieutenants, along with other top hoods in Chicago, Kansas City, and Milwaukee, enjoyed monthly deliveries of cash stolen from Las Vegas casinos. Scalish also had other earnings. He operated Buckeye Vending, along with his brother-in-law Milton "Maishe" Rockman and associate Frank Embrescia.

By having his own independent sources of income, John Scalish was less concerned with the viability of the Cleveland outfit. As older members died off, he was reluctant to induct new ones. He kept his trusted inner circle small, allowed certain underlings to operate without kicking up a percentage of their profits, and forbid certain activities. For example, when mob soldiers Eugene Ciasullo and Pasquale "Butchie" Cisternino wanted to organize sports bookmakers and enforce an operating fee, the answer was no. Scalish didn't want threats or violence bringing heat from the law. It was a style Shondor seldom avoided. As a result of Scalish's hands-off approach, the bookies, loan sharks, and other racketeers, like Tony Panzarella, operated independently.

Panzarella, known as "Tony Panz" was a respected member of the Cleveland mob and was once engaged to John Scalish's sister. "Had he married her," Shondor told an FBI agent, "he would have wielded more influence."

With Scalish having little interest in a mostly black racket, Panzarella was left to operate the numbers business as his own. He did so largely in alliance with Birns but was smart enough to attract far less attention from the law and the media than Birns.

Not long after Shondor's rant about the Cleveland mob, the FBI bug again caught Hymie Martin and George Gordon in Miami chatting with Birns about him losing money that had been loaned to him. Shondor emphasized that he paid his debt, even though he lost money. He spoke again of having threatened numbers operator Donald King, and a friendly cop giving him advice.

"Let me ask you another question," Shondor said. "Hymie, you don't have to answer this if you don't want to. Did I give you twenty thousand dollars? Was I stuck seven thousand? I grabbed this money from these people to bring it down to you. You know how I got the seven thousand dollars?"

"Tell me your story, Shon," Martin said.

"I grabbed King and told him, 'You cocksucker, you fuck my business up, and you fuck me up. I need my fucking money.' I says, 'You make me lose my money, I'll bust your fucking head.' He got scared and started running. I muscled the guy for the money and brought it down to Hymie. That's the truth. It wasn't given to me on no fucking silver platter."

"I wish I had known this earlier," Gordon said.

"He got scared," Shondor continued. "He said he was quitting and wasn't gonna get in no trouble. The next day I got a call from the copper. He said he got a request for two men to watch him. Copper said, 'They're scared of getting hurt. They're scared of you.' Copper told me if I want to do something, to take it out in the country. So I says OK. I wasn't going to go to that extreme."

Shondor had more to be concerned about than stale news about meddlesome associates. Mervin Gold's trial for possessing stolen bonds moved forward. The Cleveland FBI, knowing that Shondor associated with Mervin, decided to question Birns who was candid.

"Gold is no good," Birns said. "If he had any class whatsoever, he would take the rap and let the others off the hook."

"What about the stolen bonds?" the agent asked. "Do you have anything to do with them?

"I'm not going to comment about that," Birns said. " But it's my understanding Gold was specifically told he should burn them."

Prosecutors presented records showing the bonds had been stolen from Canadian banks. They called Gold's former secretary as a witness. She testified to seeing him wearing gray suede gloves and handling a large number of the securities.

When the trial ended, Gold was found guilty of possessing $55,000 worth of stolen bonds and using them as collateral to obtain bank loans. Before sentencing Gold, Judge Battisti asked him if he had anything to say.

"Only that when the trial started, I pleaded not guilty," Gold said. "And I still know that I am not guilty."

"I heard all the testimony, weighed it well, and found that you were guilty," Battisti countered.

Judge Battisti sentenced Gold to eight years and fined him $20,000. He allowed Gold to remain free on bond, pending completion of a presentence report. Mervin, sensing that he might be headed for prison, devised a plan. He prepared a document, made several copies, and sealed them in envelopes. He gave one to his wife.

Mervin called his conviction a railroading job. "They set out to pin it on me all alone," he told journalist Forrest Allen. "There wasn't anyone else they wanted. Why? Somebody was very happy to keep that figure down to $55,000—they'd settle for that. Then with me convicted, the whole stolen securities business could be swept under the rug."

Referring to the testimony of Gold's former secretary that Mervin was wearing gloves while handling bonds, Allen said, "I asked him if these were the stolen bonds. But his answer was typical Gold hyperbole and evasion. There were always generalities and confusion about important points but detailed memory on inconsequentials. Gold always fielded the tough questions from this or that 'posture.'"

"That was a long time ago," Gold told Allen. "At that time, I was handling hundreds of securities—stock certificates and bonds—all sorts of paper, so from this posture of being in the midst of complicated developments, I couldn't say what my secretary might have seen me counting in March 1961."

Allen asked Gold if he ever counted bonds or anything else in his office while wearing gray suede gloves.

"Now as to that, I don't know whether they were gray but there was a time along in there—the prescription will show the date, and I can produce it—I had skin trouble, and I would grease my hands and then wear gloves in the office. I can prove that with evidence."

Allen pressed Gold for answers to simple questions. "Did you ever count Canadian bonds, gloved or ungloved, in your office?"

"I am still in jeopardy in trials to come, and I can't answer that."

Allen asked Gold whether he got the bonds from Shondor Birns.

Gold said, "I testified that my secretary went to my attorney, George Zimmerman, in the Republican headquarters and got $34,000 worth of bonds that were pledged at Continental Bank."

"And where did Zimmerman get the bonds in the first place—from your office after you counted them with gloves on?" Allen asked.

"All I can say is this: someday it will all come out as to where the bonds came from."

"You know," Allen said to Gold, "there were uncashed interest coupons on these bonds that were past due. Didn't that indicate to you that somebody was afraid to submit them for cashing because he knew that the Canadian banks would sound an immediate alarm?"

"That just didn't occur to me," Gold said.

Allen said, "I asked Mervin if it was a coincidence that the period Shondor Birns practically became his shadow—March 1961 to the time he fled in August—was the same period the stolen Canadian bonds figured so prominently in his life. 'I considered Shondor Birns a friend—and an adviser on restaurant investments,' was the reply that didn't answer my question."

Three months after Mervin Gold's conviction on the stolen bonds case, his trial for manipulating the assets of Cosmo began. Merle

McCurdy prosecuted the case. He was appointed by President Kennedy and was the first black US attorney in the Northern District of Ohio.

Shondor's longtime lawyer, James Willis, defended Gold. In his opening statement, Willis said his client had left the country because of his health. "While he was gone, the officers of Cosmo, all experienced businessmen, blamed their business problems on Gold," Willis argued. "They made him a sacrificial lamb."

Shortly after the trial got underway, Mervin walked into Willis's office. Shondor was there discussing ways he might negotiate a settlement for his delinquent taxes. Mervin asked Birns whether he would take a message to one of the Cosmo officers.

"I told him I would only deliver it if he would put it in writing," Shondor later told an FBI agent. "I did that because Merv would say one thing and mean several others. He typed out a note promising to exonerate the individual for fifty thousand dollars. Mervin wanted me to hold the money until he carried out his promise. I delivered the note but said I was only acting as messenger."

As Gold's trial progressed, Mervin testified in his own defense. He pleaded victim status, claiming that he acted on the instructions of Cosmo's attorney and shareholders. "Everything I did at Cosmo was done at the direction of its officers and stockholders," he testified.

When questioned about the passport he had replaced, Gold said he thought it had been destroyed then later found it in his wife's luggage.

As the trial wound down in late May 1963, it took a bizarre turn. A juror asked to be excused from the case. She claimed she was ill. Halfway through deliberations, she commented to fellow jurors that she had already formed an opinion before entering the jury room. The vote was eleven to one for conviction, with her being the holdout.

Then the juror claimed she never took the oath when Judge Battisti swore her in. The jury foreman notified the bailiff. The eight-day trial quickly unraveled.

Judge Battisti called in the FBI and met with two agents in his chambers. He told them that Gold knew that the jury asked for a clarification of law while they were deliberating. Only Battisti and the jurors should have known this. Battisti believed that the juror had been influenced by Gold or an associate.

Battisti gave Gold the opportunity to let eleven jurors decide the case. Birns pressured him to do so. Holding out for his constitutional right to twelve jurors, Gold refused. The next morning, Battisti declared a mistrial. He ordered an investigation.

The FBI agents questioned the juror, who admitted raising her hand while the oath was administered but claimed she never actually took it. Judge Battisti ordered her arrested and charged her with contempt of court.

Jury tampering was a concern in any trial with Shondor Birns's interests at stake. The juror denied that anyone approached her to influence her service. During the contempt hearing, Judge Battisti pointed out the expense of holding a trial. He noted that she sat silently through eight days of testimony.

"You trifled with the court," Battisti told the juror. He sentenced her to one year in jail and set a date for Gold to be retried.

Gold went to Birns for attorney fees for the new trial. Birns refused.

"I already paid for the first trial. You should have let the eleven decide," Birns said.

Jim Willis was concerned he might not get paid in full. Then he heard Gold was talking about cutting a deal with the government. The attorney didn't want to defend Gold if it was part of a deal to implicate others, who might include Willis's clients. He told the court vehemently that he did not want to represent Gold any longer. Judge Battisti ordered the attorney to continue.

When the Cosmo retrial began, Gold stonewalled the prosecution. Judge Battisti had exhausted his patience in the first trial. He sent the jury out then laid into Gold. "I have had to conduct more examination in this case than any other that has come before," he snapped. "Now you listen to Mr. McCurdy's questions, and you answer them."

After one week, the trial ended. The jury found Gold guilty of three counts of misapplication of $44,000 in Cosmo funds. He was released on his existing bond, pending a presentence report. Jim Willis filed a motion for a new trial, arguing that Gold should have been tried in another jurisdiction because of the heavy news coverage. Judge Battisti denied the motion. Willis said he would appeal the conviction.

Shondor turned to lawyer Jerry Gold for an opinion.

"Do you think Mervin has a shot on appeal?" he asked.

"Ninety-nine percent of federal convictions stand on appeal, Shon."

"Well, this guy is dangerous."

Mervin Gold was indicted again—this time for obtaining the federal loan of $150,000 fraudulently. He was out of money to pay for his legal defense, so he called for repayment of some smaller outstanding loans. One of them was for $5,000 to Dominick Bartone. Bartone avoided Gold's calls.

Desperate to avoid prison, Gold telephoned Birns.

"Did you speak to that fat ex-friend of mine?"

"Now, just a minute," Birns said. "I'm getting photostatic copies of the liens and having them delivered, understand? He wants to pay the five, but he wants to talk a lawyer and get legal clearance, a guarantee that he won't get pulled into your IRS issues."

"He wants a guarantee? When I telephoned his lawyer, he wouldn't—he ducked out on me. And when I tried to get in touch with him in November, he ducked out on me. He's a lying no-good rotten bastard."

"Look, Merv, if you tell me what's wrong, we'll take one step at a time. I mean, eh, sure, he's no good in the first place, but you're nuts for lending him the money. You got yourself involved, so what do you want?"

"Why doesn't the no-good rotten bastard call me? I'll cut his heart out."

"Oh, well . . . I wouldn't talk like that. We want to get clearance from the legal thing so we don't get double jeopardy."

"There's no guarantee that he can have, none whatsoever," Mervin said. "He gets as much guarantee as I did when I went ahead and gave him the money."

Gold's biggest concern was continuing to pay for an attorney.

"I'll tell you what the situation is," he told Birns. "Your lawyer says point blank, I'm dropping you Monday unless I have my money."

"I'll call him at eleven thirty," Shondor said. "You be in the office. As a matter of fact, if necessary, I was just contemplating whether I ought to jump in there or not. I think the way you keep calling me, I'd better jump in and consider guaranteeing payment to him."

Birns then implied that Gold might have to serve some time if he got convicted.

"Now let me ask you another question as long as we are on the phone," Shondor said. "Now, say you go down in this case. You gotta go for an appeal, right?"

"Here's the way it is, Shon. I know what you're asking. If I go down on the case, yeah, we're going for an appeal, and the lawyer tells me the government has a tough case."

"All right. Just a minute," Birns said. "It's a question of getting money for the attorney? Now if you go down, if things go in reverse, then you've got to go down. Can you get some help for yourself on money?"

"I'm trying to help myself. But if I can't . . . if these rotten no-good bastards who owe me money and who are looking for me to go to the can so they don't have to—"

"Now, wait a minute, I don't want to hear that—" Birns started to counter.

"I know you don't want to hear that, Shondor," Gold said. "My answer is this: on this case, I'll help myself. If I can't help myself, then I want you to help me, because my problems, sir, are as numerous as yours."

At this point, it was clear to Shondor: His scheme to nudge Mervin into a role of sacrificial lamb for the stolen bonds and the Cosmo debacle had unraveled. Mervin Gold was not going down alone, and their conversation further deteriorated.

"Now just a minute," Shondor said. "You want me to fight your case all the way to the Supreme Court? I see myself getting in hock right down the line. Is that what you want me to do? You're not gonna sell me a bill of goods that you ain't got no money, Merv. I'm not going to buy that."

"I need legal help on this particular case," Gold said. "And as long as they dealt me out, as long as I got a way to come back under appeal, schmappeal, or anything else, I expect to have help from my friends. I will do everything I should do as a man, but I want my friends to act the same way."

"OK, pal. I wish you'd acted like a man before, but you thought you were so smart. You know all the answers. You know, Mr. Gold, you're the smartest man in the world. But I think you're the dumbest."

"The dumbest?" Gold said. "It might look like it, but I'll say, my friend, as far as discriminations are concerned, there are a lot of deals I made that I didn't want to. Just remember that, Shon. Sometimes I did things to accommodate other people."

"You didn't accommodate me. Because you were told not to."

"I was? You've got a hell of a memory, my friend."

"Now look, don't give me that fucking shit," Birns said. "Listen, Merv, you gonna keep talking to me like that? You think you're talking to a fool? I'll come up there and make you talk the way you're supposed to talk."

"I'll tell you something," Mervin said. "I'm glad you said that."

"Yeah?"

"Yes because here's what I've done, point blank, Mr. Birns. Listen to me carefully. Every last drop is down on twenty-three sheets of paper. Notarized, signed, sealed, and delivered."

"Yeah?"

"And distributed," Mervin said. "Just in case you get the clever idea of getting cute. Don't ever threaten me again."

"Oh, well, we understand each other now," Shondor said.

"All you do is give me the necessary help. Don't worry about me, my friend."

"Don't worry about you?" Shondor said. "The way you're talking, I don't care nothing about ya."

"The way I'm talking?" Mervin said. "Well, I'm not going to back up against the wall and play dead for you."

"Goodbye, Mervin."

"Hello. Hello. Wait a minute. I'm not quite through."

"Now, wait a minute," Shondor said. "I don't want to be hanging on. I don't know where you're talking from. Number one, you're too cute for me."

"I'm too cute for you? Now, what's going to happen with the man tomorrow?"

"You worry about tomorrow yourself."

"I worry about tomorrow myself, Shon? Haha. In other words, you throw around threats and don't think I'm smart enough to stay ahead of you? Now I'm going to call you tonight at six thirty."

"Why?" Shondor asked.

"Why? Because I want to know about the general subject of money regarding this lawyer and myself and these circumstances."

"Look I'll be up there tomorrow. And if you ever—look, Merv. I know you're cute. You're too smart for your own good."

"Don't try to hurt anybody," Mervin said. "You'll only end up hurting yourself."

"Ahh, look, look, Merv. If you'd only listen to people sometime. You think you're the smartest man in the world. You ain't gonna put me up against a wall."

"I'm not going to do anything to you, my friend," Mervin said. "You're going to do it yourself. Point blank. Don't get cute with me. I don't frighten easily."

The conversation ended. As he did with many of his business calls, Gold had been recording it. Later in the day, he telephoned Birns back.

"Hello, Shondor. How are you?"

"All right," Shondor said.

"Well, did you cool down a little bit, I hope?"

"No. You think threatening me with written statements doesn't upset me?"

"I didn't threaten you. You threatened me," Mervin said.

"I just asked a civilized question, and you got all excited about it. Well, anyway, that's neither here nor there. I talked to the attorney."

"I presume that you had a satisfactory conversation with him?" Mervin asked.

"Satisfactory—where you're concerned."

"Now listen . . ."

"I don't want too much conversation, Mervin."

"I understand. I'll talk to you in a couple of days," Gold said.

"OK."

"OK, kid. Bye-bye."

154

***

Wednesday, July 3, 1963

Mervin Gold was still not getting the help he expected. He appeared before Judge Battisti for his arraignment. Gold owed James Willis several thousand dollars and missed a final deadline for payment. As a result, Willis petitioned the court to withdraw. Battisti insisted that Willis remain as Gold's attorney so that the arraignment on the fraudulent loan indictment would not have to be postponed.

When the hearing concluded, Gold left the courthouse toward Short Vincent and walked into Kornman's. Birns was there having lunch with an attorney. Gold walked right over to Birns, who remained seated but offered his hand. Mervin, a six-foot, two hundred and ten pounder, grabbed Shon's hand and started shaking it aggressively in mock gratitude.

"Thank you, Mr. Birns, for all of your help."

Birns was not amused. Gold was unfazed. He complained loudly that Jim Willis requested permission from the court to withdraw from his case for nonpayment.

"I paid Willis twenty-five hundred dollars, and I don't owe him more," Gold said.

The attorney admonished Gold to settle down. After a few moments, Gold walked away.

That evening, Shondor and Ellie, his schoolteacher girlfriend, arrived at Kandrac's, a steakhouse across from a suburban police station. Shondor and Ellie walked in the front door, and he turned right and led Ellie into the bar room. He preferred that section to the roomier and carpeted dining area to the left.

During Birns's first visit to the restaurant six weeks earlier, he had introduced himself to owners Frances and Ed Kandrac. Shondor liked the atmosphere and the food. Soon he was dining there twice weekly, often with Ellie.

Numerous customers waved hello to Shon. A few approached and shook hands and a couple of them also greeted Ellie. The waitress perked up. Serving Mr. Birns guaranteed an overly generous tip.

Shon selected a booth at the end of the bar, near the jukebox. Ellie sat and got comfortable while he remained standing and bought a round of drinks for his acquaintances. While standing between the bar and the booth where Ellie remained seated, Shon chatted for several minutes then joined Ellie. It was a Wednesday evening, and they were the last dinner customers. Frances Kandrac took their orders. She returned with salads rather quickly.

"Don't rush me," Shon told her pleasantly. "I want to have a couple of drinks before I eat. After I eat, I don't drink."

Shon ordered a Scotch. Sinatra, Elvis, and 1940s dance band hits played on the jukebox. Shon alternated between sitting with Ellie and standing by the bar until their entrees arrived. She had whitefish. He had frog legs, which Frances noticed as a departure from his favorites of veal cutlet or lobster tail.

Meanwhile, at the Gold residence, the children were in bed. Mervin and Lily were watching *77 Sunset Strip*, a television series about a private detective. Mervin started dressing to leave.

"Where are you going?" Lily asked.

"I want to see Shon," he said.

"Why so late?"

"He's having dinner with someone. He said he would be home by nine thirty, but I'm giving him a half hour more."

"Why don't you just end it?" Lily asked. "Take whatever jail time you get. End it. We'll be all right. I'll go to work, and you can serve whatever time you have to."

"Remember my cousin who died of cancer?" Mervin said. "Remember how hard she fought to live? I'm of the same family. And I'm a fighter."

Lily continued to watch TV. One of the characters was arrested for a serious crime. Mervin was in and out of the room. He noticed a small stain on his pants. Moistening a towel and rubbing away the spot, he pointed out the area to Lily. She looked at it and said she would press the pant leg the next day.

"I'll be back in an hour," he said.

"Take your credit card," Lily said. "You'll probably have to buy gas. There was only a quarter tankful when I got back from taking the children to the doctor."

Mervin didn't answer. He was focused on the television. The man who had been arrested told his partner he needed help.

"I bet his partner doesn't believe him," Mervin said.

Toting a thin file folder, he walked out the front door.

Lily finished watching the *77 Sunset Strip* episode. Mervin's prediction was correct.

***

Thursday, July 4, 1963

It was 2:30 a.m. when the baby started crying. Lily Gold woke up immediately and noticed that Mervin wasn't home. He never stayed out that late. She tended to the baby, and when he fell back to sleep, she telephoned Shondor's house. There was no answer. She tried several more times, then fell asleep. Three hours later,

Lily awoke and Mervin was still gone. She redialed Shondor's house. There was no answer. As the sun rose over Ohio, she kept trying.

At Jane Birns's house, the telephone rang at 9:30 a.m. It was Shondor.

"Jane, I have to go to Columbus last minute," Shondor said. "Will you let Fury out and feed him?"

Jane agreed. About an hour later, she arrived on Judson. While tending to the Doberman, she heard Shondor's telephone ring and answered. It was Lily. She told Jane that Mervin had not come home. Lily wondered if he was with Shondor. Jane told Lily that Shon had called her an hour ago from Columbus and said he would be back the following day.

At 10:40 a.m., Lily called the Pepper Pike Police Department and reported Mervin missing. She said he left around 9:30 p.m. to meet with Shondor Birns and never came home. The police sent out a statewide alert for Mervin and his car, a white and salmon Mercury.

At 2:30 p.m., just over 140 miles from Columbus and 100 miles from Cleveland, Shondor Birns walked into the Town House Motel in Toledo in northwest Ohio. He told the clerk he didn't know how long he would be staying. After registering, Shon made small talk. He asked the clerk when he went off duty. The clerk replied that his shift was almost over, and then he would be having dinner with his fiancée in the Aku-Aku Room. The young man noticed Birns's right thumb was bandaged and asked what happened.

"I closed it in a car door."

Shondor went to his room. Later he wandered into the Aku-Aku, which was attached to the motel. The Polynesian-themed nightclub had been opened two years earlier by Irving "Slick" Shapiro, a bookmaker and Mafia associate. The Aku-Aku attracted a diverse clientele, including well-known mobsters. It featured name entertainment and excellent meals.

Shondor saw Slick sitting in the Aku-Aku, eating with his wife and children. The two men exchanged greetings then spoke privately for a few minutes. When they noticed the clerk and his fiancée enter the dining area, Shapiro called him over.

"Mr. Birns is a good friend of mine. Take care of him, if you can."

Birns walked away with the clerk. He told him he had been having marital problems.

"I'd appreciate it if you could change the registration time," Birns said. "Can you show that I checked into the motel at eleven o'clock last night?"

The clerk thought for a moment.

"I can't do it," he said. "The registration transactions run consecutively. Any change will be obvious."

Shondor and the clerk discussed it briefly and decided not to make the change. Shondor thanked him, and the clerk went back to his table with his fiancée. Birns paid for their meal.

Shondor relaxed at the pool. He spent time chatting with Slick Shapiro and Ray Gentile, a Toledo organized crime and gambling figure and operator of the Bunkhouse Restaurant.

Back in Cleveland, US Attorney Merle McCurdy assumed Mervin Gold had left the judicial district. He requested that the FBI search for him.

"If he can't be found, a fugitive warrant will be issued," McCurdy said. "Nothing would surprise me as far as Mervin Gold is concerned. We cannot rule out violence or foul play. Living the kind of life he did, and the people involved, anything could happen."

Lily Gold was interviewed by police and reporters. She said Mervin had recently been very busy and seeing many people. He felt that everyone was double-crossing him.

"What chance do I have against all this power?" he asked her.

On the day he went missing, Mervin had been in a happy mood, Lily reported. He was home in the morning and mailed a letter for her. Around 12:30, he ate lunch. Lily served vegetable soup and sardines. Mervin had an appointment with an attorney at 2:00 p.m. Lily needed the car to take the children to the doctor for a checkup, so she drove Mervin to the rapid transit. He didn't know whether he could get a ride home. Lily told him to call her at the pediatrician's office if he needed her to pick him up.

While at the pediatrician, Lily received a message that Mervin would not need a ride. She went directly home and started cooking. Mervin arrived as Lily was taking the chicken out of the broiler. While the chicken cooled, she chopped cucumber, tomato, lettuce, and green onion. She diced the chicken, added the vegetables, oil, and vinegar, and made chicken salad. With corn and string beans as side dishes, the family ate dinner.

Afterward, while Lily scrubbed the broiler pan, Mervin took the kids to Dairy Queen. When Lily finished in the kitchen, she went out into the humid evening to water the shrubbery. When Mervin returned, he was down to the bottom of a small vanilla ice cream cone. The baby was still trying to finish off a Dilly Bar. Much of the ice cream and chocolate was on his shirt and face, so Lily ran him through the sprinkler.

Around 8:00 p.m., Lily gave the baby a bath and put him to bed. She bathed the girls, then they watched *The Flintstones*. Mervin lay on the sofa. One of the girls tickled his feet, and he teased her in retaliation. After Lily put the girls to bed, she and Mervin chatted and watched *77 Sunset Strip*. Then Mervin got dressed to leave.

***

In Toledo, Shondor asked the Town House Motel clerk for directions to Al Cook's Men's Shop. Before he went shopping, Birns called Slick Shapiro and said he needed a doctor because he had slammed his thumb in his car door. Shapiro telephoned a doctor, who came to the hotel. He cleaned the laceration, prescribed Terramycin antibiotic capsules, and told Birns to soak the injury in Epsom salts. The doctor instructed Birns to meet him later at his office for a tetanus shot to prevent lockjaw.

On Sunday, Birns's thumb was still giving him some difficulty. Dr. Rayman went to the hotel and cleaned and treated the wound. Afterward, Shondor spent the day playing cards with Ray Gentile.

Back in Cleveland, police continued to search for Mervin Gold.

CHAPTER EIGHT

Monday, July 8, 1963

On Monday morning, Judge Battisti issued a bench warrant for Mervin Gold for fleeing the court's jurisdiction. It was now four days since Lily had reported Mervin missing. At the Gold residence, Lily retrieved the envelope Mervin had left for her months earlier. She then telephoned the office of Merle McCurdy. Ninety minutes later, two FBI agents arrived at her front door. Lily told them she was afraid Mervin had been harmed. She left the room and returned with four large manila envelopes neatly sealed with scotch tape. Then she started crying.

"Mervin is the victim of politicians regarding his financial handlings," she told the agents. "He's been taken of advantage of by them. And some of his own business partners have property that was taken from our house while we were in Israel."

The agents asked what persons Lily meant, but she declined to name anyone. She handed them the envelopes. "I don't want you to open them here. I think there might be something in them that explains what happened to Mervin."

The agents gave Lily a receipt and left.

That afternoon, Bentleyville Village police received a complaint about an abandoned car that had been parked for two days near the Chagrin River. The rural location was in Solon Village, just inside Cuyahoga County on the border with Geauga County. A patrol officer checked the license plate against the latest bulletin of stolen cars. It was not listed. He assumed the car belonged to a fisherman working the nearby river for trout. Reaching inside the open driver's window, he turned on the parking lights. It was something the officer had done before as a courtesy to make it easier for fishermen to find their way back after dark.

Late in the afternoon, Solon police received a complaint about the same car. It was described as a pink-orange and white Mercury. Chief John Vondracek went to check the car personally and recognized the license plate as a match for a missing person alert. He peered in the passenger side window. No key in the ignition. An infant seat with a toy steering wheel on the front passenger side. Children's clothing on the back seat. A spare tire was lying on the rear passenger seat. A pile of papers strewn about the back driver's side floor and covered with cigarette ashes.

Another police officer had been following the newspaper coverage. He told Vondracek he believed Gold would be found by the water, the victim of a suicide. Chief Vondracek organized a search party of eleven police officers and firefighters. Spreading out about a quarter of a mile, they started walking slowly through the woods and brush down toward the river. When they reached the riverbank, they found nothing.

The chief and another Solon police officer returned to the car and looked through the window at the tire sitting on the back seat.

"An odd place for a spare tire," the chief said.

He pulled up on the trunk. It was locked.

Vondracek went to a nearby house and asked to use the telephone. After dialing the FBI, he informed an agent that he had found Gold's car and searched the area. He mentioned the spare tire in the back seat and that the trunk was locked. The agent suggested that it be opened and said he would be en route to the scene.

The chief went back to the car, opened the rear door, and pulled the seat-back loose. Peering through a small opening into the trunk, he saw another spare tire. Then something caught his attention.

At the chief's direction, firefighters used a pry bar and forced open the trunk. They were greeted sharply by the pungent odor of bodily decomposition. It was a middle-aged white man, face down on top of a maroon blanket and mostly covered by a pink blanket. The legs were jammed against the spare tire to the side. The head was near the middle of the trunk. An arm was extended toward the back of the rear seat, allowing the hand to be visible by Chief Vondracek. One end of the blanket had been tied to the man's belt. There was minimal blood in the trunk. Vondracek pulled a wallet from a rear pants pocket. Inside was an identification card. It belonged to Mervin L. Gold.

When FBI agents arrived, Vondracek reported his findings. He said he was going to remove the body to a waiting ambulance, but the agents suggested that he contact Cuyahoga County Coroner Samuel Gerber before disturbing anything.

With spectators gathering, Chief Vondracek ordered the car towed to the fire station and summoned Dr. Gerber to meet him there. Then he telephoned the Pepper Pike Police Department and asked them to drive Mrs. Gold out to view the body and make a positive identification.

In the meantime, a local radio station broadcasted that Mervin Gold's car had been located in Solon. A friend of the Gold family telephoned Lily to inform her. Lily called the police to confirm the report. Since the dispatcher could not be sure of Lily's identity, she refused to provide any information. A moment later, Lily Gold's phone rang. She answered, and the caller asked if it was true that her husband had been found dead. Lily hung up. A few minutes passed. Someone knocked on her front door. It was a police officer, and he told her Mervin's car had been found in Solon and she was needed there. When she arrived, Dr. Gerber introduced himself. He brought her over to identify the body. She looked at the body, the head covered by the pink blanket.

"Do you recognize any of the clothing?" Dr. Gerber asked.

"The pants," she said quietly. "They are the same ones Mervin was wearing when he left the house."

She began crying hysterically and nearly collapsed. The police officer helped her to the front passenger seat of the car, where she slumped over and sobbed.

After a few minutes, she spoke again with Dr. Gerber. He asked her if Mervin smoked or drank. Neither of them smoked, she said, and Mervin hadn't drunk alcohol in two years, excepting an occasional glass of brandy.

***

In his office, Merle McCurdy opened the envelope obtained from Lily Gold. Inside were two legally prepared affidavits signed by Mervin Gold, one two pages long, and one twenty-three pages in length. In the two-page document, Gold wrote that between November 1960 and January 1961, he provided Shondor Birns with loans totaling $10,000. When Mervin called for repayment, Shondor provided him Canadian bearer bonds as collateral to continue the loans. Gold's twenty-three-page affidavit was turned over to the FBI, and a multi-agency search for Birns began.

***

Tuesday, July 9, 1963

On the morning of July 9, Birns was still at the Townhouse Motel in Toledo. He asked the housekeeper to make up his room. Noticing the bandage on his right thumb, she asked him what happened.

"I hurt it shooting firecrackers on the Fourth. I wanted to be a kid again."

Birns's thumb was still swollen, infected, and throbbing. He visited Dr. Rayman's office in the afternoon and again received treatment.

Meanwhile, newspaper headlines and stories abounded.

The *Plain Dealer* led off with MERVIN GOLD FOUND SLAIN and "Police Hunt Shondor Birns."

The *Washington Post* covered the crime with "Police Find Body of Convicted Stock Handler."

News of the murder quickly reached Tel Aviv.

"Mervin Gold, Who was Deported from Israel, Was Found Dead in his Car in the US," read the *Haboker Daily Newspaper*.

Cleveland reporters sought out informed sources for comments.

"If Birns is living, he'd usually be showing up about this time after bad trouble like this," said Carl Delau, now a lieutenant in charge of the homicide bureau. "It's very strange. I wouldn't be surprised to hear that Shondor was found lying in some ditch."

"We're all anxious to talk to Birns," said Merle McCurdy. "Our only interest is his connection, if any, to the stolen bonds. We can only speculate about him being alive. There have been so many things happening, nothing would surprise me."

Wilson Hirschfeld, writing for the *Plain Dealer*, described Mervin Gold as a "man of talents with a mind as quick as a hair-spring trigger; an actor, a great strategist with a great command of the language; an operator lacking what most folks know as simple honesty. His worship of the quick buck warped his thinking."

A Gold relative commented, "When Mervin gets in to something, it's like the kiss of death."

Meanwhile, Cleveland police detectives obtained a search warrant for Shondor's house. When they arrived, Fury was barking and straining to get loose from his chain and doghouse. Detectives notified the dog warden's office, and two animal control officers responded. Jane Birns arrived at the same time and calmed the Doberman. While detectives searched and photographed each room, a small crowd of curious neighbors gathered outside. Several youngsters leaned against Jane's robin's egg blue Thunderbird, and a reporter asked them about Shondor. They spoke admiringly and said he passed out quarters and dollars on Halloween.

Inside, detectives confiscated a bloodstained bed sheet, a rifle, a revolver, a container of bullets, an adding machine, a throw rug, and a locked filing cabinet. Using a dolly, they rolled the cabinet down the front steps and into a truck. Jane took Fury inside, and the officers brought the evidence to the police station.

While detectives applied for an separate search warrant to open Shondor's filing cabinet, a tip came into Cleveland police and the FBI. They sought the assistance of their counterparts in Toledo, who began conducting surveillance of the Town House Motel. The clerk at the Town House said he had last seen Birns around 1:30 p.m. in the dining room. He was watching the all-star baseball game being televised from Cleveland.

When the *Cleveland Press* came out, there was an editorial about Gold.

The Mervin Gold trial and the 33-year-old man's conviction was spectacular in itself—but it is only a curtain raiser to a far bigger and more spectacular, and a much more sordid international finance crime than has been disclosed so far . . .

Before they saw him, Shondor spotted police and FBI agents at the motel. He didn't want to spend the night in a Toledo jail, so while

167

some of the officers were looking at his Cadillac, he walked around to the other side of the motel and to a payphone. He called a friend and got a ride back to Cleveland.

***

Wednesday, July 10, 1963

Dr. Gerber and his assistant worked overnight to complete a post-mortem examination of Mervin Gold. The lack of significant blood on the blanket Gold was wrapped in indicated that he was killed elsewhere then placed in his car. At least two men, perhaps using the blanket like a stretcher, carried the body to the trunk.

"Mervin Gold was struck about the head and face up to 15 times," Gerber reported. "He used his hands to ward off the blows. He suffered fractures to three fingers on each hand, and his wedding ring was bent oval. A plastic clothesline was knotted tightly around his neck, and he had been shot four times, apparently from a .38-caliber revolver. Three of the slugs coursed around the skull, exited at the neck, and settled into the blanket. However, none of the slugs pierced the skull."

Gerber was sure that the cause of death was strangulation. He also found that heart disease had cut Gold's life expectancy short.

***

Thursday, July 11, 1963

Shondor was back in Cleveland. In the morning, he telephoned Sheriff McGettrick's chief deputy to surrender. They agreed to meet near the Castle Arms Restaurant in Garfield Heights. Birns emerged from behind a building, and the sheriff and deputy took him into custody.

At the county jail, a physician examined Shondor's thumb and gave him a shot of penicillin. Several officials questioned him about his recent whereabouts.

"I never saw Gold that night. I was home entertaining a woman of fine character. And she'll testify, if necessary."

Dr. Gerber questioned Birns, who stated he could account for his whereabouts during the murder. Shondor said he would not discuss the matter further and did not want to embarrass his friends unnecessarily. The coroner was determined.

"I asked Shondor if he could help in resolving the murder or give any information," Gerber said. "He said he knew nothing. I told him he should know something because Gold's wife said Mervin went to see him at nine thirty that night. He said he couldn't help me. I said there would have to be an inquest and I would subpoena him as a witness. What Shondor calls cooperation is not what I call cooperation."

Jim Willis defended Birns's silence.

"Why should he say anything?" the attorney told a reporter. "The police are not interested in solving the crime. They're more interested in trying to incriminate Birns. If Birns said he was dining in a monastery, the police would be out there trying to corrupt the monks."

When Carl Delau met with Birns, a heated exchange occurred.

"You strangled, shot, and beat your best friend," Delau said.

"I resent that. I have no comment on anything you ask me. I don't want to talk to you. I am not going to talk to you. You've been trying to send me to jail for thirteen years."

"You're crazy," Delau said. "Any time you get jammed up, you blame somebody else."

"You picked me up to cover your own dirty stuff. You've got nobody on Short Vincent fooled."

Delau later told a reporter, "Shondor has never liked me. Most recently, he accused me of breaking into his home and taking a rifle and pistol. As a matter of fact, I was off when the guns were taken in an official search with a search warrant. He has accused me of trying to get him through stoolies. He doesn't like me because he has wanted to run over the city unmolested. When I accused him of killing his best friend, that really set him off. But Shon usually talks more when he's mad. He loves the publicity. He is a vain, hot-tempered con man and refuses to act his age. Over the years, it has been fashionable with some people to look up to Shondor. I can't understand that. He's a hoodlum, just a hoodlum."

FBI agents joined the investigation into Gold's murder and interviewed Birns at the county jail. He denied knowing anything about the stolen bonds or owing Gold money.

"In fact, Mervin owes me about five thousand dollars," Shondor said. "I have a note that was due in March that he never paid. And he owes me fifteen hundred dollars from playing gin rummy."

Shondor told the agents that Gold was offered $25,000 by several persons connected with Cosmo. They said they would pay Mervin if he promised to tell the truth in court. When the agents asked who the individuals were, Shondor refused to identify any of them. After various law enforcers questioned Birns, news reporters were given a shot.

"Where was I," he said to a *Plain Dealer* reporter. "I'm telling you the same thing I told the rest. No comment."

A reporter asked him why he left his car and clothing in Toledo.

Birns grinned. "I didn't want to."

Another told Birns that another *Plain Dealer* reporter had been looking for him in Toledo.

"I wish he'd found me," Shondor said. "I needed a ride back to Cleveland."

Headlines screamed as newspapers reporters covered every angle of Gold's murder, the stolen bonds, and Birns's arrest.

BIRNS LINKED TO BONDS BY GOLD

HOME WHEN MURDER OCCURRED, BIRNS SAYS

George Barmann of the *Plain Dealer* suggested that despite Birns aging, he was still dangerous.

"If you ran into Shondor on Short Vincent, you'd see a man of 57, dressed in pretty fair taste—dark, well-put-up suit, flashy tie, cool but not offensive, and suede and leather shoes," Barmann wrote. "Maybe he'd be wearing a hat and maybe he wouldn't. Sometimes he's with glasses, other times not . . . On close notice, his face lacks strength . . . It hides the man who is capable of quick violent retaliation."

***

Friday, July 12, 1963

Carl Delau had Tony Panzarella and Dominick Bartone on his short list of potential suspects that he wanted to question about Gold's murder. After ducking detectives for several days, Panzarella finally walked into police headquarters. He was interrogated and denied knowing Mervin Gold or having been in recent contact with anyone in Toledo. He was detained for additional questioning until Jim Willis obtained a court order for his release.

The Cleveland FBI learned Bartone was in Miami. They requested that the Miami field office interview him "thoroughly regarding all financial transactions he had with the late MERVIN GOLD and whether or not he ever made any bonds, Canadian or otherwise, available to GOLD, as well as Bartone's whereabouts on the evening of 7/5/63."

But four months earlier, FBI headquarters had instructed Miami not to interview Bartone in connection with another investigation, one with a potential relationship to the stolen Canadian bonds and Gold's murder. That case involved Jimmy Hoffa and Babe Triscaro and their possible intent to make Teamster funding available to their Mafia friends to provide arms for anti-Castro forces. The Miami field office sent a request to Washington for permission to interview Bartone on behalf of their counterparts in Cleveland.

The FBI also received information from a confidential tipster that Birns's associate Angelo A. Amato, a cement contractor, made a trip to Buffalo that involved the stolen bonds. The information was in connection with a Toronto cigarette hijacking. Agents interviewed Amato, who denied any knowledge of Gold's murder or the bonds. He admitted meeting Mervin two years earlier when he was referred to him for a loan.

Meanwhile, the *Cleveland Press* offered a $10,000 reward for information leading to the capture of those responsible for Mervin Gold's murder.

The Press makes it clear that it holds no brief for Mervin Gold and his own crimes. It holds no brief, in fact, for anyone or any influence which in any way, shape or form figures in this brutal murder. Its only concern is that an especially brutal crime has been committed in Greater Cleveland. It was accomplished in such a fashion that the law enforcement agencies are confronted with a particularly difficult challenge in solving this crime and bringing its perpetrators to justice. Such obvious gangland murder and violence puts the entire community in jeopardy. The Press' concerns is for the law-abiding people whose security transcends any other consideration . . .

Carl Delau was encouraged.

"I hope that this reward offer leads persons who have no connection with the case to pass along any tiny clue they may have," he said. "This is a case in which even the slightest scrap of information could be of extreme importance and help to us."

Dr. Gerber set his the inquest date, subpoenaed Shondor, and required him to post a $50,000 bond to ensure his appearance. He also summoned Ellie Leonards.

Shondor was in Judge William K. Thomas's courtroom twice on July 12.

In a morning appearance, he won his freedom from the filing of a writ of habeas corpus. The judge's decision was without objection by county prosecutor John T. Corrigan, since Birns was under the bond set by Dr. Gerber.

In an afternoon session, Judge Thomas heard a motion by Willis, protesting the bond requirement. The courtroom was packed with spectators as the defense lawyer argued for a personal bond.

"The worst thing that could happen is my client might not show," Willis said. "Mr. Birns fully expects to appear at the inquest, but if he didn't, he'd only be guilty of contempt of court. There is no charge against him. He is held only for investigation, and there is no such crime."

Corrigan presented three witnesses. A police records room clerk presented Birns's rap sheet—forth-two entries, including a few convictions. It took her fifteen minutes to read it into the record. A deputy sheriff testified to Birns's refusal to answer questions. Dr. Gerber described the injuries on Gold's body and that he was to meet with Birns on the night he went missing.

Judge Thomas ruled that Dr. Gerber's bond amount of $50,000 would stand. Birns secured bond. It cost him $2,500 for the bondsman's fee.

In Police Chief Richard Wagner's office, Carl Delau and several other officials gathered to execute a search warrant on Shondor's filing cabinet. They located two revolvers and several notes and papers of interest. Several had to do with money owed Birns, such as a three-cent-per-ton commission from the sale of stone. The notes included persons to contact for help with collection, apparently for Ellie's information in case something happened to Shondor.

Investigators were particularly interested in two items. One was a note documenting $3,000 owed to Shondor from Mervin Gold. The other read: *To Plead: $17,000; If They Receive Probation; $17,000. If They Are Found Not Guilty: $34,000.*

In the meantime, a *Plain Dealer* reporter tracked down Ellie and visited her at home. Bright-eyed and wearing a black blouse and calf-length pants, she agreed to answer a few questions.

The reporter asked Ellie about her knowledge of Birns's history.

"Before this Gold business, I never read or heard anything about Shondor," she said. "Maybe I was too young at the time. I am glad I never did read anything about him, because sometimes when you meet someone in person, he is entirely different from what you may have read about him. I know Shondor as a perfect gentlemen and a very fine person."

When the reporter pressed for details about Ellie's personal relationship with Shondor and their whereabouts on the night of Mervin Gold's murder, she politely refused to answer.

***

Monday, July 15, 1963

As the inquest approached, it was learned that, in the weeks leading up to his death, Gold had been talking to police and reporters and "threatening to tell all he knew" about the stolen Canadian bonds he claimed to have received from Birns. Mervin reportedly told Birns he wanted him to raise $150,000 from the people who knew about the theft of Canadian bonds as a fund to care for his family while he was in prison. Then he planned to leave the country after his release from prison because he had money stashed abroad.

Meanwhile, Shondor rented a hotel room for Ellie to stay in, so that she and her mother could escape the phone calls and visits from investigators and reporters. The couple was seen dining at a steak-house outside of Akron. When Shondor returned her to the hotel, he left her a bottle of peroxide to lighten her hair.

At the Gold residence, Lily located a satchel of Mervin's business papers. Concerned they might contain information like the affidavit her husband wrote implicating Birns and afraid someone might invade her home to steal the documents, she turned them over to the Cuyahoga County Probate Court. Lily and her three children were the beneficiaries of a $60,000 life insurance policy on Mervin Gold. Because she declined to administer her husband's estate, a probate judge assigned an attorney to handle the case.

Later that day, an investigator monitoring Shondor's phone line traced a call to Ellie. She didn't get a chance to use the peroxide Shondor brought her. Just after midnight, a coroner's agent, accompanied by two local detectives, knocked on her motel door.

"I've been expecting you," she said.

She accepted the subpoena to appear at the coroner's inquest.

Meanwhile, Dr. Gerber, Prosecutor Corrigan, and Sheriff McGettrick listened to Mervin   Gold's phone call recordings. In particular was the one with Birns that escalated to a clash.

Birns: "You didn't accommodate me. Because you were told not to."

Gold: "I was? You've got a hell of a memory, my friend."

Birns: "Listen, Merv, you gonna keep talking to me like that? I'll come up there and make you talk the way you're supposed to talk."

There was much interest from the media in the Gold murder case, and *Cleveland Press* editor Louis Seltzer recognized the opportunity. As a so-called political kingmaker, he had Dr. Gerber's ear.

The newspaperman was opposed to the closed nature of a grand jury investigation. An inquest, however, would be open to the public and covered by reporters. And that would sell newspapers.

Coroner Gerber called for an inquest. It was held in a Cuyahoga County Common Pleas Court civil branch courtroom. He agreed to let a local radio station run a microphone line and make it available to any radio or television station. Adjacent to the courtroom, a temporary control room was set up. Two microphones covered the action: one directed toward Dr. Gerber and one aimed at the witness chair.

The primary witnesses called in the inquest included Shondor, Ellie Leonards, Tony Panzarella, Lily Gold, and Ed and Frances Kandrac.

The Kandracs testified that Shondor and Ellie had dinner at their restaurant on the evening of July 3. They remembered that Shondor ordered the frog's legs and that the couple left at approximately 10:00 p.m.

Gerber questioned Tony Panzarella about the record of a phone call between his home and Birns's hotel room when Shondor was in Toledo. Panzarella denied talking with Birns at the time, but admitted being in contact with Birns's crony Ray Gentile. Tony said the call pertained to money that Ray owned him.

"Why didn't you tell the police that when they talked to you?" Dr. Gerber asked.

"If I would have told Delau that, he would have thrown me in jail."

Gerber took offense. "Police don't throw innocent men in jail, Mr. Panzarella. They detain them for investigation. You're excused for now, but stay in the county. I'm not satisfied with your answers."

Dr. Gerber asked Lily Gold about her husband's business activities. She said she was sometimes very curious about his affairs, but he

176

made it a rule not to bring business home. Lily identified William Kahan and George Zimmerman as two of Mervin's associates.

Gerber asked Lily if Mervin and Shondor were business partners.

"Oh, no, not that I ever knew of," Lily said. "We knew him as a friend. A good friend. I met Shondor in May of 1960. The first time he came to the house, our car was broken down. He let me use his Cadillac to go shopping. I saw him several times. Once we had dinner at the Somerset Restaurant with him and his wife."

Dr. Gerber asked about the last night Lily saw her husband.

"I asked Mervin whether he was worried. He said, 'Don't be silly. If I was worried, I wouldn't have come back from Israel.' He said he was going out about nine thirty. I asked why so late and he said he wanted to see Shon, but he was having dinner with friends and wouldn't be available earlier."

"Did you get any of Mervin's property back?" Gerber asked.

"I got his wedding band back and his lucky money clip."

"What was the condition of the wedding band?"

"It was all bent."

"Since your husband's death, Mrs. Gold, have you received any telephone calls from Shondor Birns or any of your husband's other business associates?"

"No."

Ellie Leonards walked into the courtroom accompanied by Shondor's attorney, Jim Willis. She was wearing a knit beige suit appliqued with brown butterflies and a white sweater. She wore white shoes and carried a white wicker purse. Once she was seated at the witness table, Dr. Gerber began his questioning.

"Miss Leonards, where was the subpoena served on you?

"On advice of my counsel, I have nothing to say at this time."

"I direct you to answer."

"I refuse to answer on the grounds that the answer might tend to incriminate me."

"What is your occupation?" Gerber asked.

"I have nothing to say."

"I inform you that your answer will not incriminate you and I direct you to answer."

"I refuse to answer."

Dr. Gerber continued for another twenty minutes. There were questions about her relationship with Shondor and his whereabouts on the evening that Mervin Gold disappeared. It was useless. Ellie had officially gone from schoolteacher to mob moll and refused to answer. In total, she invoked her Fifth Amendment constitutional right against self-incrimination seventy-five times.

Dr. Gerber asked if she believed in the US Constitution. Ellie refused to answer. On the verge of sending her to jail for contempt of court, he turned his attention to Jim Willis. "Did you advise her to refuse to answer these questions," Gerber asked.

"I don't take the Fifth Amendment," Willis said. "I claim the privilege of confidentiality of lawyer and client."

"Talk the questions over with Miss Leonards," Gerber instructed.

Willis stood. "Dr. Gerber, I am governed by my view of the canon of lawyers' ethics and not by yours. If you differ, you have a remedy."

Gerber ordered Ellie jailed as a recalcitrant witness and set a bond of $10,000. Willis promptly secured her release. Ellie walked out of the courthouse confidently, much to the frustration of Gerber and other officials.

After a break, Dr. Gerber called Shondor to the witness stand. They immediately began sparring.

"Your name?" Gerber asked.

"Before I give you my name, I'd like to ask a question. Are the—"

"Just give us your name."

"Are the reporters recording this?" Shondor pointed to the microphone placed in front of the witness chair. "If so, I want to object."

"In this case, I'll have it turned off," Gerber said.

He walked over and turned the microphone away from Birns. He ordered reporters to turn off the tape recorders in the next room.

"How can I be sure?" Shondor asked.

"You'll just have to take my word for it."

"I do."

"Your name?"

"Al Shondor Birns."

"Where do you live?"

"Judson Drive, Cleveland."

Dr. Gerber got up and put the microphone on the floor behind the bench. "Just to make sure," he said.

"It cost me twenty-five hundred dollars to appear here," Shondor said, referring to the bondsman's fees for the $50,000 bond.

"That was your fault," Dr. Gerber said.

"No, your fault."

"How long have you lived in Cleveland?"

"All my life, excepting seven months."

"Please explain.

"I refuse to answer that. On advice of my attorney, I take the Fifth Amendment."

"Why are you refusing to answer?

"I refuse to answer any questions on the ground that it may tend to incriminate me."

"Where were you on July 3, 1963, after you left Kandrac's restaurant?"

"I refuse to answer."

"Did you take a bottle of peroxide to Miss Leonards so she could dye her hair in the past few days?"

"I refuse to answer."

"You are here as a witness to help resolve the manner of the death of Mr. Mervin Gold and your answer is that you refuse to answer?

Birns was silent. Gerber turned up the heat.

"Mr. Birns, do you know the circumstances of Mr. Gold's death? Do you know that he was beaten over the head and that a plastic rope was tied around his neck and he was asphyxiated? Did you know that another blanket was wrapped around his body and that he was shot in the head three times and once in the back, and his body was then dumped in the rear of an automobile? Did you know that, Mr. Birns?

"I take the Fifth Amendment and refuse to answer."

"Mr. Birns, I certainly can't thank you for your cooperation. I certainly can't."

"That's what you get for making me spend twenty-five hundred dollars for nothing."

"I expect you to remain in Cuyahoga County until such time as you are called in the future. You are excused."

Shondor had stood firm on the stand, but as he strode out of the courthouse, hands in pockets and eyes downcast, he looked as if he felt every bit of the verbal barrage that Gerber had leveled at him.

As for Gerber, he was frustrated.

"I'm hoping all who read the newspapers about the inquest are filled with the same disgust aroused in me by some of the witnesses who wouldn't cooperate and help solve the crime," he said.

"Miss Leonards is much too educated to have such hostile attitude," said Carl Delau. "I do not believe that she is uncooperative out of fear but out of a misplaced loyalty and friendship with Birns. It is a shame, but Birns is using her to gain respectability. I can't understand why she will not go past ten thirty in outlining Birns's alibi that night. She owes it to law enforcement to tell us everything she knows. She evidently is sticking by Mr. Birns, but how long will Birns stick with her?"

"I feel sorry for her," said Prosecutor John Corrigan. "She doesn't realize how much trouble she might be in. She will probably lose her job, and it will be hard to find another teaching position. Neighbors will likely hold her in contempt. And then there's her family. This has probably caused her mother a lot of grief. She will most likely have to pay expensive legal fees. Her troubles are just beginning."

A few days after the inquest, Lily Gold opened a cabinet and found the wire attachments she believed Mervin used to record his phone conversations.

"I want to turn this over to the sheriff or somebody," she told a visiting newspaper reporter. "It is not a good thing, and I don't want it around the house."

Carl Delau believed that Birns either committed the murder of Mervin Gold or was close by when it occurred. He discussed the possibility that a professional hired killer had been used.

"A professional would have just shot him in the head and left. He would not have bothered with the blankets in which Gold's body was found. And Gold would not have gone into a building with a complete stranger."

Meanwhile, the Cleveland FBI received a reply from Washington that their request to interview Dominick Bartone was denied. Bartone's attorney said his client was in Miami on the day that Gold was killed.

It was a good bet that Mervin Gold had gambled against Shondor Birns and his associates, but seriously miscalculated the odds. Reporter Doris O'Donnell had a source who told her it was in a garage where Gold was murdered by Shondor Birns, but no evidence developed to pursue the lead.

The fabled Theatrical Restaurant on Short Vincent Avenue, Cleveland.
(Photo credit: Cleveland Public Library Photograph Collection)

Saxophonist Carmen Leggio performs for a packed Theatrical house.
(Photo credit: Cleveland Public Library Photograph Collection)

No doubt Shondor had a smile like this
when he met Ellie Leonards.
(Photo credit: Cleveland State University Cleveland Press Collection. Photo by Clayton Knipper)

Allene "Ellie" Leonards in her college
days before she fell for the charms of
Shondor Birns.
(Photo credit: Kent State University Libraries.
Special Collections and Archives)

Shondor in a 1957 mug shot.
(Photo credit. Cleveland Police)

Mervin Gold—husband and father.   Mervin Gold—con man and racketeer.

(Photo credits: Cleveland Public Library Photograph Collection.)

Dominick Bartone, mobster, arms trafficker, con man, and associate of Shondor Birns. Bartone was deeply involved in a plot to utilize stolen Canadian bonds for funding the purchase of weapons to influence the Cuban Revolution.

(Photo credit: Author's collection)

Mervin Gold's house in the affluent suburb of Pepper Pike—an impressive home, while it lasted.

(Photo credit: Cleveland Public Library Photograph Collection. Photo by Richard J. Misch)

Carl Delau of the Cleveland Police Department, longtime nemesis of Shondor Birns.

(Photo credit: Cleveland Police Museum)

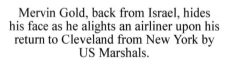

Mervin Gold, back from Israel, hides his face as he alights an airliner upon his return to Cleveland from New York by US Marshals.

(Photo credit: Cleveland Public Library Photograph Collection)

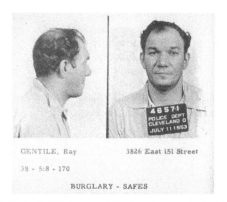

GENTILE, Ray   3826 East 151 Street

38 - 5:8 - 170

BURGLARY - SAFES

STITMON, Fred P.   2684 East 53 St.

MUSCLEMAN - POLICY

Ray Gentile, Cleveland and Toledo associate of Shondor Birns.
(Photo credit: Cleveland Police)

Birns enforcer Fred Stitmon.
(Photo credit: Cleveland Police)

Bentleyville Police Chief Lester Peterman guards Mervin Gold's Mercury while a group of police officers and firemen fan out toward the Chagrin River in search of Mervin.

(Photo credit: Cleveland Public Library Photograph Collection. Photo by Robert Quinlan)

Officials review phone calls recorded by Mervin Gold. Left to right: Cuyahoga County Prosecutor John T. Corrigan, Cuyahoga County Coroner Dr. Samuel Gerber, Cleveland Police Lieutenant Carl Delau, and Cuyahoga County Sheriff James McGettrick.

(Photo credit: Cleveland Public Library Photograph Collection. Photo by Marvin L. Greene)

Jane Birns, looking perturbed at being drawn into the public scrutiny of Shondor's criminal issues, waits outside his house while police search inside in connection with a murder investigation.

(Photo credit: Cleveland State University Press Collection. Photo by Bill Nehez)

Shondor conceals his injured thumb from photographers following his arrest in a 1963 murder investigation.

(Photo credit: Cleveland State University Cleveland Press Collection. Photo by Clayton Knipper)

Merle McCurdy, the second black lawyer to be appointed as a US Attorney, and the first black US Attorney for the Northern District of Ohio, with Attorney General Robert F. Kennedy.

(Photo Credit: Kent State University Ashtabula Library)

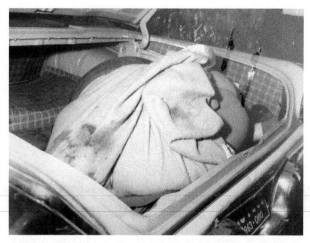

After a search party returned to Mervin Gold's car, police opened the trunk and made a disturbing discovery.
(Photo credit: Cleveland Public Library Photograph Collection)

Cleveland Press photographer Clayton Knipper persisted and got a shot of Shondor's bandaged thumb.
(Photo credit: Cleveland State University Cleveland Press Collection. Photo by Clayton Knipper)

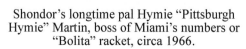

Shondor's longtime pal Hymie "Pittsburgh Hymie" Martin, boss of Miami's numbers or "Bolita" racket, circa 1966.

(Photo credit: Avi Bash Collection)

A fan cools the room as suspects face heat at a July 1963 murder inquest called by Dr. Sam Gerber, county coroner.

(Photo Credit: Cleveland Public Library Photograph Collection. Photo by Richard T. Conway)

Edward Keeling, numbers operator and close associate of Shondor Birns.

(Photo Credit: Cleveland Police)

Anthony "Tony Panz" Panzarella, Shondor's Cleveland Mafia ally in the numbers racket, in 1963.

(Photo credit: Cleveland Public Library Photograph Collection. Photo by Richard J. Misch)

Ellie Leonards appears amused, perhaps delighted, with
the attention as she chats with Shondor and attorney James
Willis during the coroner's inquest into a murder for which
Shondor is under suspicion.

(Photo credit: Cleveland Public Library Photograph Collection)

PART 3

CHAPTER NINE

A s the intense reporting of President Kennedy's assassination transfixed the nation, the Mervin Gold murder investigation, less than five months old, faded.

The conspiracy indictments against most of the other Cosmopolitan Small Business Investment Company investors, including Gold's brother-in-law, Nathan Lipsyc, were dismissed. US Attorney Merle McCurdy said the investigation into the complex case showed that only Gold benefited financially from the manipulation of Cosmo funds. (In a later trial, George Zimmerman and Leonard Luxenberg faced a charge of aiding and abetting Gold in fraudulently securing a $28,000 federal loan. Lawyers Jim Willis and Fred Garmone testified that Gold, during his Cosmo trial, once promised to plead guilty and exonerate Zimmerman and Luxenberg in exchange for concurrent sentencing and his choice of prison. Ultimately, Luxenberg was convicted, fined, and placed on probation. Zimmerman was also convicted. After lengthy appeals, he went to prison and was paroled after serving part of an eighteen month sentence.)

Dr. Gerber released Shondor and Ellie from their witness bonds.

"Although I am closing the inquest, I can reopen it any time if we come upon any new information or evidence," Gerber said.

"We had eight happy years," Lily Gold told a reporter. "He was a good husband and a good father. That is the way I will remember him. That's the way I want the children to remember him. . . You know, at the outset I didn't care whether they ever found out who killed my husband. But now I hope and pray it will be solved. Then it will be over. And as the years go by, the children won't have to be reading, 'Mervin Gold was killed a year ago . . . two years ago . . . every anniversary'. The story will never end until the murder is solved, will it?"

"We're hopeful we can solve this crime someday," Carl Delau said.

It was a relief for Birns, but pressure on the fifty-eight-year-old mounted. Cleveland police and the Internal Revenue Service aggressively pursued cases against him. He and Ellie headed down to Miami Beach. Shon visited with Hymie Martin several times and saw Cassius Clay defeat heavyweight champion Sonny Liston while FBI and IRS agents kept taps on him.

When Shondor returned home, the IRS summoned him to a hearing. He learned that he might be charged with perjury for making false statements when trying to arrange a settlement. A grand jury investigated and even subpoenaed Hymie Martin, ostensibly to ask him about his financial connection with Birns. Martin flew to Cleveland and waited for three days to be called as a witness. He was represented by Fred Garmone, one of Shondor's lawyers. Martin was in the grand jury room about two minutes—enough for him to identify himself and refuse to testify.

"Mr. Martin has his constitutional rights, and he exercised them," Garmone told a reporter.

When the story hit the papers, Mafia capos James Licavoli and Tony Delsanter reacted to the news.

"I hear Shon is going to get it again for income tax," Licavoli said.

"Again?" Delsanter said.

"Yeah. They want to know how much he paid for this and that."

"You know, Jack, at times you gotta give the poor son of a bitch credit. He takes all kinds of chances. The only thing I don't like about him is when he took over the numbers and he don't go in and tell Johnny."

"Well, I'll tell you, he don't step on nobody's toes," Licavoli said.

Jane would have disagreed.

To facilitate his trysts will Ellie, Shondor rented her an apartment. Jane had enough. She charged gross neglect. Shondor didn't contest the divorce.

Jane took up residence in Cleveland Heights with eleven-year-old Michael. Shondor continued living in the Judson Drive house but searched for a bigger home.

As for Ellie, her relationship with Shondor was more about loyalty and care, and less about fidelity. No doubt she loved him. But she, too, wanted sexual freedom. Her plays for other men, always younger, irritated Shondor and led to arguments. He told a confidant that he couldn't get rid of Ellie because she was his alibi witness in the Mervin Gold murder.

When it came to business, Shondor's capacity for reconciliation with business associates outshined that of marriage. So it was that Donald King, survivor of birdshot to the head courtesy of Birns seven years earlier, became a Birns enforcer. King would even occasionally be seen driving Shondor's new white Cadillac.

"Whenever Shondor needed anything done involving the blacks, he got Donald King to carry it out," said a clearinghouse operator.

Shondor was back in the numbers racket. But it was no secret. When investigators noticed Birns's repeated trips to suburban Parma, they set up surveillance.

On an afternoon in July 1964, Cleveland and Parma detectives observed Shondor entering a two-story building. He was wearing a sports shirt and carrying a small paper bag. Fifty minutes later, Edward Keeling, thirty-seven, a well-known numbers figure who had long been an associate of Shondor, arrived and walked inside.

The police moved in. In a small windowless office, they surprised both men, who were using adding machines to tabulate bet revenue, and arrested them. The space belonged to Vulcan Basement Waterproofing Company, which was run by Birns's associate Fiore Bucci. Vulcan was a front for Bucci's other businesses, including burglary and gambling. He was also suspected of being one of Birns's explosives men. Detectives located Shondor's checkbook register, which showed a balance of $2,300. They confiscated it. Eventually the IRS emptied the account and applied it toward Birns's tax bill.

Birns and Keeling were indicted for running a clearinghouse game. Shondor's attorney felt the case was weak and that the police should have had a search warrant. Still, Shondor wanted better odds. While out on bail, he asked Clarence Bennett, a Parma detective, to meet him at the Beef and Bottle Restaurant. When they settled in, Birns asked about his family.

"How many kids do you have?"

"Five. And my wife is pregnant," Bennett said.

"What's your salary?"

"Sixty-eight hundred a year."

"How can you support five kids?" Shondor asked. "I make twenty thousand a year from a Canadian ore company and have difficulty raising one kid."

Birns placed twenty ten-dollar bills on the table.

"What's this for?" Bennett asked.

"It's a present for your wife and five kids."

"Come on, Shondor, I know better than that. What's the money for?"

"Look, I'm going to beat that gambling charge on a motion of illegal search and seizure, but just in case, I want any information the police may have."

"Shondor, it looks like I'm getting into something and it reminds me of Mervin Gold," Bennett said. "You know they found him stuffed in a trunk."

"Don't worry about Gold. You'll never be as low as he was."

Detective Bennett was wearing a hidden microphone that was transmitting to a receiver monitored by his partner in a car outside the restaurant. As a result, Birns was indicted for bribery. The uncertainty of this case's outcome would hang over Shondor's head for quite some time.

Meanwhile, Shondor increased his workouts and steam baths at the Executive Club. He often ate breakfast there with Frank Brancato. He might meet George Gordon, when he was in town, at the Executive Club or the Somerset Motel in Shaker Heights. When the FBI learned of Gordon's visits and meetings, they placed a hidden microphone in his room. On one occasion, they overheard Gordon tell someone, "Shon got away with a headache." Agents suspected it was a reference to the murder of Mervin Gold.

In the evenings, Shondor was putting in nightly appearances at La Scala Restaurant. When he was in the house, guests might hear an employee call out over small group jazz music, "Shondor! Telephone call from Pittsburgh." During the same period, Birns invested in a cocktail lounge called Don Antonio's and a black nightclub called the Apex. He also put up cash for an associate to provide loans and sports booking for dockworkers with the okay of waterfront boss Danny Greene. Danny provided longshoreman jobs for some of Shondor's friends.

Greene ran the union with an iron fist. He also began associating with city racketeers, thus drawing the attention of the FBI. As part of their mission to combat organized crime, FBI agents were tasked with developing confidential informants. Anyone with access to inside knowledge was a candidate. But convincing someone, especially an insider whose reputation and life could be at stake should they be outed, was some feat. It was an Irish-American agent who convinced Danny Greene to work with the FBI.

Greene's grip on the docks didn't last long. When longshoremen complained about unfair management practices, a tenacious *Plain Dealer* reporter went to work. His exposé sparked a federal investigation and resulted in an indictment. A trial followed, and Greene was convicted of falsifying records and embezzling over $10,000 in union funds. He was fined $10,000 and barred from participating in any labor union business for five years. He appealed the conviction and continued to operate as a valued FBI informant.

From there, Danny became a driver and enforcer for Frank Brancato. In the months to follow, Danny took on a similar role for Shondor Birns.

***

In early 1965, Shon and Ellie moved to Orange Village, a rural bedroom community just outside of the Cleveland city limits. The $31,500 ranch was put in the name of Shondor's sister, Hermina Cooke. The house sat on a 1.5-acre lot at the top of a low hill. The interior had an open design with a living room and formal dining area that led to the kitchen. A recreation room featured a fireplace in which Shondor installed a grill. Off the kitchen was a laundry room, and next to that was an extra room where Shondor worked out on heavy and speed bags. For his age, he was swift and powerful. Also in that room were kennels for Fury and a second Doberman pinscher that Shon named Satan.

One day, Birns had just returned from a workout at the Executive Club when a reporter visited. Shondor sipped Tang, an orange vitamin drink, from a tumbler and chewed on a cigar while he showed the reporter and a photographer around his property. He stopped to give them a peek at his new Cadillac, titled to his brother-in-law, and a new tractor. The reporter asked Shondor if he would pose on the mower. He declined.

"The revenue boys would really like to see that," Shon said. "You know, one of the reasons I stay in shape is to keep up with my troubles."

***

Shondor and Ed Keeling moved their operation to an east side apartment. They had 140 writers and runners, many of them women working out of their homes. Up to $8,000 came in daily for their new big bond game which originated in Pittsburgh.

The big bond accepted higher wagers and featured bigger payouts, thus it was in competition with the other clearinghouse games. The big bond game paid winners 600 to 1, and the regular bond paid out at 500 to 1. Winning numbers were determined by a formula using daily bond price figures in the financial section of the newspaper. The new stock game paid 400 to 1, and the old stock game paid 300 to 1. Those winners were determined officially by various columns and combinations of the stock market's daily closing "advances, declines, and unchanged" figures as published in the Wall Street Journal. Clearinghouse players were eager to check the newspapers daily to see if they "hit the number."

"The numbers racket in Cleveland is big," said a numbers writer, a foreman in an assembly plant, in 1972. "You can play at [certain] pizza houses, smoke shops, beverage stores, haberdasheries, factories, hospitals. . . You can play in Cleveland Heights, you can play in Parma. The game is everywhere."

Major numbers operators included Bill Seawright, and Virgil Ogletree. Seawright was a politically-connected entrepreneur who invested his gambling profits in land and legitimate companies, such as construction firms, a travel agency, and a nightclub called the Music Box. Ogletree, at the height of his success, captured nearly half of the city's numbers action. He drove a custom Cadillac.

"In the numbers business, you have to drive a fancy car," Ogletree said. "It is necessary to have an impressive image. People will not go to a shabby numbers bank."

Bill Riedthaler, a former detective for the Cleveland Police Department, investigated gambling extensively. He explained how a typical clearinghouse operation worked.

"The bettors would place their bets with the writers," Riedthaler said. "The writers would turn in the bet slips and cash at the station. The station workers checked the slips to make sure they were written correctly and that they matched the money turned in. Once the deadline was reached, an hour prior to the stock market closing, the bets were charted to determine how much was wagered on each number. Originally this was done by hand, then it became computerized. A worker faxed these figures to the office or sub-office. Each operator knew how much of a hit he could take if a heavily played number won. If need be, he would lay off to a bigger operation by wagering a certain amount on that number."

Riedthaler explained another system which clearinghouse operators used to reduce risk.

"At certain times, certain numbers might be played especially heavy, like 2-1-4 on Valentine's Day. To increase the odds in favor of the house, such numbers would be 'cut' and the payoff reduced. Players would be notified in advance by cut cards being distributed in the neighborhoods served by the particular operation."

Shondor Birns, like Benny Mason thirty-five years earlier, touted his game as a benefit to the community.

"If I got out of numbers," he told a cop, "thousands of people would be on charity."

Birns cornered most of the layoff action for the clearinghouse racket thus insuring operators from catastrophic losses. He sent these wagers, and those of his own operation, to Kelly Mannarino. Kelly and his brother Sam were Mafia bosses in New Kensington, Pennsylvania, and allied with the Pittsburgh mob.

Tony Grosso was the top operator and financier in the numbers racket in Pittsburgh. The city was considered by some experts to be the national headquarters for illegal lotteries. Shondor often went through Joseph W. Harper, a black numbers money man who raked in big profits behind the scenes by exclusively handling layoff bets. Harper's success provided him with a home in Pittsburgh and a penthouse suite in Park Centre, a high-end downtown Cleveland apartment complex.

Several weeks after relocating his numbers operation with Ed Keeling, Shondor was on Vincent Avenue near the Theatrical when he ran into an FBI agent. Sensing that Shondor was in one of his typical chatty moods, the agent suggested they sit down. Shondor was not unfriendly with friendly feds. He was open but of course cautious to tell the agents only what he was fairly certain they already knew.

The men ducked into a nearby health club. Shondor told the agent that he had married Ellie recently in Florida, but he was preoccupied with his tax difficulties and another pending indictment. In addition, after the IRS warned officials at Ontario Stone that they would garnish Shon's wages, the company took him off the payroll.

"I want to get it settled once and for all with the IRS so I can work legitimately for Ontario Stone. I'm not getting five cents from Ontario right now. They forced me back into the numbers. Then I wanted to open a college fund for my son, but an accountant told me the IRS could steal that from me too."

The agent asked about the clearinghouse business.

"Here is the real problem with the numbers. There are too many independent operators, and there is no organization or control," Shondor said. "The blacks feel they should control everything themselves and no whites should be involved. They're all fighting among themselves, and none of them have a sufficient bankroll to pay winners if they get hit bad."

***

The 1964 indictment for bribing the Parma detective weighed heavily on Shondor. He anticipated going to prison and was concerned about the bad press that might follow.

"If I get another conviction, the papers will murder me," he told a friend. "Life is just a jungle . . . Every time something happens, I'm blamed. They blame it on a Birns sergeant or lieutenant. What do they think I have, an army?"

In the meantime, another legal matter took center stage. In November 1965, Shondor's trial for making false statements to the Internal Revenue Service began. During a break, Birns leaned on a banister and chatted with journalist Michael Roberts. A couple of judges passed by, smiled, and waved, "Hi Shon."

"If I'm the city's biggest crook, why do they all want to be my friend?" Shondor said. "I'll tell you why. Most of them are worse than I am, and they know that I know. Write that sometime."

Roberts did write it—in a story for *Cleveland Magazine*, a new monthly that became a source of in-depth investigative pieces about organized crime.

Roberts observed, "It was a generation of newspaper reporters, more than anyone else, who had given Shondor Birns one of the things he had sought the most: notoriety."

In early December 1965, Shondor was convicted of having made false statements to the IRS, in 1961 and 1962, about his assets. It was success for the feds. Shon appealed.

A few weeks later, it was success for the locals.

BIRNS FOUND GUILTY OF BRIBERY read the *Plain Dealer* headline on December 23, 1965.

It was a one-two federal-state punch for Cleveland's most-arrested and least-convicted racketeer who might have also been dubbed "slowest convict to commence time." Birns remained free as both cases worked through the appeals process.

Eight months later, Shondor was still on the streets, seen with Danny Greene in tow almost daily. With two cases closing in, Birns anticipated prison time. Greene would protect his numbers business and keep payments coming in to Ellie.

In the meantime, Shon and Ellie enjoyed his freedom. They dined out frequently. A couple of times, they invited Danny and his wife, Nancy. Clothing, especially considering their similar sizes, was a subject of conversation for the wives. When Nancy voiced admiration for her pantsuit, Ellie made a gift of it.

Almost two years after his dual state and federal convictions, Shondor exhausted his appeals in the bribery case. Prosecutor John Corrigan filed for an arrest mandate, and Carl Delau waited eagerly. James Willis needed a little more time. He telephoned Judge Angelotta, who was out of town, and obtained a temporary stay of execution from the arrest.

Corrigan fumed. "It's a delay tactic. I was angry and I covered the waterfront with the judge," he told a reporter.

Birns would have to appear before Judge Angelotta the following week. Willis finalized his legal maneuvering. He sent his associate, Charles Mosely, to see Angelotta just before the hearing was scheduled to begin. Moseley told the judge that he could not ensure Birns's appearance. As a result, Angelotta ordered Birns arrested. It was the moment Carl Delau had long waited for. He dispatched a team of detectives to snatch Birns.

Before they even reached their unmarked cars, Delau's crew was too late. Willis had already surrendered Birns at federal court. Shondor, at least for now, would avoid the Ohio Penitentiary and serve time in the relative comfort of federal prison. He was sent to Terre Haute, a newer institution on the Wabash River in Terre Haute, Indiana. After a few months, he was transferred to the US Penitentiary at Atlanta, Georgia. Jim Willis continued to argue that improper evidence went to the federal jury.

With Shondor locked up, one numbers operator increased his pay-out on winners to boost business. Danny decided to send a message. He lit a stick of dynamite and started cruising toward the man's storefront. The fuse was burning faster than Greene expect-ed. He tried to throw it out the passenger window, but it hit the door and bounced back in. Danny opened his door to escape. He was halfway out when the dynamite exploded. When police arrived, he claimed someone drove by and tossed the dynamite through his window. Danny was lucky. His car was heavily damaged, but he was relatively unscathed. He would, though, forever be hearing impaired from a shattered right eardrum.

These were violent times in Shondor's world, and perhaps in some respects he was better off locked away in prison. Increasingly, reporters were covering street violence. Racially-charged riots brought civilian and police deaths. And in the underworld, power plays brought offensives to maintain reputations and control. In the years following the killing of Mervin Gold, several murders occurred within Shondor's circle of associates.

Shondor's old buddy, Abe Zeid, had established a reputation as a Pittsburgh gambling figure and mob enforcer. In 1965, his body was found on a farm stuffed in a shallow grave covered with weeds. Zeid had been beaten and shot in the head. It happened just hours after he was convicted in a $12,000 blackmail scheme.

Perhaps the most notorious Cleveland mob murder of the 1960s was that of Perino "Pete" DiGravio. He was partnered in a legit-imate money lending operation in Little Italy. It was a "6 for 5" system: borrow $500 and pay back $600; borrow $5,000 and pay back $6,000. DiGravio prided himself on being a tough and successful businessman who operated independently of the mob, even though he was well-acquainted with top players.

DiGravio was golfing in rural Geauga County. He was at the sixteenth tee lining up his swing when a rifle shot cracked off and echoed across the course. Mortally wounded, DiGravio fell as a sniper hidden in adjacent woods fired two more times to be sure his job was complete. A reputed hitman named Bob Boggess was questioned. The murder went unsolved, but motives persisted. One had a mob power infuriated over DiGravio's reply to a newspaper reporter questioning his friendship with alleged mobsters.

"I need the Mafia like I need cancer," he said.

It was also rumored that DiGravio refused a loan to Shondor's pal Frank Brancato.

***

Jim Willis was earning an impressive reputation in the appeals arena. An appeals judge agreed that evidence of Birns's criminal history should not have been included in documents provided to the trial jury. In May 1968, Shondor's conviction was reversed. He was released by US District Judge Thomas Lambros and given ten days to confer with Willis about a retrial. Birns's temporary release from federal custody was secured by a low bond of $1000 because the US attorney felt the aging racketeer was a low risk.

"It's the first time anybody's been kind to me," Birns told a reporter as a court clerk prepared paperwork for him to sign. "I'm going to keep my copy of the bond and frame it—I've had higher bonds for doing nothing."

The reporter asked Shondor about his time at the federal penitentiary in Atlanta.

"Believe me, it was no holiday camp," Birns said. "They had three killings and fifteen knifings. That's something you never hear about."

Shondor signed the bond form and the clerk asked for his telephone number.

Birns declined to provide it. "I'm not going to be home anyway," he said.

"Well, I might want to call you for a tip on a football game," the clerk joked.

"Look, I'll give you the best tip right now," Birns said. "Keep your money in your pocket."

Cuyahoga County Prosecutor John Corrigan found no amusement in Shondor being freed for ten days.

"Birns has been sentenced to the Ohio Penitentiary, and that is where he'll go," he said. "The fact that he is a federal prisoner does not give him immunity from what the state wants to do with him. We'll take him down to Columbus just as soon as we can legally do so. That could be within ten days, the length of stay granted by Judge Lambros."

A few days later, the US attorney decided against retrial. He knew Birns had state time to serve, so he dismissed the federal case. As a result, and despite the best efforts of his attorney, Shondor was moved in 1968 to the Ohio Penitentiary. Also serving time there was burglar Charlie Broeckel.

"That's when I got close with Shon," Broeckel said. "He was an old guy coming through and didn't know shit from shinola at the pen. I got him the right cell, the right job. Whatever little connections there were, I made for him to make things better. I respected him and took care of him whenever I could."

Shondor was eventually transferred to Ohio's Marion Correctional Institute. There he was put in charge of the commissary. And he became assistant to the Catholic chaplain, Father Frederick Furey. Furey remembered Birns as an inmate worker who was honest, generous, and admired.

"There was never even a stick of gum missing when Shondor ran the commissary," Furey said. He would walk through the prison yard and command respect. He was an arbiter. If an enforcer was after a guy, Shon would try to help the poor fellow."

Furey once told Shondor that he would have been top dog anywhere. "Why didn't you go into a business?" the priest asked the racketeer. "You would have been a millionaire."

Shondor was rarely reflective about his past. But he did tell Father Furey that he had tried to go straight during his Alhambra days. "But when they get you down," he complained, "they don't let you go straight."

Back in Cleveland, Danny Greene managed Shondor's numbers operation and made regular payments to Ellie. She took care of the house and Dobermans and occasionally visited her mother. Ellie was a regular customer at Albert and Louis Salon, where she became good friends with her beautician, Sandy. They went out regularly for drinks and dinner—the Highlander, the Theatrical, the Blue Grass, and the Proud Pony were favorites.

Sometimes Sandy's fiancé would go along. Ellie might bring Danny.

"One night we were out for dinner with Ellie and Danny Greene," Sandy recalled. "When we left the restaurant, me and my fiancé were supposed to go to a party. We couldn't find it, so we went to Ellie's house. Danny was there. Ellie had changed into a robe. She and Danny were sitting on the sofa. Close. They were being playful and teasing each other. A few days later, Ellie showed me a present that Danny gave her. It was a teddy bear. Green."

Ellie visited Shondor in prison frequently. She brought him food, and he shared it with fellow inmates. On his birthday, she paid for Hough Bakery to send a truck to cater a party. This sort of team spirit was also present on the softball field where Shon's team won the prison's softball championship.

Birns served his time with a generally lighthearted attitude. One year, he sent out Christmas cards featuring Santa Claus behind bars telling his lawyer, "It's some ridiculous thing about breaking and entering."

***

Shondor's parole hearing came up in the summer of 1971. With a clean prison record, his odds were favorable. He had a job offer through Sam Miller, vice president and treasurer of Forest City Enterprises, a rapidly expanding real estate development firm. Miller had a history of providing jobs to paroled convicts.

With employment secured, Shondor received parole, but for five years, not the one year he was expecting. He was convinced his attorney could get it reduced after he was released.

On July 1, 1971, Alex Shondor Birns walked out of Ohio's Marion Correctional Institution. He was coming home and had a new job. And that was valuable ink for newspaper reporters. But Birns as a Forest City employee was a problem for the respected company. When the story hit, the offer was withdrawn.

"Shondor Birns will not have any job, directly or indirectly, with Forest City," announced Sam Miller.

Shon understood. He was sensitive about causing embarrassment for his legitimate business friends. Years later, Miller revealed to author John Tidyman that his job offer to Shondor had been in return for a favor.

"I ran numbers for him when I was a kid," he said. "I had to give him a job."

Not only did Shondor need a job, he also needed a new wardrobe. A friend referred him to a downtown store called Buddy Lewis's Fashions for Men. Lewis, a mobbed-up businessman, gave Birns the platinum treatment and they became friends.

Shondor also found an ally in probation officer Henry Stoken, who initially found Birns to be cooperative. Stoken filed his report and requested consideration be given for a reduction in Shondor's parole.

While Birns waited for a decision, he renewed friendships and business associations with numbers operators, bookies, loan sharks, labor union officials, ex-cons, fix attorneys, fix judges, hitmen, and burglars. Still running in such circles, Shondor seemed unlikely to die in a rocking chair.

He also seemed unlikely to give up his insatiable desire for much younger women, even though he was now sixty-five, complaining of backaches and gall stones, and with his once fiery red hair thinning and graying. So it was that Shondor renewed a relationship with Mary "Janie" Jarus.

She was only twenty-two. The green-eyed brunette had met Birns as a teenager while dabbling in prostitution. She graduated to serving one client at a time—as long as his money lasted. In addition to men with disposable funds, Janie fancied the biker type, including members of the Hells Angels Motorcycle Club, with whom she socialized.

Meanwhile, the parole board made their decision. Henry Stoken went to Birns's house to give him the news.

"I arrived in the morning," Stoken said. "I told Birns his parole period remained unchanged. It would remain at five years. At first, he showed no surprise. Then he started getting angry."

"I'll file through Jerry Messerman [a well-known attorney]," Shondor said.

If Shondor thought he could still get his parole reduced, his behavior during Stoken's first visit did not help his case.

"The more we talked, the more angry Birns became," Stoken recalled. "He became very foul in his speech and cursed our department with various four-letter words."

Satan stirred and whined in his kennel. Stoken suggested Birns was overreacting.

"Then he said he wanted to take a trip to Las Vegas," Stoken recalled. "He was quite upset when I told him he would need a travel permit. He said he would no longer cooperate when he had a year completed. He said he would do as he pleases and travel without permission. He shed his sheep's clothing and showed what might be termed his old self—aggressive and hostile. Almost threatening."

Birns's efforts to reduce his parole were without success. Another parole officer, Harry See, was eventually assigned to Birns. See was twenty-six with an imposing but nonathletic frame. During his first visit to Birns's house, Satan came running in attack mode. The dog hit the door and startled See, who reached for his gun. During subsequent visits, See waited in the car until Shondor or Ellie put the Doberman in his kennel.

See wasn't the only one who had a problem with the Doberman. Jim Willis never felt at ease around him.

"I was sitting in Shon's living room," the lawyer said. "Every time I shifted in my chair, that dog lifted his head and stared at me. I said, 'Shon you got to do something with that fucking dog. It could be on someone in a second.' He said the dog wouldn't bother me. I told him all someone had to do was throw it a big piece of meat. Shon said it would only take food from him or Ellie."

***

212

The FBI kept tabs on key underworld characters by conducting spot checks at known haunts like the Theatrical, and the Lancer Steakhouse on Carnegie Avenue. The Lancer was a favorite gathering spot for black politicians, businessmen, and racketeers—their version of the Theatrical Grill. Confidential informants, which FBI agents increasingly cultivated, also reported on the movements of local hoods. Shondor was often observed with Frank Brancato.

Brancato had been under indictment along with his henchman, New Jersey import Carmen Semenoro. Semenoro's bond was reduced, and he was released from jail. He and Brancato awaited trial. Three months later, Semenoro was seated in his suburban ground-level apartment repairing a lamp when he was shotgunned through the window. A well-placed law enforcement source said Brancato believed Semenoro was going to testify against him, so he ordered his murder.

Brancato was also busy with gambling operations and a scheme to organize local rubbish haulers. The latter had brought New York mobsters big money. He used Danny Greene as an enforcer. The assignment brought Danny in direct conflict with friend and rubbish hauler Mike Frato. When Shondor learned of the issue, he told Greene, "Don't mess with the Italians. That's not good."

But Danny wasn't one to respect the rules. Though apparently unknown to Shondor, Danny had already proven his indifference to boundaries with Ellie. Naturally Ellie kept that quiet, but she did tell Shondor about hairdresser Sandy and her husband. Shon wanted to meet them.

The two couples struck up a friendship and went out for dinner often. Shondor preferred to take his own car. He would have Ellie drive but give her instructions like where to park. Along the way, sometimes, Shondor would make a stop to drop off or pick up an envelope. Neither Sandy nor her husband would ask any questions, and Shondor liked, even respected that. After dinner, he always picked up the tab. Later, Sandy's husband helped Birns remodel his house.

Perhaps, like games of handball with health club acquaintances, Shon found a sense of normalcy in time away from scheming racketeers and kiss-ass wannabes. Or perhaps Birns strategically used straight arrows as a cover of legitimacy—sort of a perpetual red herring.

There were times that Shondor revealed his tendency to be abusive to Ellie. He would rebuke her for a minor error with a verbal put-down. Occasionally he would punctuate it with a smack to her face. It was an infrequent but uncomfortable scene for Sandy and her husband. And Birns could be heartless. When Ellie got pregnant, he insisted that she have an abortion. He paid but sent her for the procedure alone.

***

After Shondor's release, Danny Greene continued doing odd jobs and enforcement work for him and Frank Brancato. But the thirty-nine-year-old Irishman as an errand boy for the aging Italian and Jew was not a good bet. Danny muscled in on local rackets. He started with fire chasers, the salesmen who monitor fire radio calls and respond to lock up the contract for repairs. When another opportunity presented itself, Danny asked Shondor for funding.

"After Shon got out, he didn't need Danny to oversee his operation," said Jim Willis. "So Danny asked him for a $75,000 loan."

Greene claimed that the money was to open a cheat spot, a nightclub that would serve liquor beyond the state's legal time limit. Birns, having invested in nightclubs and bars before, agreed and made arrangements with Mafia associates in New York City for Greene to receive the loan.

Meanwhile, Shondor slid right back into the numbers racket. The other big operators were Virgil Ogletree, Richard Drake, and Donald King. King was the owner of the New Corner Tavern, where he brought in entertainers like B. B. King and Erroll Garner. Drake inherited the business when his father, Arthur, died. Shondor took Richard under his wing, and the two became partners. Some in the black community believed there was a deeper connection between the two men.

Richard's light complexion and reddish-tinged hair fueled a persistent rumor that his father was actually Shondor Birns.

In addition to his operation with Drake, Shondor continued to serve as an administrator of finance and enforcement with the goal of keeping the numbers business running smoothly and profits steady.

"But Birns remained somewhat legendary, and somewhat of an anachronism, two ingredients that cause vulnerability," wrote Michael Roberts.

For a white man in a black racket, no doubt there would be challenges. In a *Call and Post* editorial, a group of black clearinghouse operators made clear their thoughts on the significance of numbers to their community.

Numbers playing is a heritage that involves exclusively black money. The numbers operation is a functional financial institution in the black community contributed to by black people to provide hundreds of jobs and support the neighborhood businesses which supply their goods and services. It employs black people who otherwise are unable to qualify or just simply barred from holding jobs in white-owned businesses. Numbers fulfill the responsibility forsaken by white banks in the community that profitably use black money, but refuse to finance or support black home and property owners and businesses by being a funding base.

Despite such a perspective, many blacks viewed the role of Shondor Birns in the numbers racket from a context of business and recognized his value.

"Black folks respect Shondor," said a numbers employee. "He's a mediator. And he can move with politicians, judges, and cops."

Those with priorities other than business threatened trouble. Shondor had employed capable enforcers like veterans Frank Cook, Fred Stitmon, and Billy Cox. But their dependability was waning.

While working as a bouncer at a bar, Frank Cook caught three slugs in his midsection before returning fire and killing his assailant. Cook survived the shooting, but his health deteriorated rapidly due to heart disease. Ultimately it was stroke that killed him. Shondor paid for his funeral.

Fred Stitmon and Billy Cox were gravitating toward the big and fast profits of drug trafficking. Younger black racketeers simply wanted Birns, an old white man, out of the numbers racket that they felt belonged to their community.

But the loyalty of others on Birns's payroll endured. They included Ronald Grier, a politically connected leader in the black community who converted to Islam and adopted the surname Bey. He was also a racketeer allied with the Mafia. Despite working in several city departments during the administrations of Carl Stokes and Ralph Perk, Bey's name was occasionally mentioned in connection with violence. He was on Shon's payroll for $200 a week.

William Barnes, who took the name Ali Khan and was prominent with the Black Panthers, also made $200 a week. If an operator raised his payoff amount on winners, or paid a runner more than 25 percent of his total bets, then Shon would get a call. He'd sit down and try to convince the operator to cooperate. If it were a failed sit-down, then Bey or Khan would step in.

***

Burglars figured prominently in Shondor's capacity as a fence. This circle included some of the most skilled thieves in the country. Some provided additional services.

Bob Boggess was notable in that regard. He took pleasure in sipping brandy. Some say he also took pleasure in carrying out mob hits. Boggess was ambidextrous and lightning quick with his trademark .45. With an unconventional style, he would allow his victim to sit behind him in a car. Suddenly Boggess would spin around and "nail 'em to the back seat," as he would say.

Boggess told burglar Charlie Broeckel that he and Mafia member Joe Gallo murdered Carmen Semenoro for Frank Brancato. Broeckel also figured Boggess for the 1968 murder of Patrick Catalano, a labor union official whose body was never found.

"Bobby is the only real killer, real hitman, I've known," Broeckel said.

Bob Boggess was like a brother to William "Moe" Kiraly, a self-taught mechanical engineer on whom some bestowed genius status. Kiraly had multiple interests, including horseracing, and even patented a new design for a sulkie. Another interest was explosives.

Frank Brancato used Boggess and his crew as enforcers for his gambling operations. One of Brancato's most popular game originated in the Middle East and was brought to the US with Greek immigrants. It was known as *Barbut*. Similar to craps, the fast-paced dice game involves two players at a time betting against each other and trying to throw winning combinations of numbers. The odds of winning in Barbut are 50:50. The house takes a percentage of the losing bets to generate a profit.

"Barbut was a gold mine," said mob associate Martin "Mutt" DiFabio. "When it was run in the Murray Hill [Little Italy] area, it was controlled by Jack Licavoli and run for him by Butchie Cisternino and two others. It took place at a location we called The Library. Jack received a weekly profit."

Frank Brancato received a percentage of the Greektown Barbut game run by John Fotoupolis, also known as John Fotos. When Fotos retired, Anastaseo "Tasso" Vrettos, a Greek coffee shop operator, inherited the operation. When Tasso stopped paying his cut, Frank warned him to shut down. Vrettos ignored Brancato's demands.

On a fall evening in 1971, Brancato summoned Vrettos to a meeting. It was 1:00 a.m. when Tasso arrived at Captain Frank's on the Ninth Street Pier.

"One word came to another, and it wasn't changing Tasso's mind," Charlie Broeckel said. "He more or less told Frank to go fuck himself. Then he walked out and got in his car."

Vrettos shifted into reverse, but another car had pulled up and blocked him in. Vrettos locked his door. He grabbed for the .38 revolver he had been recently carrying. The man approaching his door had a pistol. Tasso didn't wait to exchange greetings. He shot rapidly through the window and felled his assailant with five bullets. But the man got back up. He shot Tasso several times and returned to his car. The driver sped off. Vrettos's car slowly drifted back across the pier and was stopped by a utility pole from dropping into the lake.

According to Broeckel, Tasso's assailant was Bob Boggess. His wheelman, Moe Kiraly, drove to the Youngstown, Ohio, area, where Boggess was treated by a doctor. Though severely wounded, he survived. Tasso Vrettos did not.

The crew that Bob Boggess and Moe Kiraly worked with included Billy Whitcomb, Sal Carcione, and Charlie Broeckel. Charlie was close with Phil Christopher, the soft-spoken, notorious bank burglar. In March 1972, while residents of Laguna Niguel, in Orange County, California, slept, Phil disabled the security system at the United California Bank, allowing him, the notorious Dinsio brothers from Youngstown, Ohio, their crew, and Broeckel to pull off the biggest bank heist in US history. They cut a hole in the roof and blasted through the top of the vault. They hammered open hundreds of safe-deposit boxes then carried away $30 million gross, mostly in bearer bonds. But they made mistakes. When the indictments came, a newspaper reporter dubbed Phil "Superthief."

After the heist, Charlie Broeckel approached Shondor to fence the bonds. He took Phil Christopher with him to meet Birns at the Theatrical.

"It was lunchtime and busy," Phil recalled. "We sat at the bar and ordered. Charlie noticed Shondor a few stools away and said hello. Shondor yelled, 'Hello, Charlie!' I thought to myself, can this guy talk any louder?"

Charlie got up and greeted Shondor. They walked to the back of the restaurant. Charlie motioned for Phil to follow.

"I waved him off," Phil said. "A lot of people watched Charlie and Shondor enter the restroom. My sandwich came, and I ate fast. I was just finishing when Charlie and Shondor came back. Charlie introduced me. We shook hands. Shondor said loudly, 'I hear you're doing pretty good.' I smiled but was thinking to myself, what an obnoxious asshole."

Shondor shook hands with Charlie and returned to his seat. Before he sat down, he said to Charlie, "I'll see you later with those things."

Charlie sat down and started on his sandwich.

Phil was pissed. "Is this motherfucker nuts talking so loud?"

"Nobody knows what we're talking about, Phil."

Phil couldn't get away from Shondor quick enough. Once outside, he laid into Charlie.

"Is that guy an idiot? Does he think he has a license to steal?"

"That's just the way he is, Phil. He's loud. But Shon's got a lot of connections."

***

Michael Birns usually visited his father when he needed money or was in trouble. And with a notorious racketeer for a role model, he found it difficult to stay out of trouble. In the summer of 1972, the nineteen-year-old was arrested for growing marijuana. He pleaded guilty and paid a one-hundred-dollar fine. In 1974, he was driving in Cleveland Heights at 1:00 a.m. when he hit a car from behind. An argument broke out. Michael slugged the other driver, who grabbed a steel bar from his car and womped young Birns in the head, sending him to the emergency room.

Meanwhile, Shondor had more problems to deal with.

"Shon obtained a loan of $75,000 for Danny Greene," explained Charlie Broeckel. "It was from the New York outfit. Billy Cox was involved. The money wound up lost in a drug operation raided by the cops. Guys came down from New York, and they wanted the juice money on the seventy-five. On a 6 for 5 loan, that's about five thousand dollars a week. Now, who is gonna pay five thousand a week for money he hasn't even got? Shondor blamed Danny for losing the money. Danny said it wasn't his fault and he couldn't pay it back."

"I got my people to help you, and you screwed them," Shondor told Danny. "You're a big man now. You want to be on your own, huh?"

"Oh fuck you," Danny said. "You're old, and you're finished. And I'm doing things my own way now."

When Shondor was at the Theatrical, he ran into one of Danny's guys. Shondor pushed a confrontation. He beckoned the man outside and slapped him. When Danny found out, he was furious.

"Shon is dead before midnight," he told an associate.

Birns had enough. He called in Bobby Boggess and said he would pay him $20,000 to get rid of Greene. While Shon waited, he employed off-duty police officers at five dollars per hour to sit outside his house. When he was out on business, Shon utilized bodyguards, including Boggess, Sal Carcione, or Ali Kahn.

Within a few weeks of Boggess receiving the order, Greene

learned he was a target. He found a bomb on his car and disabled it. He vowed to return the explosive to the "old bastard" who had it placed.

Boggess suspected it was a newer crew member who informed Danny: Billy Whitcomb, who lived in Collinwood near Greene. He decided Whitcomb had to go.

According to Charlie Broeckel, Boggess's crew dug a grave in a wooded area of Oakwood Village, not far from the Mayflower Motel and Tavern, in preparation for the hit. Bob Boggess and Moe Kiraly picked up Billy under the guise of casing a location for a burglary. Kiraly drove, and Boggess sat next to him. A pistol lay at Boggess's left hand. Carcione sat behind Kiraly and Whitcomb behind Boggess.

When Kiraly turned onto a secluded access road, Boggess eased the pistol from his left hand to his right. Whitcomb realized he was about to be murdered. He pulled his gun just as Boggess spun around. Shots were fired. It was chaotic and lasted only seconds. Whitcomb and Boggess were dead. Carcione was seriously wounded.

Later, Carcione told police he had been shot while in a phone booth. Due to the angle of his bullet wound, they deemed his story implausible. Neither he nor Kiraly ever talked to investigators. And the details of the shootout and double murder remained mostly unknown.

Meanwhile, longtime Birns enforcer Billy Cox was indicted for trafficking in heroin and cocaine. Shondor visited him at Cuyahoga County Jail and paid his bond so he could be released. Charlie Broeckel was also there, facing twenty years for burglary. Shondor brought both men cigars.

When Cox failed to appear for his drug trial, Shon had him run him down to get back $2,500 in bond money.

"They're both on junk, and I'm through with them," Shondor told Janie.

Cox was angry with Birns for allowing him to be arrested, for not letting him go with the bond money, and for taking his wristwatch. Other young black racketeers were increasingly dissatisfied with Shondor's position of influence in black organized crime and spoke of taking over Birns's role as overseer of the numbers racket.

In the meantime, the approach of the Ohio state lottery was of little concern to clearinghouse operators.

"There hasn't been a state where numbers has been hurt," said one writer.

The Ohio Lottery Commission's first game, the three-digit Buckeye 300, debuted in 1974. But the neighborhood clearinghouse remained an attractive game of chance, especially in black communities. There were higher payoff odds, no IRS reporting of winnings that generated taxes, and perhaps the option for some trusted players to gamble on credit. Eventually, numbers operators abandoned the stock and bond figures to provide a winning number. Instead, they conveniently utilized the Ohio Lottery drawings. In effect, it was an arranged marriage of their illegal operations to the state lottery, which they even used as a layoff source.

"The street numbers game continued to function—if not flourish— even after the state tried to snatch it away from the men who had run it for decades," wrote *Plain Dealer* associate editor Phillip Morris.

Any potentially negative impact to clearinghouse by the state lottery was further mitigated by the decline of policy. In Cleveland it was nearing extinction, with games down to an area of five blocks around Shondor's old neighborhood, East 55th and Woodland Avenue, known as the policy belt. Bets were picked up at night. Games were "floated" to different locations. The recording of policy wagers might be was done on nitrocellulose, known commonly as flash paper and used by magicians for special effects. In the event of a police raid, it could be ignited and would burn away in an instant. Similarly, rice paper could be used with a pot of boiling water at the ready to instantly reduce it to mush. And instead of operators allowing large crowds at the drawings, they limited attendance to three or four monitors who spread the word of the winning numbers. Running a policy game became more cumbersome than ever, so many operators announced their retirement. As a result, clearing-house gained new players.

CHAPTER TEN

Parole Officer Harry See continued to supervise Shondor. Birns referred to the young man as "kid." See was not intimidated.

"You might call me 'kid' in your house," he told Birns. "Anywhere else, I'm Officer See."

When See visited, Ellie was often home.

"She was the opposite of the tough broad you might expect Shondor would attract," the parole officer said. "She seemed sensitive, maybe even oversensitive, and the protected or sheltered type. Ellie was polite and would always offer me coffee and a roll. She kept the house immaculate."

Like Shondor, See raised Doberman pinschers. Consequently, the dogs became a topic of conversation, and Shondor or Ellie would let Satan and Fury out of their cage. The well-trained dogs would stay by Shondor's side. If Ellie were home, Satan would shadow her. If she went to the bathroom, the dog would lie down outside until she emerged. See suggested that Shondor take one of the dogs with him when he went into unsafe neighborhoods.

"Nobody will mess around with your car as long as that Doberman's in there," See told Birns.

During this time, Shondor remained on travel restriction. He needed approval to travel outside the Parole Authority district.

"Sometimes he would want to go to Youngstown," See recalled. "I knew the Mahoning Valley was a hotbed for organized crime activity. I'd tell Shondor, 'I don't approve.' He wouldn't get angry but would try convincing me that it would be okay. Then he wanted to travel to Las Vegas. I said to him, 'I doubt that will fly. It will be a waste of time and paper.'"

"Put my request through," Birns told See.

"Shondor, it's alleged that you deal with organized crime, and organized crime built Las Vegas."

"Put it through, kid. I told you I'm gonna stay out of trouble. I promised the parole board and you that I won't be any trouble. I don't break any provision of parole. I'll tell you why. If I go back to jail, I'll die there. I'm not going back to jail. It's a little entertainment. Gambling is legal there and I can see some old friends. Just put it through. And if it doesn't get approved, I'm calling Jerry Gold [a well-known attorney]."

See told his supervisor of Shon's request.

"He wants to go where?" the man said.

See marked the request "Submitted with reservation" and put it through. However, Birns's ability to influence local, county, and state officials was usually a good bet. Harry See and his supervisor got a surprise. Birns's travel request came back. He received approval for the trip to Vegas. See didn't begrudge him the good news.

"He was classy," See said. "He treated me with respect and was a model parolee. I felt he was back in the rackets, but I never had any proof to revoke his parole."

Shondor maintained a respectful relationship with his parole officer out of common sense. But with uber-youthful courtesan Janie Jarus, strained emotions often sparked quarrels. Despite their rocky relationship, Shondor paid bills for her and her family and even bought her a new Pontiac. They would also spend some late evenings at the apartment of Richard Drake, Shon's numbers partner.

Shondor's endless quest to enjoy life's pleasures, live up to his legendary notoriety, and stay relevant within his social circles filled his time. He often spent the day crossing the bridges spanning the Cuyahoga River, which split the city between east and west, in his newly leased aqua blue diamond fire Lincoln Continental. The luxury car had a vinyl landau top, power sunroof, and power seats. In the morning, he might pick up doughnuts and visit his friend, owner of Buddy Lewis's Fashions for Men.

Shondor frequented top-shelf restaurants and some blue collar joints on the east side and west side. During this period, at least one other woman beckoned Shondor's interest. It was at the Seven-Thirty Club, at 730 Vincent Avenue, that Shon met Clevetta "Christy" Schuler. She was an attractive blonde thrice divorced. Christy and her last husband, a third-string racketeer, had owned a bar. With a renewed ambition to operate a tavern, Christy bought a go-go joint called Jack and Jill's, renamed it Christy's, and installed outdoor signage sporting mud-flap-girl-like silhouettes of shapely female forms.

The bar and grill sat at the northwest corner of Detroit Avenue and West 25th Street, across from St. Malachi Church, the anchor for one of the city's original Irish settlements. Christy's, with its front door on Detroit Avenue, was at the easterly end of a nearly block-long series of brick multiuse buildings. Apartments on the second and third floors overlooked the businesses below. It was a busy location—with an access ramp to a highway, the Cleveland Memorial Shoreway, off West 25th Street and bordering Christy's parking lot, which ran along the rear of the buildings. A walkway led customers from the rear parking lot to the side door of Christy's.

Some say Shondor provided Christy partial funding to buy the bar. She partnered with her brother, Del Hudson, owner of another joint called Party Time. Del was a heavy-drinking womanizer who kept his own party time suite above Christy's.

Christy's three-sided bar had fifteen stools on the long side and five on the short ends. The bar ringed an elevated platform with a mirrored backdrop. The stage featured go-go dancers clad in miniskirts and high boots grooving to the jukebox. When the music went silent, the girls solicited male patrons for quarters or fed the machine from a jar behind the bar. To encourage a festive atmosphere of flowing booze, Christy and Del kept a steady supply of watered-down liquor for employees. If the sibling partners wanted the good stuff themselves, they would signal the barmaid.

When Shon was at Christy's, he usually bought a round of drinks for the house and tipped the barmaid $20 or $30. His drink of choice was Hennessy cognac, and Christy kept a bottle exclusively for him under the counter. Shon usually sat at the short end of the bar closest to the front of the room while chatting with Christy or Del. When he left for the night, Del would walk him to his car.

***

It was lunchtime one day in 1974 when Shondor was at the Theatrical sitting with Jim Willis.

"An acquaintance of ours came in," Willis recalled. "He told us that Charlie Broeckel was going to testify in federal court. Shon looked at me. He said, 'I gotta see this.' We walked over to the courthouse. We sat there listening to Charlie. After ten minutes, Shondor got up. He didn't say anything to me and just walked out of the courtroom. I listened for a few more minutes then went to find Shon. I asked him why he left. 'I felt like I was going to throw up,' he said."

Facing twenty years for burglary, Broeckel flipped and went to work as a federal cooperating witness. He implicated the notorious Laguna Niguel, California, bank burglars, and two corrupt Cleveland police supervisors.

As a fence, Shondor was so concerned about Broeckel's testimony that he paid an acquaintance $200 a day to listen and take notes. The insider testimony was part of a new organized crime dynamic. While Shondor had reason to worry, an even greater threat was hanging over his head.

With Bob Boggess gone, Shondor's contract to kill Danny Greene fell to Moe Kiraly. He placed a package on the Irishman's Toyota. Danny found the bomb and promised to return it to his former mentor. Although he once walked in the shadow of Shondor Birns, Danny pushed forward to find his own niche.

In the fall of 1974, loan shark and former burglar James Zimmerman was found shot to death and dumped in the Cuyahoga River near downtown.

"A week after Jimmy Z was murdered," wrote *Cleveland Magazine* reporter Terence Sheridan, "Danny Greene had his book and was contacting his customers."

Meanwhile, as Shondor waited for his contract on Greene to be fulfilled, he and numbers partner Richard Drake would stop in the Lancer Steakhouse two or three times a week to meet with various associates.

Shondor had previously felt at home at the Lancer. But while he was imprisoned, the civil rights movement sparked a period that would significantly change the dynamics of the streets.

Michael Roberts summed it up in a *Cleveland Magazine* piece. "The nature of crime was changing, and the era which Birns symbolized was giving way to drugs and a resentment of white influence in a city where blacks were seeking independence in every walk of life," he wrote.

On a night in February 1975, Shondor and Janie Jarus were leaving Richard Drake's apartment. A yellow car with two men approached. One of them had a handgun and he fired twice. Neither Birns nor

Jarus was hit. Janie believed the shots were meant for her, not Shon.

Not long after, Shondor was with Janie, Richard Drake, and bodyguard Ali Khan at the Lancer. There was an altercation, and it escalated quickly. Several men yelled and cursed at Birns, and one displayed a gun in his waistband. Khan countered with a glimpse of a small machine gun under his coat. Drake hurried Janie outside.

"You shouldn't have to hear this," he told her.

Not long after the Lancer incident, Janie Jarus told Birns that she was in a downtown bar when she overheard a conversation that he was going to be killed. She warned him, but Shondor was dismissive.

"If you're talking about Greene, I'm not afraid of him or anyone else," he told her. "There's not a man brave enough to come up and shoot me. Danny doesn't have the guts."

"No," Jarus said. "It's going to be a bomb."

The conversation must have given Birns pause. What were the odds that Janie happened to overhear men planning his murder, including a key detail?

***

At the time, the use of bombs to murder and settle underworld disputes was increasing. Explosives were stolen from mines, quarries, and construction sites. An explosion, the thunderous and violent expansion of energy at an unfathomable 25,000 feet per second, is a terrifying force. Depending on its size and design, a bomb may instantaneously sever human limbs, disintegrate an entire body, mangle a car, or even level a building. It is an intensely frightening means to warn or an effective method to kill.

The belief that all evidence is destroyed in the blast was thought a great advantage by bombers. Post-blast investigations continued to improve, with many investigators having gained experience in the military. Meticulous examination would often uncover, at a minimum, the detonating system and type of explosive.

With their perceived advantages as tools of murder, bombings could go wrong due to their potential imprecise targeting. An explosive wired to a vehicle starter would be lethal to the person turning on the ignition. But that unfortunate might not be the intended victim. And if he were, there was no guarantee he would not be in the company of his wife, child, or other nonplayer. And for an explosive set with a timer, the bomber could not know for sure that an innocent person might not happen by at the wrong second. Bombers themselves risked instantaneous death by accidental detonation while "placing a package."

In January 1975, someone left a bomb, concealed in a suitcase, outside a house. Police believed it was intended to explode outside as part of a battle between outlaw motorcycle clubs. A resident unwittingly carried it inside, where it detonated. It was the wrong house. Three people, including a child, were killed.

The following month, someone left a gift-wrapped package outside the home of Richard Moss, a businessman with ties to organized crime figures. Richard picked up the box and called to his wife. Before she could answer, the package exploded.

The day after Moss was killed, Shondor was at the Theatrical Grill when Carl Delau approached.

"Pretty sad about your buddy Moss," Delau goaded.

"The son of a bitch probably deserved it," Birns said.

"Well at least he went faster than Mervin Gold, isn't that right, Shon?"

Shondor grinned. "You know how to hurt a guy, don't you?"

***

Apparently, Shondor did not feel indebted to Janie for her warning about a bomb ending his own life. He held onto the relationship for the desires she satisfied, but in early March he told her that her bills were getting to be too much. Then he dropped the subject.

Janie told a friend she was trying to break it off with Shondor, but he was refusing. As weeks went by, though, he spent more time with Christy, and consequently his relationship with Janie further deteriorated. It hit a low when they argued and Shondor smacked her several times.

Janie told her friend, dancer Carol Goan, that she needed time alone to think. She flew to California. A week later, Janie returned to Cleveland. She needed money, so she sold the Pontiac Shon gave her. Then she flew with Carol to Clearwater, Florida, saying it was to get away from Shondor. According to Carol, FBI agents drove her to the airport.

Two weeks later, Janie returned to Cleveland. On Good Friday, Jarus left for Florida again. Carol accompanied her. Janie checked the Cleveland newspapers daily. Carol asked why.

"Shon's always in the news about something."

***

On Holy Saturday, Shondor woke up with a cold. He dressed in maroon pants, a white turtleneck sweater, and a burgundy sport coat. He left the house, picked up a dozen doughnuts, then drove downtown to visit with Buddy Lewis. The men chatted. Shondor said he was leaving for Florida on Tuesday. He would be seeing Eugene Ciasullo, a Mafia enforcer, and other friends.

Shon brought a few items for his trip then left Lewis's store and drove to the Theatrical. While there, he overheard an acquaintance, a trash hauling executive, mention that his car was out for repair.

The man needed to get to the Silver Quill restaurant. Since Shon planned on heading there later, he offered him his car. Shon said he would get a ride to the Theatrical. Declining the offer, the man said he would take a taxi. Shon insisted, and the man relented.

They walked outside, and Shon showed him how to disable his theft alarm. He handed him the keys to the Lincoln. Later Shon got a ride to the Silver Quill from an Iron Workers Union official and friend. The rubbish hauler returned Shondor's keys and thanked him.

Shondor sipped on a cocktail and chatted with a close associate. For several minutes, he was overheard ranting over his Danlys Honduran cigar.

"That no good fucking psychopath. I put the umbrella over him a couple years back and saved his worthless ass and he just keeps it up. Tell that cocksucker, I'll meet him anywhere, face to face."

The friend gestured for Birns to lower his voice and calm down.

"I'm not going to mess with him," Birns said. "Three different groups want to take him out. They're looking for him now."

Shondor stayed at the Quill until 5:45 p.m. then headed to Christy's, where he parked in the rear as usual.

"Hi, Shon!" several patrons called out as Birns entered the go-go bar. Shondor waved to his admirers, and Christy greeted him with a hug. She poured him a generous shot of Hennessey, and he bought a round for the house. There were a few seconds of cheers and numerous "Thanks, Shon."

He and Christy sat at the bar and chatted. As he dabbed his nose with his handkerchief, he told Christy that he was leaving for Miami on Tuesday and that the Florida weather would help his cold. He was even thinking about retiring and told Christy that he just wanted to be left alone so he could enjoy his remaining years.

"I don't want to die in any rocking chair, though," he said.

Shondor got up and headed for the payphone. He called Janie's friend, Carol, and asked her where Janie was staying. Carol knew there was a conflict between the two and that Shondor was angry with Janie.

"I don't know where she went, Shondor."

For over fifty years, Shondor, now sixty-nine, had survived life in the underworld. He was the target of ambitious local, state, and federal law enforcers. He was defended by the most capable criminal lawyers. He was shot at, and he was shot. He survived attempted coups by key associates. He served time in prison. Cops believed he got away with murder. Five decades of experience in surviving the perils of the streets. He knew. There was no way that men planning his assassination had permitted an outsider to overhear their plans.

"She better watch her trips," Shondor told Carol.

After Shon got off the phone, Christy asked him for help. The vacuum closing unit on the front door had disengaged, and the door would not open. Shon and another customer worked on it. A few patrons approached outside, and Shondor motioned them toward the side door. Ten minutes later they fixed the door. Shondor returned to sipping his Hennessy.

Around 7:30 p.m., Shondor telephoned Carol again. He said he wanted her to take a job dancing at Christy's and told her she could make eight dollars an hour during the day. Carol agreed to discuss the offer at Christy's on Monday afternoon.

As dusk crawled across the region, some two hundred Catholics were across the street from Christy's, climbing the steps to the front doors of St. Malachi Church for a special mass. It was Holy Saturday—the solemn commemoration of Jesus's death, coming between Good Friday when he was crucified and Easter Sunday when he rose from the dead. Father Paul Hritz, a theology professor well known for relating his homilies to current events, checked on final preparations for the outside procession, slideshow, and mass.

Inside St. Malachi, the lighting was low. A small group of musicians played entrance music. A portable projection screen sat at the foot of the altar. The centerpiece for the mass was the special paschal candle, adorned with five grains of incense representing the resurrection of Christ and the five wounds in his side, hands, and feet. One or two at a time, the congregants lit their handheld candles using the holy flame.

Some of the worshippers opted to stay inside. The majority filed out into the sacred night. With cupped hands shielding their flames, they followed Father Hritz and the paschal candle in silence around the outside of the building. After the procession, they filed back into the darkened church. Father Hritz started the slideshow. The theme was "Creation." Brilliant color photos of the earth, sun, moon, and heavens flipped by to a serene background of recorded symphony music. The slides would be followed by readings from the book of Genesis, then Fr. Hritz would begin mass.

Some one hundred yards across West 25th Street, Shondor paid his tab. He gave Beverly a thirty-dollar tip. Since Del was in the upstairs suite, Christy asked a thirty-one-year-old regular named Ed Kester to walk Shon to his car. Ed was friendly with Shondor and happy to oblige. He persisted even as Birns begged him off.

Shon bid Christy goodbye. They hugged, then he walked out the side door with Ed Kester in tow. They turned left at the corner to the parking lot and to Shondor's car. While Shondor got seated, Ed stood at the open car door, and the men exchanged pleasantries then shook hands. Shondor pulled the door closed. Ed turned back toward the corner of the building.

Inside Christy's, there was a momentary and collective shock. A thunderous boom rattled the building.

"Oh my God. Shondor!" Christy yelled.

She ran toward the side door.

Ed Kester had been knocked to the ground by the blast wave. By rounding the corner of the building toward the side entrance, he escaped death by two seconds. Slightly dazed, he got back on his feet and turned back toward the parking lot. Hellish fire raged and smoke billowed from the shattered and twisted remains of Shondor's Lincoln Continental.

Ed peered inside the front seat, but it was empty. He turned back toward the side door and ran into Christy, who was running toward the parking lot. He restrained her. Determined to save Shon from burning to death, Christy pulled free. She moved in close to the fire.

"Get him out! Get him out!" she screamed.

Inside St. Malachi, the large screen had just been moved off to the side. Mass was about to begin when the jolting boom brought a halt. Seconds of silent stillness ticked away. Father Hritz motioned to a guitarist, a nun, and she moved toward a side door. She opened it, took a tentative peek, and then stepped outside. Grabbing his army fatigue jacket, Hritz followed. Many of the worshippers moved out the main doors and onto the steps. The site of their holy day procession was now a confusing, unhallowed scene—haze in the air and debris floating to the ground, the smell of smoke, flames in the parking lot across the street, and a car horn going on and off.

Father Hritz and numerous worshipers hurried across West 25th to get a better look. They joined astonished patrons from Christy's in taking in the devastation. There was a blob enmeshed in the chain link of the fence looking back toward St. Malachi. It looked like chicken fat, someone observed. If any of the curious thought the devastation might have been from a bomb, none of them considered the possibility that they might be in grave danger from a second device.

The burglar alarm on a nearby Cadillac Eldorado was sounding. Shadows from the car's flashing lights blended with the flames, fanned by the winds off Lake Erie, and danced to the pulsating horn. The blast had shattered dozens of windows along the back of the building. Shon's crackled windshield rested on a fire escape. Broken glass and pieces of Shon's Lincoln—and Shon—littered the ground. His upper half, clothing blown off except for his tee shirt, was lying next to the opened passenger door of the burning car.

"I saw his head and shoulders," Christy would later say. "I pulled him out. I thought I had all of him, but that's all that was left. I was stumbling over parts of his arms and legs on the ground."

Shondor had died instantaneously, his body ripped in two at the midsection.

Flames licking nearby nudged Father Hritz back to reality. There was more of the victim's body at a safer distance. The priest knelt beside a severed leg and performed the last rites. As distant sirens wailed louder, a bystander noticed Shon's wallet on the ground. He looked inside and found a driver's license.

"Looks like he was from out of town," he shouted. "Some place called Orange, Ohio."

A fire truck pulled in. A police car pulled in. Fifteen minutes later, two Cleveland homicide detectives arrived. The uniformed officer approached them.

"Well, I guess we won't see Shondor Birns anymore. It's him on the ground there," the officer said while motioning to several spots.

Detectives swarmed Christy's, identified witnesses, and gathered information. Across Greater Cleveland, the telephones of ranking cops and racketeers rang late into the morning as word spread. Down in Florida, Janie Jarus happened to wake up at 3:00 a.m. She called someone in Cleveland and learned of Shondor's murder.

The explosion that instantaneously terminated the legendary racketeer's life reverberated through Cleveland's street and square worlds. Northeast Ohio newspaper readers woke up to the *Plain Dealer* headline: SHONDOR BIRNS IS BOMB VICTIM.

It took Easter morning sunrise and a second shift of crime scene investigators to collect all of Shondor's remains. Birns would have regretted being the cause for detectives working on a holiday. St. Malachi parishioners in their Easter finest observed from a distance as the cops placed the pieces—some identifiable and very personal, and others unrecognizable chunks, shreds, and globs—in plastic bags for transport to the Cuyahoga County coroner's office. They collected dozens of burnt and tattered bills—twenties and fifties— fluttering on the ground. A paper shopping bag of new clothing items managed to survive. It read, "Ladies Will Love You When—You Wear Buddy Lewis's Fashions for Men."

By Monday morning, Cleveland police were tracking down friends and criminal associates of Birns. Ellie hastily made arrangements for a funeral. On Tuesday morning, about three hundred persons gathered at Berkowitz-Kumin, the city's venerable Jewish funeral home, to comfort family members and pay their last respects to Shondor. There were attorneys like Jim Willis and Charles Mosely, friends and associates, including Virgil Ogletree and Tony Panzarella, and vending company representative John Conte. Richard Drake arrived in his silver Mercedes-Benz with two men—his brother John, an associate —and a woman—Janie Jarus. When approached and questioned by WKYC/NBC's Brian Ross, Drake remained silent.

Reporters mingled and sought comments from the mourners.

"I think he was killed over some broad," one man said quietly.

Funeral home employees made repeated attempts to shoo them from the building.

"Why don't you leave the man in peace?" one man pleaded with several newsmen.

From across the street, police investigators made a list of license plates and took long-distance photos from an undercover surveillance van.

The mood was more one of a farewell than of mourning as Rabbi Rudolph Rosenthal officiated.

"Shondor had the capacity to make friends and to keep friends," he said. "I knew him for many years and we often played handball. I knew more Hebrew than he did. But he knew more handball."

The line drew no reaction. Rosenthal spoke of Birns's generosity.

"It is important we recognize the many acts of charity not publicized. These were aspects of Shondor's life he wanted kept private and personal. When I served on the Cleveland Crime Commission and asked for help from Shondor, he gave me advice. However, he would not name names, not even those unfair to him.

"Our friend would not want us to present him as a saint," he said. "He was not a saint. Few of us are. Significant of his life is what we, his friends, families, and associates, personally and privately know about him. The Lord alone passes judgment on us. We're sent into this world not to stand in judgment but to recognize all of us are fallible. Shakespeare said if each one of us got our just deserts, none of us would escape a whipping."

Only a handful of the mourners joined the procession to Hillcrest Cemetery in suburban Bedford Heights. Ellie sobbed quietly as her husband's casket was carried into a mausoleum building. There, in a marble-fronted crypt next to a stained glass window scene of Jesus and Mary, were laid to rest the shattered earthly remains of Alex S. Birns.

CHAPTER ELEVEN

Informants contacted their police and FBI handlers with bits of information about the dramatic demise of Shondor Birns. Anonymous tips came in. A confidential source told a reporter from the *Call and Post*, Cleveland's black weekly, that the bomb was placed under Birns's car. The explosive was then detonated by a remote control device, possibly a Genie garage door opener.

Reporters scrambled to obtain key interviews.

"I didn't think anyone would dare," said lawyer Jim Willis.

"I will not talk with anyone about anything," said Ellie Birns.

Ellie met with Richard Drake at the Lancer Steakhouse to discuss the situation. During the evening, she drank so much that she had to be driven home. She worried about more violence against those closest to her, especially Danny Greene, and telephoned attorneys and asked who might want to hurt the Irishman for whom she still had intimate feelings. She gave one of her Doberman pinschers to him for protection.

Employees and customers at Christy's were questioned. Dozens of detectives from the Cleveland Police Department's homicide, intelligence, and scientific investigation units fanned out across the city. They searched for potential suspects or persons of interest. The US Bureau of Alcohol, Tobacco, and Firearms joined the case and sent a sample of explosive residue to their Washington, DC, lab for analysis.

Leonard Kater, Shondor's nephew, told investigators that Birns was more like a father than an uncle. Kater was upset and said he had never trusted any of Shondor's friends because he feared something like this might happen. He said he often met Birns for lunch or dinner but never discussed business with him.

Ali Khan told investigators he had met Birns only two months earlier and was introduced to him by Ronnie Bey. When it came to questions about him working as a strong-arm for Shondor, he was evasive. Khan said Birns's murder was a loss to the black community but refused to offer any additional information.

Henry Crosby, who had inherited his father's numbers operation, was interviewed by detectives, as were many others known by law enforcement to be in the numbers racket. His storefront had recently been bombed, and he and his son had been shot at.

"My father made it a firm rule not to get involved with Birns, and I've followed that rule," he said. "I've got my own man, and it's good enough protection."

With Birns gone, Crosby didn't think much would change in the numbers business.

"Shondor just created himself a job that many people disliked. When he was in jail, clearinghouse and policy continued to run smooth. He was a parasite. In fact, I think it was probably Birns who was responsible for the bombing and shooting. It was a warning for me to join his club."

Ronnie Bey arrived with his attorney, Jerry Gold, at police headquarters. He told detectives that he worked as a manager for a fire chasing company and denied ever being employed by Birns. He said on the night Shondor was killed, he got a call from his boss asking if he heard about a bombing at Christy's.

"My boss knew I was close with Shon. Knowing Birns was often at Christy's, I called there and learned that he had been killed."

In the meantime, a witness came forward, claiming to have seen two suspicious vehicles before and after the bombing. A regular in the West 25th and Detroit Avenue area, the man told detectives he was sitting at a window across from Christy's when he noticed that approaching customers could not get in the front door. At the same time, he witnessed a black Cadillac slowly cruising up the freeway ramp behind Christy's to enter the westbound Shoreway. The man kept watching and saw a green Cadillac park in front, and the driver was able to get in the front door. He came out of Christy's a short time later and left. About fifteen minutes later, he returned to Christy's and stayed about a half hour.

Detectives continued to question persons of interest. One of them was burly Keith Ritson, Danny Greene's chief enforcer. He claimed that he had met Danny five months earlier and hadn't seen him for two months. Ritson said he was unemployed but previously worked for a fire chaser. There was a lot of money in the business, he told detectives, and it was usual for the black salesmen to handle the black business and for the white salesmen to work with white customers. He said he still went to fire scenes and solicited repair contracts then sold them to the highest bidder.

Ritson said he had met Shondor six months earlier and claimed he forgot who introduced him. He said he heard on the streets that Birns was killed as a result of his involvement in the numbers business in the black community. Detectives asked if they could schedule him for a polygraph test. He agreed.

Danny Greene arrived at the police station as requested and accompanied by his attorney. Investigators asked him about his relationship with Birns. He told detectives that he hadn't seen Birns for a year.

"We broke off relations a long time ago. We don't see eye to eye," Danny said. He would not elaborate.

Greene stated he got up at ten o'clock Saturday morning, went to his downstairs gym, and worked out. For much of the afternoon, he was on the phone in his home office and received several visitors. He gave one an Easter ham that he wanted to be delivered. Danny said he left his office around 6:10 p.m. alone, in his green Lincoln Continental, and drove to the Charter House hotel and bar in suburban Euclid. At 8:30 p.m., he left there and drove directly to the Red Coach restaurant on the top floor of the twelve-story Howard Johnson's Motor Lodge, just east of downtown and overlooking Lake Erie. He said employees would remember him because he asked how raw oysters are opened. A waitress took him into the kitchen, and the chef gave him a demonstration. Danny said he left the Red Coach at 10:00 p.m., went directly home, and was there the rest of the night.

The officers asked Danny whether he would take a polygraph exam.

"He will not," his attorney said.

Police detectives and FBI agents questioned Charlie Broeckel, now a government witness, about Shondor's murder.

"Danny Greene's got a bomb party going," he said. "And it's off to the finish."

Reporters continued to seek comments.

"Danny Greene, that son of a bitch, has a death wish," said a knowledgeable source. "He muscles in wherever he can. Fire chasing, rubbish hauling, numbers—you name it. Sure there's a lot of guys feeling bad about Shon, but some of them owed him money. Now they don't have to pay."

A man who knew both men gave his theory. "Shondor and Danny had been feuding for a long time. It was just a matter of who got who first. It will be interesting to see if Greene can make it without a godfather. He kicked ass, but he used Shon's name and Frank Brancato's name while doing it."

Some black numbers associates disagreed with the information Ritson provided police.

"It's dumb to talk about blacks killing Shondor," said one. "They needed him. He had downtown connections. Years ago, anyone with a little bread could get in the numbers. But not now. It takes a lot of money. That's why blacks and whites will always be partners in the numbers. Since Shon died, people been waitin' for the bell to ring, but it's all over."

A black numbers associate weighed in. "Ain't no white guy coming with a bomb or gun to strong-arm the numbers no more. A guy like Danny Greene pull that, and he'd get his ass shot off. He's not Shondor, and he's not needed."

***

Detectives questioned Janie Jarus, who was working at an appliance store. She admitted that she and Shondor often argued.

"But we had a love for each other right to the end," she said.

When asked who she thought killed Birns, Jarus said her number-one suspect was Danny Greene. If the Irishman had any involvement, then he had set up a solid alibi just like his former mentor would have. Detectives visited the Charter House motel and the Red Coach restaurant. They interviewed employees, who confirmed Danny's story about raw oysters.

Investigators scoured the remains of Birns's Lincoln and located what appeared to be a piece of clothing in the trunk. It was entangled with the charred carpeting. The cloth section, burned on its edges, was the left side of a pair of blue knit pants. The lining of the pocket survived and was full of cash. There was $843 in various denominations.

Another rumor emerged from the streets: A professional hitman from Toledo had murdered Shondor. Investigators learned the man was eating lunch with Birns a few days before the bombing. They identified him as Jerry Leirer, an aluminum siding salesman and ex-con who had met Shon in prison. Leirer said he met with Birns to borrow $500 since he was not doing well in the siding business. Birns wasn't thrilled to see him, so he decided against asking for the loan. Investigators found in Leirer's possession instructions for making gun silencers. A polygraph test was inconclusive, but there was no evidence to charge Leirer with a crime.

Detectives called in Richard Drake and his lieutenant, George "Gorgeous George" Moore.

"Word on the street, Richard, is that you and George have received threats," the detective said.

Drake admitted receiving a threatening phone call. "You're next," the caller had said then hung up.

"Do you believe you're about to be killed?" the detective asked.

"If I was sure, I'd be in Mexico," Drake said. "But then again, they can get me anywhere, so what's the use of running?"

"I hear a lot of people are worried about someone putting a package on their car," the detective said."

"A lot of people are walking lately," Drake said.

The detective asked Drake about a rumor that Danny Greene and Ron Bey were involved in Shondor's murder and that they were going to take over his operation.

"I asked Ron about that very rumor," Drake said. "He got very upset and denied that he would have ever turned over on Shon. Me, Ron, and George laughed at the thought of Danny taking Shon's place."

"Of all the persons close to Shon, you would be the one he would confide in," a detective said.

"Shon knew someone was after him," Drake said. "But he never told me when he was in trouble."

"Well, what do you think happened?"

"The reason Shon was killed was not numbers, narcotics, money, or power," Drake said, his eyes moistening. "It was done by someone who hated Shon, and for no other reason."

Meanwhile, detectives were anxious for Keith Ritson to schedule his polygraph examination. After he consulted with an attorney, he changed his mind.

***

A week after Shon died, Ellie summoned Birns's friend, clothier Buddy Lewis, to her house.

"I walked in the room, and there was Ellie and the top guys from Shon's number's circle," Lewis recalled. "Virgil Ogletree, Richard Drake, and a guy from Don King's office were there, along with Ali Kahn and Ronnie Bey. We sat down and started talking. I asked what I was there for."

"Everyone seems to think you can handle this," Ellie said. "You were close with Shon, and you run a business. We want you to take over what he was doing and handle the payroll."

Lewis acted like he knew what was needed. He agreed to the proposal, and the meeting quickly ended. After the others left, he sat down with Ellie and asked specifically what she wanted him to do.

"She explained to me how it worked," Lewis said. "She knew it backward and forward—all the details of who got paid what to keep the whole clearinghouse business running smoothly. So we made a deal and started right from there. We took over Shon's peacekeeping operation. I started learning more and more. It was about lending money too—more or less like loan-sharking. When an operator got hit hard with a winner and ran out of money, we would loan him cash."

Buddy Lewis got to work and kept Shon's operation going. In the meantime, the Internal Revenue Service claimed the $843 found in Shondor's trunk and applied it to his tax balance.

**

For months after the former Public Enemy Number One was blasted out the sunroof of his Lincoln in pieces big and small, the print news coverage and dramatic features continued. Officials from the US Bureau of Alcohol, Tobacco, and Firearms announced that the explosive that had killed Birns was military grade and called C-4.

"Boom. And the bomb blew his penis off. It was in the Coroner's Office. A circumcised penis in a plastic bag—fate's final slap in the face." That's how Terence Sheridan opened his *Exit Magazine* piece, which came out fourteen weeks after Shondor's murder. "The Death of Shondor Birns and the Rise of Danny Greene—The End of Cleveland Gangland Gothic" was an excellent and concise chronicle with quotes from well-placed sources.

About the same time, journalist Roy Meyers dropped another bomb in the saga of Shondor Birns when he reprised the Mervin Gold murder case in a *Cleveland Press* piece about President Gerald Ford's Rockefeller Commission. Chaired by Vice President Nelson Rockefeller, the committee was charged with investigating reported abuses of authority by the CIA and other intelligence agencies. Meyers wrote that his source, a Clevelander involved in the Gold investigation twelve years earlier, provided the commission with documents linking the unsolved murder with the Mafia in the CIA's failed Bay of Pigs invasion of Cuba. A spokesman for the Rockefeller Commission confirmed receipt of the information but declined further comment. Meyers believed that information to be Mervin Gold's twenty-three-page affidavit that was turned over to the FBI a few days following his 1963 murder. Such information about the CIA's involvement in Cuba would have surely made its way to US Attorney General Robert Kennedy, Meyers theorized.

"At that time, the Bay of Pigs fiasco was a major blot on the Kennedy record," Meyers wrote. "If it also became known that the CIA was dealing with organized crime, it would have been catastrophic for that administration."

"For that reason," the unnamed source told Meyers, "the Gold murder investigation was halted on orders from Washington."

When Mervin Gold came into possession of the stolen Canadian bonds, he tried to keep the lion's share, Meyers believed. If the bonds were meant to finance arms trafficking as part of the CIA's unholy alliance with organized crime against Fidel Castro, then Gold's actions put a target on his back.

"When Gold returned from Israel, he was a marked man—in two ways. He knew too much and had to be eliminated. But first, those he betrayed wanted to find where he had stashed the bonds and cash. That could explain why he was beaten before being killed."

Meyers felt that the alleged CIA-Mafia collaboration in Cuba also could explain why an intense murder investigation fizzled after only six months.

"One more unsolved murder would be a small price for keeping such negotiations secret," Meyers wrote.

Roy Meyers detailed a viable motive in the slaying of Mervin Gold. Meanwhile, detectives trying to solve Shondor Birns's murder were coming up short on evidence. But the cops and those in the know were nearly certain of the culprit. Richard Drake brought Ellie the news: Word on the street was that Danny Greene killed Shon. The young widow was overcome with grief then consumed by anger.

"Ellie felt that of all the people who might have wanted Shon dead, Danny would have had more respect for her and not done it," said Jim Willis.

Ellie didn't seem like the type that would go for Shon, but there was a fierce loyalty there—perhaps more like a daughter's bond with her father rather than a wife's love for her husband. Either way, she took Shondor's death very hard. She fumed and started drinking heavily.

"Ellie was told the Italians were already planning to kill Greene to get even for him killing Shondor," said Buddy Lewis. "But she couldn't wait. She was very unassuming and quiet, but Ellie could be a mean bitch when you got her mad. As many times as she was told just wait, relax, it's gonna be taken care of, she couldn't wait. She cowboyed it."

It had been an ironic end to a life of celebrity-like status for Ellie's man—the killing of a Jewish public enemy, across from a Catholic church during Holy Saturday mass, in a former Irish settlement and by an Irish-American former protégé who also happened to be a former lover of the man's wife.

While the young widow seethed for revenge, news stories chronicled the highlights of Shondor's life of crime. In a *Plain Dealer* editorial, Howard Preston questioned the morality of presenting Birns as a social lion instead of the outlaw that he was.

"I know a number of hardworking and honest persons who are bewitched by hoods," Preston wrote. "They want to rub elbows with them. To be on a first name basis with outlaws is their heart's delight . . . I understand Birns was newsworthy even though he was civic blight. But I censure those social crawlers who distort the rational scale of human values by idolizing outlaws when society has so many legitimate examples to emulate."

Whether Ellie Birns was bewitched by Shondor or she personally idolized the elder outlaw, the loyalty she had for her husband and provider and her desire for revenge eclipsed any leftover feelings for the handsome Irishman.

Meanwhile, some of journalist Terence Sheridan's sources predicted doom for Danny.

A policeman said, "It would not surprise me to pick up my morning paper and read that Greene has been blown away."

He wasn't blown away, but the KABOOM! that jolted Collinwood residents at 3:50 a.m. on May 13, 1975, did level Greene's compact two-story brick apartment building on Waterloo Avenue. Like the other attempts on his life, Danny, this time with a very young girl-friend, walked away, both nearly unscathed.

The blast was courtesy of Moe Kiraly. Kiraly's payment was courtesy of Ellie Birns. Kiraly was reportedly assisted by Joe Gallo, an up-and-coming Mafia member under Angelo "Big Ange" Lonardo. Moe placed two bombs to be sure he got rid of the Irishman. The second and larger one malfunctioned.

In the aftermath, Danny returned to the scene of the bombing, look-ing immaculate in a white shirt and jeans, to survey the destruction and pose for a news photographer. He appeared unfazed by the car-nage, and if his eyes could have betrayed any other feelings, they were well hidden by dark glasses.

Within a few weeks, the rubble had been cleared away. Danny brought in two trailers, one for a home and one for an office. The tiny lot was his hill, and he planted the Irish tricolor. During the sunny summer afternoons, he often sat shirtless under the flag—his impressive physique glistening with tanning oil. He was in full view of passersby as a dare for his enemies to return. He tooled around Collinwood in his green Lincoln, handed out green ink pens, and presented his closest friends with gold Celtic crosses.

Emboldened by surviving the Waterloo Avenue blast, Danny moved in on the vending business. Mountains of untraceable coins for cig-arette or candy machines were a natural for mob control and were reminiscent of the nickels and dimes that fed the early numbers rack-et. Vending clients could be muscled to host machines supplied ex-clusively by a certain company. If the operator had friends in labor unions, he had additional leverage. Uncooperative restaurant and bar owners might experience a costly slowdown of crucial deliveries like food, alcohol, or linen. For the most stubborn cases, some mobbed-up vending owners resorted to violence, even murder.

Greene attempted to take over the washer and dryer accounts at numerous apartment buildings. They were held by Mafia lieutenant Tommy Sinito. Sinito was drawn into the conflict with the Irishman when he found a bomb on his car. Other vending machine dealers weren't so lucky.

John Conte was an associate of Sinito and had been of friend of Shondor Birns. He told his wife he was going to meet with Danny Greene. Later his badly beaten body was found outside a motel in Ohio's Mahoning Valley. Police theorized that Conte may have been killed in Greene's trailer. Danny denied having met with Conte the day he disappeared. He was never indicted.

In 1976, the US Drug Enforcement Administration investigated a suspicious purchase of phenyl acetic acid, a precursor for the manufacture of methamphetamine. Meth was a profitable drug of abuse trafficked by biker gangs like the Hells Angels, with whom Greene's crew was associated. Federal agents traced the sale to a company believed owned by Greene. He abandoned his plans, and the investigation fizzled.

***

For several years, John Scalish had been plagued by heart problems. In May 1976, the Mafia don died during surgery. Before he was even laid to rest, many in the underworld and law enforcement communities were asking, Who is in charge of the Cleveland outfit now?

James Licavoli emerged as the new boss, but ambitious and well-positioned players wanted a shot at the top. Among them was John Nardi, key labor union racketeering contact for the mob.

"Your enemies are my enemies," Nardi told Greene.

Danny, who was never a fan of Italians unless there was a personal benefit, felt that the Irish mob should reign supreme. Nevertheless, he partnered with Nardi, who knew how the Mafia operated. Danny had a crew of street soldiers and utilized Hells Angels members for some enforcement work. The Nardi/Greene combine launched an aggressive offensive, and soon a full-scale war was underway. Bombings were attracting increasing attention from law enforcement.

Tony Liberatore, a politically influential labor union official, was another rackets figure hoping to benefit from the change in underworld order. He maneuvered for a favorable position and was inducted into the Cleveland outfit, along with a Licavoli lieutenant, in the basement of a Little Italy restaurant. The newly minted made guy stayed friendly with Greene while conspiring to have him whacked. Lib supplied two ex-convicts who would serve as a backup hit team. Most remarkably, he was the star actor in a historic penetration of FBI security, having successfully bribed a clerk to steal a list of confidential informants. At the top of the list were national Teamster union president Jackie Presser, and Danny Greene.

The bombs continued to blow and demonstrated the possibility that explosions could go awry. Greene's crewmembers wired the car of a Licavoli soldier. When a neighbor moved the vehicle, he was killed in the explosion. A Hells Angel member, hired by Greene's enforcers to place a package on the car of a Mafia soldier, died when it prematurely detonated.

"The Bombing Business is Booming Here" led off a *Plain Dealer* story. To deal with the problem, the US Bureau of Alcohol, Tobacco, and Firearms designated Northern Ohio as a district headquarters. They tripled staffing. Following an investigation featuring an undercover investigator posing as a bomb buyer, ATF agents celebrated the arrests of two men who made and sold bombs.

The explosions continued.

Journalist Edward Whelan called the attempts to kill the Irishman a "byzantine plot."

"Only one thing is for certain," he wrote. "Not one man, not the present head of the Cleveland mob family, not even the best Cleveland intelligence cops and federal agents, knows the whole story of what is taking place on the streets of Cleveland. Because there are so many characters with so many different motivations, the story does not lend itself to easy interpretations."

Danny Greene was still looking for the big score. And perhaps for a way out. It was in the form of a Texas cattle ranch, of all things. He planned to buy a struggling beef farm to start a discounted meat program for labor unions to offer their members. Danny underestimated the costs to renovate the ranch, and some observers wrote the plan off as a pipe dream.

Meanwhile, Moe Kiraly was arrested and tried for the bombing of Greene's apartment building. He was convicted and sentenced to five to twenty-five years. Kiraly's alleged conspirator, Joe Gallo, was a fugitive for one year before he was arrested, tried, and acquitted.

Greene and Nardi survived several murder attempts by Licavoli's soldiers. When a remote-controlled bomb inside a car parked next to Nardi's was detonated, Nardi was killed. Danny was more cautious than ever. He packed a Browning Hi-Power pistol and regularly switched cars with his henchmen.

A few months later, after getting a loose filling repaired, Danny reached to open his car door in a medical building parking lot when the vehicle next to him exploded. Like his mentor-turned-archenemy thirty months earlier, Greene died instantaneously.

Journalist Terence Sheridan called Danny Greene "the kid who always wanted to be Shondor Birns." And just like Shondor's death, Danny's was front-page headlines.

Shondor's Mafia friends rejoiced but laid blame on Shondor for the rise of the Irishman. An FBI wiretap caught Jack Licavoli and a lieutenant lamenting the war with Greene.

Licavoli: "Johnnie Nardi. That cocksucker. And the fucking Irishman."

Lieutenant: "How the hell did this guy ever come into the picture?"

Licavoli: "He thought he got so big. They created a monster. And all of the headaches we used to have."

"They" no doubt included Nardi, Frank Brancato, and Shondor Birns. And more headaches were coming. They included a series of blunders by Licavoli's soldiers, courageous eyewitnesses, and outstanding police work. In the months and years that followed Greene's murder, law enforcers collaborated to nearly decimate the Cleveland mob. Jack Licavoli was a top target. The feds offered him leniency if he would cooperate. Jim Willis presented the deal to him.

Licavoli said, "Jimmy, we'll be friends for a long time provided you don't come to me with no more deals from the government. If I'm going down, I'm going down with the ship."

And he did. Licavoli was convicted federally of racketeering in connection with Danny Greene's murder. Sentenced to seventeen years, he was shipped off to prison, and the Cleveland outfit was left in shambles.

Angelo Lonardo became the acting boss. Joe Gallo, Lonardo's lieutenant, lamented the state of the outfit. He blamed John Scalish's closed-book policy for the loss of experienced middle managers.

"See, there should be people between us," Gallo explained to an associate. "But they didn't do nothing for all those years. They just let it go dormant. Angelo's gonna be seventy. We're missing the guy that's sixty. And we're missing the guy that's fifty. It's all the way down to me at forty. That hurts us, see?"

With the hope of rebuilding the Cleveland mob, Gallo and partner Tommy Sinito merged with a west side drug ring leader named

Carmen Zagaria. Ironically, Gallo's and Sinito's new associates included remnants of Danny Greene's crew who, after the murder of their boss, went to work with Zagaria. Within a couple of years, the combined operation was grossing $15 million a year, mostly from sales of cocaine. For collection work in their drug transactions, they employed a Hells Angel named George Rothrock.

When key players started robbing and killing associates, lawmen turned up the heat. Seven murders later, the first indictments were issued. Zagaria turned himself in to police at his mother's grave. He made a deal and went to work for the feds.

Across the country, a perfect storm was brewing. In its path were the Mafia and its racketeering associates. The FBI and US attorney were leading the fight with a new collaboration among federal, state, and local law enforcement agencies, stricter drug laws, new wiretap legislation, and technology. The federal Racketeer Influenced and Corrupt Organizations Act was being used regularly to eliminate the buffering of bosses previously insulated by henchmen. In effect, the law made it a crime to benefit from membership in a criminal organization. Forfeiture legislation stripped away illegally acquired cash and property.

Under the pressure of tougher justice, the culture of loyalty and adherence to omerta was fading quickly, along with a generation of street-hardened men. Once the US Marshals proved they could successfully relocate and protect criminal turncoats, the Department of Justice's Witness Security Program was an increasingly attractive option. There was a new strategy for racketeers—making the best deal to reduce lengthy sentences.

In the once-mighty Cleveland Mafia, wide-ranging convictions toppled most of the remaining players and produced an unlikely turncoat. He was an early member of the old Mayfield Road mob alongside Shondor Birns. He was convicted of drug racketeering and murder and sentenced to life. After two years in prison, he flipped, causing angst for top mobsters across the country. If Shondor had been physically ill at Charlie Broeckel testifying against fellow burglars and bent cops, he might have dropped dead at Angelo Lonardo singing for the feds.

Big Ange's testimony helped cripple Mafia families in Los Angeles, Kansas City, Milwaukee, and New York City. At the time, he was the highest-ranking Mafioso to betray the Sicilian code of silence.

Amidst the fallout, a defense attorney scoffed, "Danny Greene died five years ago, and he's still fucking with us."

"Don't mess with the Italians," Shondor once told Danny.

EPILOGUE

In the years following Shondor's murder, Janie Jarus continued to weave a life of drama. Her new man was George Wesley Rothrock, whose acquaintance with Jarus dated to the time that she was struggling to part ways with Birns.

Rothrock was the owner of a small company that repaired hydraulic cylinders for trash compactors and garbage trucks. He also worked for former members of Danny Greene's crew, collecting cash from drug transactions while occasionally bragging about driving the late racketeer's green Lincoln Continental.

George Rothrock was also a founding member of the Hells Angels Motorcycle Club (HAMC) in Cleveland. They were known as the "Dirty Thirty," and Rothrock was dubbed Dirty George. He carried a large-bore pistol tucked in his HAMC-buckle belt. And like former HAMC member Enis Crnic, Rothrock liked explosives. He may have been the club's most prolific bomb maker.

On one occasion, Janie witnessed George in an upstairs bedroom of her house assembling a bomb. Another time she happened upon a metal box that he had hidden in her basement. She opened it to find blocks of plastic explosive and sticks of dynamite.

"The more I learned about George and his activities, the more scared I got," she said.

Despite her fear, Janie stayed with George. In 1981, they had a son. Rothrock lived with Jarus, their infant son, her teenage son and daughter, and her mother. To casual onlookers, their domestic arrangements belied George's criminal activities. Their west side home was a neat, three-story yellow bungalow with a full-length front porch. The living room had two sofas, two chairs, and a stereo with tall speakers. A formal dining room held a table and featured a window seat with drawers.

Like her relationship with Shondor, Janie's time with George was tumultuous. She complained that he spent too much time with his fellow Angels and not enough with his family—not understanding that George considered the Angels his family.

In late 1981, things came to a head. Rothrock and two other Hells Angels were under indictment by a federal grand jury for possession of illegal firearms and explosives, including a .30-caliber machine gun, four hand grenades, and an antitank rocket. On the way home from her job as a barmaid, Janie stopped at McDonald's and picked up dinner. When she got home, Rothrock was there. According to Janie, he was heavily intoxicated. She offered him food.

"We already fucking ate," he said.

Janie noticed that he had placed his Llama .45 atop the homemade, three-tier cement-block bookshelf in the living room. She sat down on a sofa to watch television and eat. Suddenly Rothrock turned the TV off and yelled at Jarus. They started arguing, and she reached for the phone to call to the police.

"George ripped the telephone off the wall, threw it at me, and was choking me with the cord," she said. "My thirteen-year-old son came running down the stairs. He was screaming at George and jumped on his back to pull him off me. George turned and went after him. I screamed at him to let him go. I grabbed my gun. I screamed again at George to stop. Then I started shooting."

Rothrock was struck in the back three times. He collapsed. Concerned that he might get up and go for his gun, Jarus handed the pistol to her son. She sent him upstairs, ran outside, got in her car, drove to a corner pay phone, and called the police.

When police and paramedics arrived, Rothrock was dead. Jarus was arrested. Prosecutors ruled the shooting was in self-defense.

Some of Rothrock's family members and friends felt she got away with murder. The root of their suspicions was revealed during a criminal case involving several Hells Angels.

In the early 1980s, three significant criminal cases appeared to have numerous Hells Angels members on the ropes. Two prosecutions were for murder. Both wound up in the courtroom of Judge James McGettrick. Back in 1963, McGettrick was Cuyahoga County's sheriff and the one lawman to whom Shondor chose to surrender when he was sought for the murder of Mervin Gold. McGettrick had launched a bid for the bench in 1972 and was elected as a common pleas judge.

In 1983, to the dismay of prosecutors and local and federal law enforcement officers, McGettrick dismissed a murder charge against a Hells Angel. The next year, the judge was having a drink in a bar. Next to him, also having a drink, was a federal agent who had worked the 1983 case.

"We really appreciate what you did for us in the murder case," the agent said to the judge.

It was a random and sarcastic remark meant to goad McGettrick, but the judge didn't recognize the agent. And worse, McGettrick figured him for a Hells Angel and the comment for genuine appreciation.

"I haven't received full payment for that," the judge said.

The agent played it cool and left space for McGettrick to keep talking.

"I stuck my neck out," the judge said. "Jerry Milano [an attorney] paid me to fix the case, but I'm owed more money."

As a result of Judge McGettrick's misdirected and untimely comments, he was charged and convicted of accepting a bribe. He was sentenced to four years in prison.

In the meantime, the Hells Angels federal weapons trial got underway. Prosecutors presented a key witness who, for ten years, had secretly provided information to the FBI. It was Janie Jarus. Her role as a federal informant dated to when she was involved with Shondor Birns and continued through her time with George Rothrock. She claimed that she provided information about Birns out of patriotic duty but was paid for her knowledge about Rothrock.

During her testimony, Jarus linked Rothrock and Keith Ritson to the murder of Shondor Birns.

"George told me that he made the bomb that Keith used to kill Shon," she testified.

It had been a murder with two separate motives—Ritson working for Danny Greene in his battle with Birns, and Rothrock, the bomb maker, having once vowed to kill Shondor if he would not break up with Janie.

***

Shondor once commented about his life of crime.

"It's not worth it," he told a reporter. "It just doesn't pay. I think I must have spent close to a quarter of a million bucks on attorney's fees, bond money, and fines. And what do I have to show for it? Not a blankety-blank thing. The guy I admire is the steady plugger, the nine-to-five guy. He'll never be rich, but think what he can own? He can buy a car, support his family, and not have a worry in the world. He probably even likes the work he's doing, too."

The racketeer is remembered with mixed opinions.

"Shondor Birns was *the* Public Enemy Number One," said author John Stark Bellamy II. "And it was a role he played to the hilt . . ."

"I'd see Shon go into his pocket and give guys who were down and out five or ten bucks," said Birns's friend Hymie Mintz. "He never asked anybody for nothing. He was always smiling. I knew him all my life. He feared nobody, and he was always in good shape. He was like steel. It took a bomb to kill him."

"Shon was the most vicious son of a bitch I ever met," said a cop. "He wouldn't stop at anything."

"Shon's word was his bond," said an old pal. "He never forgot a guy. And he never forgave a guy."

"I'm not going to say a good thing about Shondor," said longtime nemesis Carl Delau. "I hate to knock the dead. What happened to him was a terrible thing, but I had no use for him. He had judges and political figures in his corner. And there is no doubt in my mind that, with the help of Fred Stitmon and Billy Cox, Shondor killed Mervin Gold."

"To the shame of those who relished being in his company, Shondor Birns was something of a celebrity," said *Plain Dealer* columnist Howard Preston. "He was something to be pointed out to visitors as one might point out the Terminal Tower. Good men and women who contribute much to the community's welfare unfortunately get far less recognition than the Birns type."

"When you'd see him at the Theatrical, he was the most pleasant, sociable guy in the world," said Judge Harry Jaffe of the Cuyahoga County Common Pleas Court. "He'd say hello to everyone. Even my wife liked him."

"Shondor wasn't no bad fella," said a black numbers associate. "He was white but it didn't make no difference. He had a black soul. He

was black through and through. Shit, there wasn't no racial prejudice in that goddamn Shondor Birns at all. He was a helluva guy.
No, no, there ain't going to be no more Shondors."

Affable Shondor Birns, in 1967.
(Photo credit: Cleveland State University Press Collection. Photo by Van Dillard)

Shondor on the move. He loved his cars and spent a lot of time behind the wheel, crisscrossing his domain, checking on operations, and meeting with associates.
(Photo credit: Cleveland State University Cleveland Press Collection)

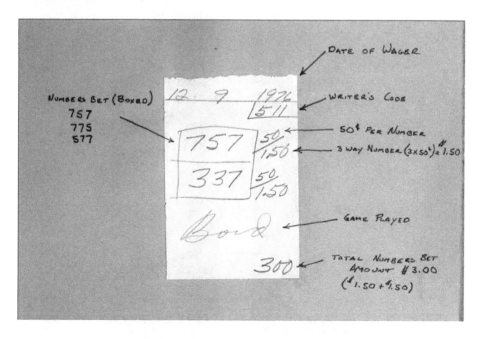

A typical clearinghouse bet slip from the 1970s, with an investigator's explanation.
(Photo credit: Bill Riedthaler)

Shondor's house in Orange Village, just outside of Cleveland, where
he took up residence in 1965 with girlfriend Ellie Leonards.
(Photo credit: Author's collection)

Michael Roberts and Todd Simon, two of the many journalists, who, through
the years, extensively covered the life and crimes of Shondor Birns.
(Photo credits: Will Richmond, and Cleveland Public Library Photograph Collection.)

Tasso Vrettos, Greek coffee shop owner, gambling operator, and Mafia murder victim.
(Photo credit: Author's collection)

Frank Brancato, an influential and respected Mafia member. He and longtime friend Shondor Birns fought orders of deportation for decades.
(Photo credit: Frank Monastra).

Joe Harper operated in Cleveland and Pittsburgh and made big money by exclusively handling layoff action.
(Photo credit. FBI & Bill Riedthaler)

265

Shondor, in handcuffs, being moved from the relative comfort of federal prison to state prison in 1968 while his attorney, Jim Willis (in background), continued to work for his release.

(Photo credit: Author's collection. Plain Dealer photo by Karl J. Rauschkolb)

Ellie Birns, circa 1973. Her smile is not as big as it was in her earlier years with Shondor.

(Photo credit: Author's collection)

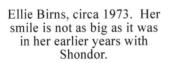

Irish-American racketeer Danny "the Irishman"
Greene, protégé of Frank Brancato and Shondor Birns.
(Photo credit: Cleveland Police Dept)

Clearinghouse operator and
entrepreneur Bill Seawright.
(Photo credit: Cleveland Police & Bill
Riedthaler)

At the height of Virgil Ogletree's
success, he captured nearly half of
the city's numbers action.
(Photo credit: Cleveland Police & Bill
Riedthaler)

In a circa 1970 photograph, numbers operator and Birns associate Richard Drake, (left) who inherited his father Arthur's business, poses with legendary boxing promoter Don King, a former numbers racketeer, and associate of Shondor Birns.

(Photo credit: Gina Drake-Busch)

Burglar Charlie Broeckel (left), associate of Birns, with pal Phil "Superthief" Christopher.

(Photo credit: Author's collection)

Bob Boggess, alleged hit man for the Mafia, and an associate of Shondor Birns.

(Photo credit: Portage County Sheriff).

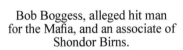

William "Moe" Kiraly, burglar, bomber, inventor, and associate of Shondor Birns.

(Photo credit: Author's collection)

A shallow hole and a bag of lime, intended for the disposal of burglar William Whitcomb's body after his murder by Bob Boggess and his crew.

(Photo credit: Oakwood Police)

Ronnie Bey, (formerly Ronald Grier), a politically-connected racketeer, Mafia ally, and close associate of Shondor Birns.

(Photo credit: Cleveland Police)

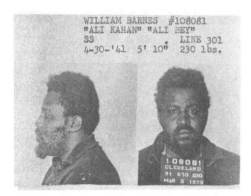

William Barnes, (aka Ali Bey, Ali Kahn), another trusted Birns enforcer.
(Photo credit: Cleveland Police)

Billy Cox, a Birns enforcer, and a drug trafficker.
(Photo credit: Cleveland Police)

Christy's Tavern (formerly known as Jack and Jill's), the go-go joint frequented by Shondor Birns.
(Photo credit: Cleveland Public Library City Hall Photograph Collection)

Clevetta "Christy" Schuler, co-owner of Christy's Tavern and close
friend to Shondor, and her brother and partner, Del Hudson.
(Photo credit: Top Hat Magazine and Author's collection)

Shondor, in 1972, during the
period that he was frequenting
Christy's Tavern.
(Photo credit: Cleveland State University
Cleveland Press Collection. Photo by
Clayton Knipper.)

Exterior of St. Malachi
Church, across from
Christy's Tavern.
(Photo credit: Cleveland Public Library NEA Photograph Collection)

Caption: Mass at St. Malachi Church, 1968.
(Photo credit: Cleveland Public Library Photograph Collection. Plain Dealer photo by Richard T. Conway)

Shondor's Lincoln Continental after a ferocious explosion that blew the windshield up and into a fire escape.
(Photo credits: Cleveland Police)

A Cleveland police detective inspects Shondor's demolished Lincoln.
(Photo credit: Cleveland State University Cleveland Press Collection. Photo by Larry Nighswander)

Richard Drake, in a light-colored suit and arriving at Berkowitz-Kumin Funeral Home, refuses to answer questions posed by WKYC/NBC reporter Brian Ross. Attending the services with him are Janie Jarus, who is clutching the arm of Drake associate Pete Mallory, and Richard's brother, John.
(Photo Credit: John Carroll University / Northeast Ohio Broadcast Archives)

Police officers stand outside the bombed-out remains of the apartment and office building in which Danny Greene again narrowly escaped death.
(Photo credit: Cleveland Police)

Danny Greene, in an act of fearless defiance, returns to the scene of his near-deadly apartment bombing and poses for a news photographer.
(Photo credit: Cleveland State University Cleveland Press Collection. Photo by Timothy Culek)

Keith Ritson, enforcer for Danny Greene.
(Photo credit: Author's collection)

George "Dirty George" Rothrock, popular and
feared Hells Angel and bomb maker.
(Photo credit: Eastlake Police)

Mary Jane "Janie" Jarus, former
prostitute who left a relationship
with Shondor Birns and wound
up with Hells Angel George
Rothrock. Jarus revealed yet
another role when she appeared
as a prosecution witness in a
federal weapons case.
(Photo credit: Cleveland Police)

WHAT HAPPENED TO THEM?

DOMINICK BARTONE Bartone served a prison term in the late 1970s for bank fraud. In 1982, he died of natural causes at age 69.

ELLIE BIRNS A few years after Shondor was killed, Ellie reinvented herself. She obtained her Realtor's license and sold houses until she died of cancer in 1996. She was 57. Business associates recalled her as quiet and professional. She had never remarried.

JANE BIRNS In the years following her divorce from Shondor, Jane Birns had a career working for a department store. She was in assisted living when she died in 2009 at age 79.

MICHAEL BIRNS Michael was 25 when he died in 1978. He was speeding and lost control of his motorcycle after ignoring an attempt by police to halt him.

FRANK BRANCATO Brancato was 76 when died of natural causes in 1973.

CHARLIE BROECKEL Charlie could not break his old habits. Even after entering the Witness Security Program, he wound up with another criminal conviction. He served time, under his assumed name, in Tennessee. Knowledgeable sources believe he died in the late 1980s.

MAXIE DIAMOND By the late 1940s, Maxie had left the rackets for the restaurant and real estate businesses. He was 73 when he died in 1971.

RICHARD DRAKE Richard died in 1995 of a massive stroke. He was 63.

MARY JANE JARUS Janie was married twice. She lived in Alabama and was 66 when she died of cancer in 2015.

DONALD KING. By the 1970s, Donald King was on his way out of the numbers racket and emerging as Don King, the fight promoter. A controversial and politically-active public figure, King, in 1983, received a pardon from Ohio Governor James Rhodes for a 1967 numbers-related manslaughter conviction in which he served four years in prison. "Don King has paid his debt to society and earned this pardon through his role in civic affairs," said Rhodes. In 2017, *New York Times* reporter Wallace Matthews wrote that King, then 86 years old, still worked with "a skeleton staff and reduced stable of boxers" in Florida. King is the owner of the *Call and Post*, Cleveland's venerable African-American newspaper.

ANGELO LONARDO Lonardo eventually left the witness security program, moved back to Cleveland, and lived in an apartment complex that was home to many Italian-American senior citizens. He continued to use an assumed name, but many of his neighbors knew his true identity. He lived to age 95 and died in 2006.

JAMES McGETTRICK McGettrick was suffering from cancer when he entered prison for accepting bribes to fix cases. He served only four months of his four year sentence when, in 1985, he had a heart attack. He died several days later. He was 68.

VIRGIL OGLETREE Ogletree was Cleveland's last major numbers operator. "Virgil made as much money, if not more money, booking the numbers than anybody ever did in the state of Ohio," said lawyer Jim Willis. "But he wasted a lot of it, burned it up, loaned it to people, gave it away." In 2003 a federal grand jury indicted Ogletree for running a multi-million dollar gambling ring. By that time, he was suffering from Alzheimer's disease and consequently was never tried. He died in 2007 at age 84.

KEITH RITSON Keith went missing in 1978. Four years later, his body was recovered in a pond west of Cleveland. He was one of numerous victims murdered in the late 1970s as part of the west side drug ring backed by the Cleveland Mafia.

BILL SEAWRIGHT Bill Seawright died in 2003. He was 96. "Throughout his self-made career, he refused to recognize roadblocks that limited other black businessmen," wrote *Plain Dealer* reporter Richard Peery. "As he moved into legitimate businesses, Bill developed a reputation for generosity toward struggling professionals and politicians."

ENDNOTES

Chapter One

Page 16   Can you get some help for yourself on money
US Dept. of Justice, Mervin L. Gold, Oct. 17, 1963.

Page 17   Shondor Birns was born Sándor Birn
Author conjecture.

Page 17   The surname Birn
FamilySearch. New York Passenger Arrival Lists 1892-1924 (Ellis Island).
https://www.familysearch.org. Accessed Feb. 26, 2018.

        Family acquaintances believed the name may have been short-
ened from Birnstein.

Michael Roberts, "Why They Blew Away Shondor Birns," Cleveland Magazine,
July, 1975.

Page 17   Hermann spoke Slovakian
U.S National Archives Administration file of Alex S. Birns. Affidavit of Emil
Gross, March 3, 1943.

Page 18   with the Birnbaum family: Samuel and Anna Birnbaum
US National Archives Administration file of Alex Birns. Deposition of Samuel
and Anna Birnbaum, Sep. 20, 1942.

Page 20   I would have won it anyway if I was here
Michael Roberts, "Why They Blew Away Shondor Birns," Cleveland Magazine, July, 1975.

Page 20   As kids in the summer
Jesse Bryant Wilder, "The Last Untouchable," Northern Ohio Live, March 1993.

Page 21   Shondor was a delivery boy
US Dept. of Justice, FBI, Mervin L. Gold, July 19, 1963, Statement of Anthony J. Kolk, July 10, 1963.

Page 22   raisin jack: Author conjecture

Page 22   Ellen Birn and still explosion
Cleveland News, Nov. 11, 1920.

Page 22   You have been sufficiently punished by the death of your wife
Cleveland News, Nov. 24, 1920.

Pages 22-23   About Camp Wise
Albert M. Brown, The Camp Wise Story, Cleveland, Jewish Community Federation of Cleveland, 1989.

Page 23   a woman fourteen years younger: This was Alice Fridman.
Cuyahoga County Marriage Record; www.familysearch.org. Accessed January 30, 2019.

Page 23   to avoid confusion: Author conjecture.

Page 23   with a US Navy anchor tattoo and tales of his experience
Michael Roberts, "Why They Blew Away Shondor Birns," Cleveland Magazine, July, 1975.

Page 24   and others criminals like him: They included bootlegger and nightclub owner Harry Berner.
Plain Dealer, Nov. 21, 1935 (Author conjecture)

Page 26   A former Mafia boss recalled: This was Angelo A. Lonardo.

US Senate. "Organized Crime: 25 Years after Valachi," Testimony of Angelo Lonardo to Hearings before the Permanent Subcommittee on Investigations, 1988. US Government Printing Office, 1990.

Page 27   Then there were the battles over corn sugar
Porrello, Rick. The Rise and Fall of the Cleveland Mafia, New Jersey, Barricade Books, 2010.

Page 28   Above all Shondor wanted to be the man among men
Michael Roberts, "Why They Blew Away Shondor Birns," Cleveland Magazine, July, 1975.

Chapter Two

Page 29   Policy was popular in New York City and Chicago and with southern blacks US Senate Kefauver Hearings, 1951, Statement of Cleveland Safety Director Alvin Sutton.

Page 30   The payout amount for winners depended on wager type
Personal interview.

Page 30   About William Thier and William Lark
Plain Dealer, Nov. 01, 1906 and March 30, 1932.

Page 31   I got no college education
Plain Dealer, March 14, 1935.

Page 31   Gambling is a game for suckers
Cleveland Press, March 14, 1935.

Page 32   Policy Blues lyrics by Arthur "Blind" Blake
Catherine Yronwode, "Policy Blues," Blues Lyrics and Hoodoo. http://www.luckymojo.com/bluespolicyblake.html, Accessed Jan. 30, 2019.

Page 33   An associate from Chicago helped organize a takeover: This was Mike "Bon Bon"Allegretti. US Senate Kefauver Hearings, 1951, Statement of Cleveland Safety Director Alvin Sutton.

Page 33   About Tommy Boyce
Call and Post, April 20, 1957.

Page 33   Seawright was not intimidated (Based on)
Brent Larkin, "Seawright Defied Odd," Plain Dealer, April 20, 2003.

Page 33   I wouldn't give you forty percent
Dave Hawkins, "Witnesses Finger Policy Trial Defendants," Call and Post, July 4, 1942.

Page 34   You better start making payments
Call and Post, July 4, 1942.

Page 35   About Louis Cadek
Plain Dealer, April 14, 1936.

Page 36   he was arrested for stabbing a man: The victim was John Van Tasko.

Page 36   a minor gangland murder that occurred in his pool hall: This was the murder of Phillip "Funny Face" Corry by Mike "the Pipe" Shrinkman. Plain Dealer, April 29, 1932.

Page 36   Diamond and several members of his crew: They included Harry "Hoot Gibson" Katz and Harvey Kater.

Page 36   Potter was killed, it was believed
Messick, Hank. The Silent Syndicate. New York, Macmillan, 1967.

Page 36   her companion took offense: This was John Consorte.
Cleveland News, July 22, 1931.

Page 36   Birn was arrested for assaulting and robbing: The owner/victim was Anna Kriz. Plain Dealer, Oct. 24, 1931.

Page 37   Shondor punched the cabbie in the face: The victim was Joseph Sords. Plain Dealer, June 3, 1932.

Page 37   Shondor Birn is the type of man who should be eliminated from society: The prosecutor was John Butler. Ibid.

Page 37   Those present included: Also John Abbey and Harry Marcus. Plain Dealer, June 27, 1932.

Page 38   I don't know what happened to him
Plain Dealer, June 27, 1932

Page 38   Surname change from Birn to Birns: According to Sadie Birn, there was a different explanation. Shondor, as a boy, added an "s" because it was easier for his fellow schoolmates to pronounce, and he continued to spell his name Birns. It should be noted that other members of the extended Birn family, in later years and for unknown reasons, changed their names to Birns.
US Dept. of Justice; Immigration and Naturalization Service, Alex Shondor Birns; Affidavit of Mrs. Herman Birn, Feb. 18, 1943.

Page 39   I had a nice little pool room and restaurant
Cleveland News, Feb. 11, 1937.

Page 39   He had prostitution houses all over Cleveland
US Dept. of Justice, Immigration and Naturalization Service, Alex Shondor Birns; Interview with Belle Herman by Inspector David W. Walters, Sep. 30, 1942.

Page 39   Some of those clients eventually became government officials
Author conjecture

Page 40   When I got to a hotel in Cleveland, I was dropped off at a house
US Dept. of Justice; Immigration and Naturalization Service, Alex Shondor Birns; Statement of Joan Johnson, Sep. 20, 1942.

Pages 41-42   About Clementina Damiano.
Plain Dealer, July 30, 1933.

Page 42   and two other members of his crew: They were Frank Rossman and Joe Ceresi. Plain Dealer, Sep. 26, 1933.

Page 43   flamboyance and desire for prominence
Michael Roberts, "Why They Blew Away Shondor Birns," Cleveland Magazine, July, 1975.

Page 43   Shon was too much of a freelancer
Ibid.

Page 43   About Rudy Duncan
Cleveland Press, July 6, 1934
Plain Dealer, June 7, 1934,
Plain Dealer, June 26, 1934.

Chapter Three

Page 46   Two prominent rackets figures from Akron: They were Louis Azar and Mike Saviolas. Plain Dealer, Sep. 20, 1935.

Page 47   Your Honor, I came to Miami to mind my own business and spend money. Cleveland Press, Feb 11, 1937.

Page 47   New leader of the East 55th and Woodland mob
Plain Dealer, June 3, 1932.

Page 48   This is Shondor Birns
Cleveland Press, Feb. 11, 1937.

Page 48   Phooey!
Cleveland News, Feb. 11, 1937.

Page 49   Them cops. Funny thing, ain't it?
Plain Dealer, Feb. 11, 1937.

Page 49   Well may Shondor Birns be boastful
Cleveland Press, Feb. 11, 1937.

Page 50   Molnar's squad located records: Shondor's name was in paper-work located in the club, but apparently there was insufficient evidence to charge him with a crime.

Page 51   Crime is more rampant
Plain Dealer, May 15, 1937.

Page 52   Someday you guys will be in lineups too
Plain Dealer, April 22, 1937.

Page 53   Indictments were issued against Angelo Sciria, Angelo Lonardo, Frank Hoge, and twenty others: They were John DeMarco, Milton Rockman, Albert Polizzi, John Angersola, George Angersola, Joseph Artwell, Nick Satulla, William Richardson, Charles Lavocco, Solly Hart, Dominic Sciria, Dominic Suspirato, Joseph Tampiro, Charles Lardomita, Victor Mannino, Elsworth Jewel, Tommy Boyce, Herbert Oliver and Larry Gaskins.

Page 53   This investigation was undertaken because we felt that this gang of racketeers Joseph M. Gambatese, "Report Expected to Hit Mayfield Road mob; 70 'talk' in racket probe," Plain Dealer, April 26, 1939.

Page 54   I'll be surprised if they don't find me guilty
Plain Dealer, Oct. 25, 1938.

Page 54   What is this, Germany or something where a man can't even walk. Cleveland Press, Dec. 16, 1941.

Page 55   Illness and death of Herman Birn:
Ohio Certificate of Death at https://FamilySearch.org. Accessed Jan. 30, 2019.

Page 56   Panting from her exertions
Plain Dealer, May 29, 1942.

Page 56   the Army said flatly and emphatically, 'No.'
Cleveland Press, Jan. 14, 1943.

Page 56   he and Birns wore identical suits
Todd Simon, "Court Rebuff Hits Cullitan in Birns Quiz," Plain Dealer, Dec. 21, 1949.

Page 57   I've been carrying that charge over my head for more than three years Anthony DiSantis, Plain Dealer, Aug. 7, 1942.

Chapter Four

Page 58   About the 1940 alien registration act
https://loveman.sdsu.edu/docs/1940AlienRegistrationAct.pdf, accessed June 17, 2019.

Page 58   he was never naturalized: The 1920 US Census record indicates Herman and Illona Birn, and their children, were naturalized, however on the 1930 census, their "NA" (naturalized) status is stricken for Herman, Alex (Shondor) and Sarah in the document image located online (https://FamilySearch.org. Accessed Jan. 30, 2019). The author found no record documenting why Shondor Birns never naturalized, nor that he naturalized then lost his citizenship.

Page 59   In Cleveland, the US attorney ordered an investigation
US Dept. of Justice, FBI investigation of Alex Shondor Birns. Report by S.A. Douglas J. Krauter, Oct. 8, 1942.

Page 59   I've known Shondor since he was a young boy
US Dept. of Justice. FBI investigation Alex Shondor Birns. Statement of C.M. Roskoph of the Union Linen and Towel Co. Report by S.A. Douglas J. Krauter, Oct. 8, 1942.

Page 61   Three agents apprehended Birns: They were Samuel E. Virden, Weldon F. Donovan, and William M. Kelly. US Dept. of Justice, FBI, Alex Shondor Birns, Feb. 26, 1943.

Page 61   Above reproach
Doris O'Donnell papers in author's collection.

Page 62   If some of the people that put me in this trouble
Louis Clifford, "Reveals details of Shondor Birns' hearing resulting in internment," Cleveland Press, undated. Located in US Dept. of Justice; Immigration and Naturalization Service, Alex Shondor Birns.

Page 63   My son is a good Jewish boy
Michael Roberts, "Why They Blew Away Shondor Birns," Cleveland Magazine, July, 1975.

Page 63   Shondor's pals threw him a two-night going away party
John Stark Bellamy II, The Killer in the Attic, Gray and Co., Cleveland, OH, 2002.

Page 63   The delivery of Shondor Birns
Cleveland Press, Jan. 15, 1943.

Pages 64-65   Our beloved President!
US Dept. of Justice, Immigration and Naturalization Service. File of Alex Shondor Birns. Handwritten letter of Mrs. Joseph Kovacs to President Franklin D. Roosevelt, Feb. 5, 1943.

Page 66   Alex: I am glad to hear that you hope soon to be relieved
US Dept. of Justice, Immigration and Naturalization Service. File of Alex Shondor Birns. Handwritten letter dated April 3, 1944.

Page 66   It was not always easy to trace Birns' influential contacts
Michael Roberts, "Why They Blew Away Shondor Birns," Cleveland Magazine, July, 1975.

Pages 66-67   By virtue of your gracious and kind heart
US Dept. of Justice, Immigration and Naturalization Service. File of Alex Shondor Birns. Typed letter from Shondor Birns to the director of the US Dept. of Justice Alien Enemy Control Unit, Edward G. Ennis.

Page 67   About the Theatrical Grill
David D. Van Tassel and John J. Grabowski, eds., Encyclopedia of Cleveland History, Bloomington, Indiana University Press, 1996.

Page 68   Wexler wrote a check to Rose Scheiner for $25,000 and bought Shondor out Ted Princiotto, "Calls Birns'$5000 Their Nest Egg," Plain Dealer, July 13, 1954.

Page 69   It is our impression
Todd Simon, "Report Names Source of Police Corruption as Molnar is Indicted," Plain Dealer, April 28, 1948.

Page 69   Molnar had virtually controlled
Call and Post, July 17, 1948.

Page 69   the cashingest family: The assistant county prosecutor was Victor DeMarco. Todd Simon, "Jury Debates 4 Hours; Motion for New Trial will be Heard Friday." Plain Dealer, July 27, 1948.

Page 70   Stop fighting, get down to business, and make some money
Todd Simon, "Numbers Figures Parade to Stand," Plain Dealer, Dec. 6, 1949

Page 71   Advertisements boasted the "finest food, wines and liquors
Plain Dealer, March 24, 1947.

Page 71   Prone to be whimsical
Cleveland Press, April 2, 1947.

Page 71   Alhambra interior
Plain Dealer, July 22, 1951 and personal interviews.

Pages 71-72   often ordered full dinners and had them delivered to his apartment via taxi Michael D. Roberts, "Why They Blew Shondor Birns Away," Cleveland Magazine, July, 1975.

Page 72-73   Get over here, Cannata
Personal interview.

Page 73   Birns stabbed by employee
Cleveland Press, Nov. 26, 1976.

Pages 73-74   About Carl Delau
Plain Dealer, Jan. 26, 1966 v
Wally Guenther, "Carl Delau, 89, headed Cleve. Police Dept.'s Detective Bureau," Plain Dealer, Jan. 15, 2008.

Page 75   Sure I took out my billfold
Plain Dealer, Aug. 10, 1948.

Page 75   You don't want to do that, Shon
Cleveland Press, April 2, 1947.

Pages 75-76   Chief, from now on these hoodlums will be plenty roughed up
Cleveland Press, Sep. 16, 1948.

Page 76   When the visit was complete, Shondor gave the guard twenty-five dollars
Plain Dealer, Sep. 21, 1949.

Page 78   The biggest names in northeast Ohio criminal defense: The other attorneys were Louis Fernberg for Amata, Fred Garmone for Artwell, and William J. Corrigan and Frank Azzarello for Lonardo.
Call and Post, Nov. 9, 1949.

Page 78   Birns is one of the slickers
Todd Simon, "Jury to Ballot in Birns Case Today," Plain Dealer, Jan. 6, 1950.

Page 78   No more gunplay and the loudmouth threat is passé
Todd Simon, "Rope Trick is Simple for Jobless Hoodlums," Plain Dealer, May 31, 1950.

Page 79   I don't want to tell you how to run your jail
Todd Simon, "Birns Blasts Amata on Jury Plot," Plain Dealer, Jan. 12, 1950.

Page 79   I would spend time with Shondor in the Alhambra office
(Based on) Todd Simon, "Girl Tells Secrets of Racketeer," Plain Dealer, April 2, 1950.

Page 80   Go ahead, give them the keys to the city
Nathan Silverman, "Jury Takes 2 ½ Hours to Reach Verdict in 8-Week Bomb Trial," Plain Dealer, May 18, 1950

Page 81   I'm going to keep my nose clean
Ibid.

Page 81   Judge Silbert, this is Shondor
Nathan Silverman, "Birns Phones to Sweeney from Chicago," Plain Dealer, May 20, 1950.

Page 81   I'm satisfied it was an honest misunderstanding
Ibid.

Page 82   Your attempt to sway a juror using that young woman
Nathan Silverman, "Birns Back in Jail; Bail Plea Today," Plain Dealer, May 25, 1950.

Page 82   Lower in reputation
Plain Dealer, Nov. 23, 1950.

Chapter Five

Page 84   An attorney purchased it: The attorney was Morris Blane.

Page 84   This will make a new man of me
Lima News, "Cupid Spurs Gambler to Life of Toil?" July 2, 1951.

Page 84   IRS officials seized Shondor's Cadillac: Other vehicles seized and auctioned belonged to Buster Matthews, Thomas J. Davis, and William Seawright. Plain Dealer, Sep. 3, 1952.

Page 85   Michael Birns born
Plain Dealer, June 4, 1953.

Page 85   It's my feeling that you can't and won't make a legitimate living
Sanford Watzman, "Shondor 'Pays' $281 in Jail on Tax Claim," Plain Dealer, July 8, 1953.

Page 86   I could go to work tomorrow if the police would quit harassing me. Plain Dealer, May 1, 1954.

Page 86   Shondor gave it to me in 1949 after we were engaged
Ted Princiotto, "Call Birns' $5000 Their Nest Egg," Plain Dealer, July 13, 1954.

Page 87   I put it in an envelope and put it in the safe for Mr. Birns
Ted Princiotto, "Blonde Springs Trap for US at Birns trial," Plain Dealer, July
17, 1954.

Page 87   Later he worked in the prison library
George Barmann, "Shondor Quiet but Capable of Quick, Violent Retaliation,"
Plain Dealer, July 11, 1963.

Page 88   Drake bombing: His girlfriend was Canis "Candy" Francis.
Geech Bell's wife was Olivia.
Plain Dealer, Sep. 12, 1955 and Call and Post, Sep. 15, 1955

Page 88   Police hauled in dozens of racketeers for questioning: They included Arthur Drake, Joe Allen, Willie Hoge, Vernial Abernathy, Willie "Buckeye" Jackson, Thomas Turk, Ira Boone, Bishop Crosby, Donald King, and
Edward Keeling. They brought in William Simms of Cleveland Heights. He belonged to a Michigan organization called United Bankers which police believed
attempted to muscle in on Drake's operation. Detectives were sent to Detroit to
question an enforcer for the group which went broke while owing over $6000 to
winning bettors. Detectives also questioned 30-year-old Frank Bonarrigo who
was in possession of dynamite of the type used in the bombing of Drake's car.
(Based on Plain Dealer and Call and Post articles.)

Page 88   They theorized that the attempt on Little Brother's life
Call and Post, Feb. 4, 1956.

Page 89   MAN WITHOUT A COUNTRY
A clipping of the newspaper article is included in an FBI report dated Feb. 19,
1957 in Birns's FBI file and is cited as appearing in the "Wash. News" (probably
the Washington Daily News), Oct. 18, 1956.

Page 89   Shondor's enjoyment of breeding Dobermans
Personal interview.

Page 90   We need to move out of Cleveland to get away from Delau and
his crew. Cleveland Press, Nov. 7, 1957.

Page 91   Headed by Tommy Boyce
Author conjecture.

Page 91   We will break the arms
Call and Post, Nov. 9, 1957.

Page 92   I know you're going to pay me
Cleveland Police Dept. Intelligence Division file, Alex Shondor Birns, undated.

Page 92   You were supposed to be killed
Cleveland News, May 20, 1957.

Page 93   They were sore because I wouldn't go along
Plain Dealer, May 21, 1957.

Page 93   I know nothing about them people
Cleveland News, May 20, 1957.

Page 94   What's there to celebrate?
Plain Dealer, Nov. 21, 1957.

Page 95   He agreed to owe
Plain Dealer, June 18, 1957.

Page 96   I was just having some fun
Plain Dealer, Aug. 20, 1958.

Page 96   Shondor in Los Angeles, and Mickey Cohen
US Dept. of Justice, FBI, Alex Shondor Birns, March 27, 1959.

Page 96   What did you do, blow out your tire?
Cleveland Press, April 9, 1959.

Page 97   Along with two detectives: They were Tom Dever and Mike
Haney.

Page 97   I jumped high
Plain Dealer, April 15, 1959.

Page 98   Go check Shondor Birns and ask what his alibi is this time
Call and Post, April 18, 1959.

Page 98   You guys got nine thousand of these already
Ibid.

Page 99   It's entirely possible that one of these days
Plain Dealer, June 24, 1959.

Page 99   You got it wrong, Carl
Author-created dialogue based on Plain Dealer, July 12, 1963. Author's conjecture on chronology.

Page 99   Bartone's associates included
Russ Tarby. "JFK in Dallas: The Syracuse Connections," Syracuse New Times https://www.syracusenewtimes.com/jfk-dallas-syracuse-connections; accessed May 17, 2017

Page 100   By the grace of God, I didn't go
US Dept. of Justice, FBI, Alex Shondor Birns; report by S.A. John J. Barrett, Aug. 3, 1959.

Page 101   We're not worried a bit
Plain Dealer, Dec. 31, 1959.

Page 101   Bartone and two others: There were Augusto Ferrando, the Dominican Republic's consul general at Miami, and Joseph Liquori, a Miami cop.

Chapter Six

Page 117   Born George C. Burslem, Gordon worked in the syndicate's first gambling joints Messick, Hank, The Silent Syndicate. New York, Macmillan, 1967.

Page 117   I can go back in anytime, Georgie
US Dept. of Justice, FBI, Alex Shondor Birns, Oct. 2, 1966. FBI wiretap transcript dated Jan. 14, 1963.

Page 118   he also had a percentage of a gambling operation in Havana:
Author conjecture
Fred Mollenkopf, "Who Shot at Alex Birns?" Plain Dealer, April 9, 1959.

Page 118   In the company of a twenty-year-old: This was Sherry Hoge,
nee Coffey. US Dept. of Justice, FBI, Alex Shondor Birns, report of S.A. Jack
Barrett, Aug. 3, 1959.

Page 118   I was going with my girl to see the Kentucky Derby
Personal interview.

Page 118   In its heyday, Short Vincent Avenue was Cleveland's
Terence Sheridan, "High Life," Cleveland Magazine, Aug., 1988.

Page 119   And there was a higher echelon of crime Brian Albrecht, "Where
the Good and Infamous Rubbed Elbows: Theatrical," Plain Dealer, April 7, 2002.

Page 119   Theatrical interior
Personal interview.

Page 120   About Danny Greene
Rick Porrello, To Kill the Irishman. Cleveland, Next Hat Press, 1998.

Page 120   He suggested the two become partners
US Dept. of Justice, FBI, Alex Shondor Birns, July 12, 1963.

Page 120   Nobody knows the bar and restaurant business like Shondor
Cleveland Press, July 9, 1963.

Page 121   Shondor introduced Mervin to Dominick Bartone: Author conjecture.

Page 121   I do what Shon does but with a pen
Personal interview

Page 121   Owned by a Cleveland councilman: This was Jack P. Russell.
Plain Dealer, July 5, 1964.

Page 122   My lawyer and I went to Mervin's office
Plain Dealer, Sep. 14, 1961.

Page 122   Leah Lipsyc, a compact woman with jet-black hair and sky-blue eyes Norman Melnick, "Gold's Widow Tell of Wartime Terror," Plain Dealer, July 16, 1963

Page 122   The Catholics were good to the Jews
Cleveland Press, July 16, 1963.

Page 122   Mervin had no money, no money at all
Norman Melnick, "Widow Tells of Wartime Terror," Plain Dealer, July 16, 1963.

Page 123   If there were ten steps to a deal, you were only in on two
Cleveland Press, Sep. 9, 1961.

Page 124   The surname Leonards: FamilySearch.org shows that Ellie's father, Leonard Leonards, also used the surnames of Deluzynski and Dluzyn.

Page 124   About Allene Leonards and Kent State University
Kent State University Chestnut Burr yearbook, 1961. www.archive.org/details/chestnutburr1961kent, accessed June 10, 2019, and personal interview.

Page 125   with prominent mob figures: These included Joe Fischetti, Joe Massei, and Tony Ricci.

Page 125   Babe Triscaro suggested that Al Naiman take Dominick Bartone
US Dept. of Justice, FBI, James Riddle Hoffa, Dominick Edward Bartone, et al; Report of S.A. Frank L. Mellott, Jan. 22, 1963.

Page 125   Shortly after Mr. Bartone came into the business, he assumed complete control US Dept. of Justice, FBI, James Riddle Hoffa, Dominick Edward Bartone, et al; Statement of Madge Kirchner; Report of S.A. Frank L. Mellott, Jan. 22, 1963.

Page 125   Forced him out of his office at gunpoint
US Dept. of Justice, FBI, Dominick Edward Bartone, Report of Michael Farrin, Feb. 28, 1961.

Page 125   Many persons Bartone dealt with in Cuba wished he would return US Dept. of Justice, FBI, William Alexander Morgan, report by S.A. Leman L. Stafford, Jr., Aug. 26, 1959.

Page 126   They made sure to thoroughly scrub off the spatters of dried cigar spittle Personal interview.

Page 126   Mervin asked me to become a stockholder in a small business company
US Dept. of Justice, FBI, Mervin L. Gold, et al, Oct. 16, 1961.

Page 126   Mervin asked me if I would invest $25,000 in this company
US Dept. of Justice, FBI, Mervin L. Gold, July 19, 1963.

Page 127   He told Schulist to hold the checks
US Dept. of Justice, FBI. Mervin L. Gold, et al, Nov. 9, 1961

Page 127   One of the Cosmo investors remembered Gold being "very pleased" Ibid.

Page 127   Everything will be all right
Plain Dealer, May 22, 1963.

Page 128   About bearer bonds
Guy Bernfeld, "Bearer Bonds: From Popular to Prohibited," Investopedia, www.investopedia.com. Accessed Feb. 10, 2018.

Page 128   We argued and Mervin became nasty
Forrest Allen, "How Gold Borrowed $20,000 on Stolen Bonds," Cleveland Press, Dec. 13, 1961.

Page 128   They issued him a replacement
Cleveland Press, Sep. 7, 1961

Page 129   THE AFFIANT
US Dept. of Justice, FBI. Mervin L. Gold, Aug. 14, 1963.

Page 129   Carl Delau and two of his detectives: They were Michael Haney
and Ray McCool. Fred Mollenkopf, "Police arrest Birns in his numbers office,"
Plain Dealer, May 27, 1961.

Page 130   Birns made a cardinal error
Ibid.

Page 130   He told me to give him $5,000 in cash, and he'd put in $15,000
worth of bonds.
Cleveland Press, Sep. 14, 1961.

Page 131   Mervin wanted me to have my daughter draw $5,000 from the
bank
Cleveland Press, Sep. 14, 1961.

Page 131   when several bank burglaries in Ontario and Quebec
Cleveland Press, Sept. 7, 1961.

Page 131   Some were found as far as Lebanon and Switzerland
US Dept. of Justice, FBI memo regarding subjects Bernard J. Ezhaya, William
W. Rabin, et al, dated April 30, 1959 and located in FBI investigative file of
Joseph R. Merola.

Page 131   Mr. Gold, your liberty is in jeopardy
Forrest Allen, "How Gold Borrowed $20,000 on Stolen Bonds," Cleveland
Press, Dec. 13, 1961.

Page 133   In Cleveland, a woman sued him for $450,000
Cleveland Press, Oct. 23, 1962.

Page 133   How much did I leave with?
Cleveland Press, Oct. 17, 1962.

Page 133   Federal agents believed Gold took with him
Cleveland Press, Dec. 13, 1961.

Page 134   I am opposed to granting citizenship to persons of questionable character. Plain Dealer, Dec. 1, 1961.

Page 134   I want to stay in Israel because it is the land of my forefathers Cleveland Press, March 1, 1962.

Page 134   If the facts are as you claim them to be, Mr. Gold Cleveland Press, March 6, 1962.

Page 135   Gold's letter and phone call to William Kahan US Dept. of Justice, FBI, Mervin L. Gold, et al, Aug. 22, 1962.

Page 136   The sharks told the goldfish be nice, don't talk Cleveland Press, July 26, 1963.

Chapter Seven

Page 137   Some in that circle said that the failure of Israel US Dept. of Justice, FBI, Mervin L. Gold, Memo Aug. 22, 1962.

Page 138   When we arrive in New York Plain Dealer, July 18, 1963.

Pages 138-139 Don't you talk, Mr. Gold.: This was Bond Commissioner Max Schiffman, US District Court in Brooklyn, NY.
Wilson Hirschfeld, "US to Return Gold Here Soon," Plain Dealer, Oct. 7, 1962.

Page 139   This will blow up ten times as big once he is brought back Ibid.

Page 139   Back in Cleveland, Gold denied that he sought Israeli citizenship Cleveland Press, July, 9 1963.

Page 139   I wanted to come back and settle up
Bus Bergen, "Gold Confident He'll Be Cleared of Fraud Charges," Cleveland Press, Oct. 17, 1962.

Page 140   He had no sense of proportion (Based on)
Forrest Allen, "Recordings Reveal Gold a Hard Man on the Telephone," Cleveland Press, July 20, 1963.

Page 140   He left little doubt in my mind
Forrest Allen, "Stolen Bonds Put the Skid to Shaky Gold," Cleveland Press, July 11, 1963.

Page 141   They said you and Panz are getting a weekly fee from numbers operators US Dept. of Justice, FBI, Alex Shondor Birns, Oct. 31, 1966. Wiretap transcript dated Jan. 14, 1963.

Page 143   Had he married her
US Dept. of Justice, FBI, Alex Shondor Birns, report by S.A. Richard J. Jones, March 25, 1964.

Page 144   Gold is no good
US. Dept. of Justice, FBI, Mervin L. Gold, memo July 9, 1963.

Page 145   They set out to pin it on me all alone
Cleveland Press, July 12, 1963.

Page 145   That was a long time ago
Forrest Allen, "Stolen Bonds Put the Skid to Shaky Gold," Cleveland Press, July 11, 1963.

Page 146   I considered Shondor Birns a friend
Cleveland Press, July 11, 1963.

Pages 146-147 Merle McCurdy prosecuted the case. He was assisted by Dominic J. Cimino.

Page 147   They made him a sacrificial lamb
US Dept. of Justice, FBI, Mervin L. Gold, memo May 20, 1963.

Page 147   He typed out a note promising to exonerate the individual for fifty thousand dollars. US Dept. of Justice, FBI, Alex Shondor Birns, July 12, 1963.

Page 147   Everything I did at Cosmo
Plain Dealer, June 8, 1963. (Based on)

Page 148   the juror claimed she never took the oath when Judge Battisti
swore her in J.C. Daschbach, "Juror is Guilty of Contempt," Plain Dealer, Oct.
2, 1964.

Page 149   I have had to conduct more examination in this case than any
other Cleveland Press, May 27, 1963.

Page 149   Do you think Mervin has a shot on appeal?
Personal interview

Page 149   Did you speak to that fat ex-friend of mine
US Dept. of Justice, FBI, Alex Shondor Birns, Oct. 17, 1963

Page 155   Battisti insisted that Willis remain as Gold's attorney
J.C. Daschbach, "Mervin Gold's Rise and Fall similar to Wayward Skyrocket,"
Plain Dealer, July 9, 1963.

Page 155   I paid Willis twenty-five hundred dollars (Encounter and dialogue based on documented summary).
US Dept. of Justice, FBI, Mervin L. Gold, Oct. 17, 1963.

Pages 155-156 At Kandracs
US Dept. of Justice, FBI, Alex Shondor Birns, Oct. 17, 1963; Plain Dealer, July
14, 1963 and personal interview.

Page 156   Why don't you just end it
Cleveland Press, July 14, 1963

Page 157   I'll be back in an hour
Plain Dealer, July 18, 1963.

Page 158   Jane, I have to go to Columbus last minute (Based on documented summary)
Cleveland Press, July 9, 1963

Page 158   Jane told Lily that Shon had called her
Cleveland Press, July 14, 1963.

Page 158   She said he left around 9:30 p.m.
US Dept. of Justice, FBI, Alex Shondor Birns, July 19, 1963.

Pages 158-159 Birns at Toledo Town House Motel
US Dept. of Justice, FBI, Alex Shondor Birns, July 12, 1963.

Page 158-159   About the Aku-Aku
The Toledo Blade, Feb. 11, 2002.

Page 159   If he can't be found, a fugitive warrant will be issued
Plain Dealer, July 7, 1963.

Page 160   What chance do I have against all this power
Cleveland Press, July 9, 1963.

Page 160   Lily Gold's description of Mervin's last day.
US Dept. of Justice, FBI, Mervin L. Gold, July 9, 1963, and Cleveland Press,
July 14, 1963, and Jan Mellow, "Last Day was Happy, Mrs. Gold Testifies,"
Cleveland Press, undated; July, 1963.

Page 161   a doctor, who came to the hotel
US Dept. of Justice, FBI, Mervin L. Gold, July 12, 1963.

Chapter Eight

Page 162   Mervin is the victim of politicians
US Dept. of Justice, FBI, Mervin L. Gold, July 19, 1963.

Pages 162-165 Search for Mervin Gold; Crime scene.
Ed Kissell, "Mervin Gold Found Slain," Plain Dealer, July 9, 1963.
US Dept. of Justice, FBI, Alex Shondor Birns, July 19, 1963.

Page 165   Gold wrote that between Nov. 1960 and Jan. 1961
US Dept. of Justice, FBI, Alex Shondor Birns, July 19, 1963.

Page 166   I hurt it shooting firecrackers on the Fourth
US Dept. of Justice, FBI, Alex Shondor Birns, July 11, 1963.

Page 166   Mervin Gold, Who was Deported from Israel
Haboker Daily Newspaper, Tel-Aviv, Israel, July 10, 1963.

Page 166   We're all anxious to talk to Birns
Plain Dealer, July 10, 1963.

Page 167   Mervin gets in to something, it's like the kiss of death
Cleveland Press, July 20, 1963.

Page 167   Execution of search warrant and Shondor's house.
Cleveland Press, July 7-10, 1963.

Page 167   Fury was barking and straining to get loose: Author conjecture.

Page 167   The Mervin Gold trial and the 33-year-old man's conviction
was spectacular. Cleveland Press, July 9, 1963.

Page 168   Mervin Gold was struck
Cleveland Press, July 9, 1963.

Page 168   He telephoned Sheriff McGettrick's chief deputy: This was John
Kocevar.

Page 169   I asked Shondor if he could help in resolving the murder
Plain Dealer, July 12, 1963.

Pages 169-170 Shondor has never liked me
Cleveland Press, July 12, 1963 and Plain Dealer, March 31, 1975

Page 170   In fact, Mervin owes me about five thousand dollars
US Dept. of Justice, FBI, Mervin L. Gold, July 19, 1963.

Page 170   Where was I?
Plain Dealer, July 12, 1962.

Page 171   If you ran into Shondor on Short Vincent, you'd see a man of 57
George Barmann, "Shondor Quiet but Capable of Quick, Violent Retaliation,"
Plain Dealer, July 11, 1963.

Page 171   thoroughly regarding all financial transactions
US Dept. of Justice, FBI, James Riddle Hoffa, Dominick Edward Bartone, et al;
Aug. 6, 1963.

Page 172   The FBI also received information from a confidential tipster
US Dept. of Justice, FBI, Alex Shondor Birns, Oct. 17, 1963.

Page 172   The Press makes it clear that it holds no brief for Mervin Gold
Cleveland Press, July 12, 1963.

Page 174   Before this Gold business, I never read or heard anything about
Shondor John Nussbaum, "Airing of Teacher's Link to Birns Sighted," Plain
Dealer, July 14, 1965.

Page 174   threatening to tell all he knew
Cleveland Press, July 15, 1963

Page 175   He left her a bottle of peroxide to lighten her hair: Author conjecture. Plain Dealer, July 18, 1963.

Page 175   I've been expecting you
Cleveland Press, July 17, 1963.

Page 175   Gold's recording of Shondor threatening him.
US Dept. of Justice, FBI, Mervin L. Gold, Oct. 17, 1963.

Page 176   Why didn't you tell the police that when they talked to you
Plain Dealer, July 18, 1963.

Page 178   I don't take the Fifth Amendment
Todd Simon, "Teacher, Birns Take '5th' at Gold Inquest," Plain Dealer, July 18,
1963

Page 181   Miss Leonards is much too educated to have such hostile attitude Plain Dealer, July 18 & 25, 1963.

Page 182   I feel sorry for her
William C. Barnard, "Allene on Stand Wins Sympathy," Plain Dealer, July 18, 1963.

Page 182   I want to turn this over to the sheriff or somebody
Cleveland Press, Aug. 2, 1963.

Page 182   Reporter Doris O'Donnell had a source who told her
Doris O'Donnell papers in author's collection.

Chapter Nine

Page 195   Attorney Merle McCurdy said the investigation into the complex case. Plain Dealer, April 21, 1965

Page 195   George Zimmerman and Leonard Luxenberg were convicted
Plain Dealer, June 24, 1965, July 12, 1967, Mar. 12, 1970.

Page 195   Although I am closing the inquest, I can reopen it any time
Cleveland Press, Dec. 31, 1963.

Page 195-196   We had eight happy years
Forrest Allen, "His 'Friends' Left Gold Barren Home," Cleveland Press, July 16, 1963.

Page 196   Mr. Martin has his constitutional rights, and he exercised them
Plain Dealer, Dec. 4, 1965.

Page 196   I hear Shon is going to get it again for income tax
US Dept. of Justice, FBI, Alex Shondor Birns, Oct. 25, 1966. Wiretap transcript of conversation held May 10, 1965.

Page 197   Whenever Shondor needed anything done involving the blacks
Cleveland Police Dept., Homicide investigation of Shondor Birns, Statement of Henry Crosby, April 8, 1975.

Page 198   Vulcan was a front for Bucci's other businesses
James T. Cox, "Police Here have Crooks on the Run," Plain Dealer, Dec. 20, 1964.

Page 199   It's a present for your wife and five kids
James, T. Cox, "Detective testifies Birns offered bribe for raid information," Plain Dealer, Dec. 10, 1965.

Page 199   Shondor! Telephone call from Pittsburgh; Shondor's nightclub investments US Dept. of Justice, FBI, Alex Shondor Birns, March 30, 1966, and personal interview.

Page 199   He also put up cash for an associate: This was Tony Buffa, a reputed fence. US Dept. of Justice, FBI, Alex Shondor Birns, report of SA John Toulan, May 23, 1966.

Page 200   It was an Irish-American FBI agent: This was Martin McCann.

Page 200   a tenacious Plain Dealer reporter: This was Sam Marshall.

Page 200   Birns's Orange Village house
Cleveland Press, March 10, 1965, "Birns Tries Suburbia," and personal interview.

Page 201   Up to $8,000 came in daily
US Dept. of Justice, FBI, Alex Shondor Birns, March 30, 1966.

Page 201   The numbers racket in Cleveland is big
Thomas J. Brazaitis, "Numbers Writer Strikes Bonanza in Poor Region," Plain Dealer, May 14, 1972.

Pages 201-202 About Bill Seawright
Peery, Richard M., "Enterprising Entrepreneur Seawright Dies at 96," Plain Dealer, April 17, 2003.

Page 202   In the numbers business, you have to drive a fancy car
Patrick O'Donnell, "King of Cleveland's numbers racket dead; Virgil Ogletree, 84, made, lost a fortune," Plain Dealer, Jan. 25, 2007.

Page 202   The bettors would place their bets with the writers
Personal interview

Page 202   If I got out of numbers
Plain Dealer, Dec. 10, 1965.

Page 203   The city was considered by some experts
Plain Dealer, Jan. 8, 1974

Page 203   Then I wanted to open a college fund for my son
US Dept. of Justice, FBI, Alex Shondor Birns; Mervin L. Gold, Nov. 24, 1964.
(Based on)

Pages 203-204 Here is the real problem with the numbers
US Dept. of Justice, FBI, Mervin L. Gold, Nov. 24, 1964.

Page 204   Life is just a jungle . . . Every time something happens, I'm
blamed Paul Lilley, "Just Want to be Left Alone," Cleveland Press, date unknown; believed to 1968.

Page 204   If I'm the city's biggest crook, why do they all want to be my
friend? Michael Roberts, "Public Enemy Shondor Birns," Cleveland Magazine,
Nov. , 1990.

Page 204   It was a generation of newspaper reporters, more than anyone
else Ibid.

Page 205   It's a delay tactic.
Terence Sheridan, "Birns May Race for Admittance to Federal Pen," Plain Dealer, Aug. 24, 1967.

Page 206   one numbers operator increased his payout on winners to boost
business: Author theory.

Page 206   In 1965, his body was found on a farm
Pittsburgh Post Gazette, June 26, 1965.

Page 207   the US attorney felt the aging racketeer was a low risk: This was Bernard J. Stuplinski.

Page 207   It's the first time anybody's been kind to me
Robert J. Holmes, "County Takes Custody of Shondor Birns," Plain Dealer, June 22, 1968.

Page 208   Birns has been sentenced to the Ohio Penitentiary, and that is where he'll go Terence Sheridan and Robert J. Holmes, "Birns Gets Bail in Prison Swap," Plain Dealer, June 21, 1968.

Page 208   That's when I got close with Shon
Statement of Charlie Broeckel to law enforcement officers, Jan. 1974.

Page 209   There was never even a stick of gum missing when Shondor ran the commissary Michael Roberts, "Why They Blew Shondor Birns Away," Cleveland Magazine, July, 1975.

Page 209   But when they get you down
Ibid.

Page 209   One night we were out for dinner with Ellie and Danny Greene
Personal interview.

Page 210   It's some ridiculous thing about breaking and entering
Christopher Evans, "Mobster Mash," Plain Dealer Magazine, Feb. 3, 1991.

Page 210   I ran numbers for him when I was a kid
John H. Tidyman, Gimme Rewrite Sweetheart, Cleveland, Gray and Co., 2009.

Page 211   complaining of backaches and gall stones
Paul Lilley, "Just Want to be Left Alone," Cleveland Press, date unknown; believed to be 1968.

Page 211   The green-eyed brunette had met Birns as a teenager while dabbling in prostitution
Personal interviews.

Page 211   I arrived in the morning
Personal interview.

Page 212   During his first visit to Birns's house, Satan came running
Personal interview.

Page 212   Shon you got to do something with that fucking dog
Personal interview.

Page 213   He would have Ellie drive but give her instructions like where
to park Personal interview.

Page 214   After Shon got out, he didn't need Danny to oversee his operation Personal interview.

Pages 214-215 Some in the black community believed there was a deeper connection Personal interviews.

Page 215   But Birns remained somewhat legendary
Michael Roberts, "Public Enemy Shondor Birns," Cleveland Magazine, Nov. 1990.

Page 215   Numbers playing is a heritage
Call and Post, April 9, 1977.

Page 215   Black folks respect Shondor
Terence Sheridan, "The Fall of Shondor Birns and the Rise of Danny Greene," Exit Magazine, July 16, 1975. (Based on)

Page 215   While working as a bouncer at a bar, Frank Cook caught three slugs. Ibid.

Page 216   If it were a failed sit-down, then Bey or Khan would step in
Personal interview.

Page 216-217   About Bob Boggess
Statement of Charlie Broeckel to law enforcement officers, Jan. 1974.

Page 217   Barbut: Also known as Barbudi, Barbooth, Barbotte, and Even-Up Craps.
https://www.barbudi.com/; accessed June 18, 2019.

Page 217   Barbut was a gold mine
Statement of Martin "Mutt" DiFabio to law enforcement officers.

Page 218   One word came to another, and it wasn't changing Tasso's mind
Statement of Charlie Broeckel to law enforcement officers, Jan. 1974.

Page 219   It was lunchtime and busy
Rick Porrello, Superthief, Next Hat Press, Cleveland, 2005.

Page 220   Shon obtained a loan of $75,000 for Danny Greene
Statement of Charlie Broeckel to law enforcement officers, Jan. 1974.

Page 220   When Shondor was at the Theatrical, he ran into one of Danny's guys: This was Earl Deere.
Ibid.

Page 220   Shon is dead before midnight
Ibid.

Page 221   Whitcomb and Boggess homicides
Plain Dealer, July 6, 1975, and Statement of Charlie Broeckel to law enforcement officers, Jan. 1974. (Based on.)

Page 221   They're both on junk, and I'm through with them
Cleveland Police Department, Homicide investigation of Alex Shondor Birns. Based on interview of Mary Jane Jarus, April 1, 1975.

Page 222   There hasn't been a state where numbers has been hurt
Plain Dealer, Jan. 8, 1974.

Page 222   The street numbers game continued to function—if not flourish
Phillip Morris, "The State Runs Numbers Now," Plain Dealer, August 19, 2003.

Page 222   Similarly, rice paper could be used with a pot of boiling water
Personal interview.

Chapter Ten

Page 224   Nobody will mess around with your car as long as that Dober-
man's in there. Plain Dealer, April 1, 1975.
Page 225   Put it through, kid. I told you I'm gonna stay out of trouble
Ibid.

Page 226   Christy and her last husband, a third-string racketeer: This was
Louis "Lumpy Lou" Raffa.

Page 226   About Christy's
Personal interview.

Page 227   An acquaintance of ours came in
Personal interview.

Page 228   A week after Jimmy Z was murdered
Terence Sheridan, "High Life," Cleveland Magazine, Aug., 1988.

Page 228   The nature of crime was changing
Michael D. Roberts, "Public Enemy Shondor Birns," Cleveland Magazine, Nov.
, 1990.
Page 229   Janie believed the shots were meant for her, not Shon
Cleveland Police Department, Homicide investigation of Alex Shondor Birns.
Based on interview of Mary Jane Jarus, April 1, 1975.

Page 229   You shouldn't have to hear this
Cleveland Police Department, Homicide investigation of Alex Shondor Birns.

Page 230   Pretty sad about your buddy Moss
Terence Sheridan, "The Fall of Shondor Birns and the Rise of Danny Greene,"
Exit Magazine, July 16, 1975.

Page 231   It hit a low when they argued (Author conjecture)
based on Cleveland Police Dept. Homicide investigation of Alex Shondor Birns.

Page 231   He dressed in maroon pants
Plain Dealer, March 31, 1975.

Pages 231-232 a trash hauling executive: This was Howard Bahm.
Cleveland Police Department, Homicide investigation of Alex Shondor Birns.

Page 232   That no good fucking psychopath
Terence Sheridan, "The Fall of Shondor Birns and the Rise of Danny Greene,"
Exit Magazine, July 16, 1975.

Page 232   Silver Quill dialogue (Based on)
Terence Sheridan, "The Fall of Shondor Birns and the Rise of Danny Greene,"
Exit Magazine, July 16, 1975.

Page 233   I don't want to die in any rocking chair, though
Michael Roberts, "Why They Blew Away Shondor Birns," Cleveland Magazine,
July, 1975

Page 234   About the Paschal candle.
https://www.catholicnewsagency.com/resources/holy-week/holy-saturday/
the-paschal-candle, Accessed June 15, 2019.

Pages 233-234 About the St. Malachi mass
Michael Roberts, "Why They Blew Away Shondor Birns," Cleveland Magazine,
July, 1975, and personal interview.

Page 235   Get him out! Get him out!
Ibid.

Pages 234-236 Description of crime scene.
Cleveland Police Department, Homicide report of Alex Shondor Birns, and
Michael D. Roberts, "Why They Blew Shondor Birns Away," Cleveland Maga-
zine, July, 1975.

Page 236   I saw his head and shoulders
Plain Dealer, April 5, 1975.

Page 236   Well, I guess we won't
Michael D. Roberts, "Why They Blew Shondor Birns Away," Cleveland Magazine, July, 1975.

Page 237   I think he was killed over some broad
Christopher Evans, "Mobster Mash," Plain Dealer Magazine, Feb. 3, 1991.

Page 237   Why don't you leave the man in peace?
Plain Dealer, April 2, 1975.

Page 238   Our friend would not want us to present him as a saint
Ibid.

Chapter Eleven

Page 239   the bomb was placed under Birns's car
Powell W. Caesar, III, "Garage Door Opener May Have Triggered Blast," Call and Post, April 5, 1975.

Page 239   I didn't think anyone would dare
Terence Sheridan, "The Fall of Shondor Birns and the Rise of Danny Greene," Exit Magazine, July 16, 1975.

Page 239   I will not talk with anyone about anything
Cleveland Police Department, Homicide report of Alex Shondor Birns.

Page 239   telephoned attorneys and asked who might want to hurt the Irishman Terence Sheridan, "The Fall of Shondor Birns and the Rise of Danny Greene," Exit Magazine, July 16, 1975.

Page 240   Henry Crosby, who had inherited his father's numbers operation: The father's name was Bishop Crosby.

Page 241   the man told detectives he was sitting at a window across from Christy's Cleveland Police Department, Homicide report of Alex Shondor Birns.

Page 241   Accompanied by his attorney: This was James W. Burke, Jr.

Pages 241242We broke off relations a long time ago.
Cleveland Police Department, Homicide report of Alex Shondor Birns.

Page 242   Danny Greene's got a bomb party going
Statement of Charlie Broeckel to law enforcement officers.

Page 242   Danny Greene, that son of a bitch, has a death wish
Terence Sheridan, "The Fall of Shondor Birns and the Rise of Danny Greene," Exit Magazine, July 16, 1975.

Page 242   Shondor and Danny had been feuding for a long time
Ibid.

Page 243   It's dumb to talk about blacks killing Shondor
Ibid.

Page 243   But we had a love for each other right to the end
Cleveland Police Department, Homicide investigation of Alex Shondor Birns. Based on interview of Mary Jane Jarus, April 1, 1975

Page 244   I asked Ron about that very rumor
Cleveland Police Dept. Homicide report of Alex Shondor Birns. Based on interview of Richard Drake and George Moore by Detective Robert Bennett, April 3, 1975.

Page 245   I walked in the room, and there was Ellie and the top numbers guys Personal interview.

Page 246   Boom. And the bomb blew his penis off
Terence Sheridan, "The Fall of Shondor Birns and the Rise of Danny Greene," Exit Magazine, July 16, 1975.

Page 246   Roy Meyers dropped another bomb in the saga of Shondor Birns
Cleveland Press, June 5, 1975

Page 247   Ellie felt that of all the people who might have wanted Shon
dead Personal interview.

Page 248   Ellie was told the Italians were already planning to kill Greene
Personal interview.

Page 248   I know a number of hardworking and honest persons who are
bewitched Howard Preston, "Why lionize social outlaws," Plain Dealer, April
14, 1975.

Page 249   It would not surprise me to pick up my morning paper and read
Terence Sheridan, "The Fall of Shondor Birns and the Rise of Danny Greene,"
Exit Magazine, July 16, 1975

Page 249   Kiraly's payment was courtesy of Ellie Birns
Personal interview.

Pages 249-250 About Danny Greene
Porrello, Rick, To Kill the Irishman, Cleveland, Net Hat Press, 1998.

Page 251   When a neighbor moved the car: The victim was Frank Pircio.

Page 251   A Hells Angel: This was Enis Crnic.

Page 251   ATF agents celebrated the arrests of two men: These were The-
odore Ricci and Richard Viccarone.

Pages 251-252 Only one thing is for certain
Edward P. Whelan, "The Life and Hard Times of Cleveland's Mafia," Cleveland
Magazine, Aug., 1978.

Page 252   the kid who always wanted to be Shondor Birns
Terence Sheridan, "The Fall of Shondor Birns and the Rise of Danny Greene,"
Exit Magazine, July 16, 1975

Page 253   Jimmy, we'll be friends
John Petkovic, "A Mobster and a Gentleman," Plain Dealer, Nov. 29, 2015.

Epilogue

Page 256   The more I learned about George and his activities, the more scared I got
Plain Dealer, Jan. 6, 1984.

Page 257   George ripped the telephone off the wall
Cleveland Police Dept, Homicide report of George Rothrock. Based on narrative summary.

Page 258   We really appreciate what you did for us in the murder case
W.C. Miller and John F. Hagan, "Barroom crack lifted lid on McGettrick case," Plain Dealer, April 22, 1984

Page 259   George told me that he made the bomb (Based on narrative summary.) John Griffith, "Shondor Birns a Ghostly Guest at Angel's Trial," Plain Dealer, Nov. 5, 1983.

Page 259   It's not worth it
John Stark Bellamy II, The Killer in the Attic, Gray and Co., Cleveland, OH, 2002.

Page 260   Shondor Birns was the Public Enemy Number One
Ibid.

Page 260   I'd see Shon go into his pocket and give guys who were down
Plain Dealer, March 31, 1975

Page 260   I hate to knock the dead
Robert Dolgan, "Cronies Call Birns 'Nice Guy' but Police Captain Differs," Plain Dealer, March 31, 1975.

Page 260   When you'd see him at the Theatrical, he was the most pleasant, sociable guy.
Ibid.

Pages 260-261   Shondor wasn't no bad fella
Terence Sheridan, "The Fall of Shondor Birns and the Rise of Danny Greene," Exit Magazine, July 16, 1975.

What Happened to Them?

Page 277   Business associates recalled her as quiet and professional
Personal interview.

Page 277   Knowledgeable sources believe he died in the late 1980s
Personal interviews.

Page 278   About Maxie Diamond
Plain Dealer, June 12, 1971.

Page 278   Richard died in 1995 of a massive stroke
Personal interview.

Page 278   Don King has paid his debt to society
"New York boxing promoter Don King has been pardoned," Jan. 5, 1983. UPI Archives.   https://www.upi.com/Archives/1983/01/05/New-York-boxing-pro-moter-Don-King-has-been-pardoned/3232410590800/; accessed Aug. 11, 2019.

Page 278   a skeleton staff and reduced stable of boxers
Wallace Matthew, "At 86, Don King is 'Semiretired' but Still Working Every Angle," New York Times, Nov. 3, 2017. https://www.nytimes.com/2017/11/03/sports/boxing-don-king-bermane-stiverne-deontay-wilder.html; accessed Aug. 11, 2019.

Page 278   He served only four months of his four year sentence
Brent Larkin, "McGettrick dies; in jail 4 months," Plain Dealer, July 18, 1985.

Page 279   Virgil made as much money, if not more money
Patrick O'Donnell, "King of Cleveland's numbers racket dead; Virgil Ogletree, 84, made, lost a fortune," Plain Dealer, Jan. 25, 2007.

Page 279   Throughout his self-made career, he refused to recognize road-blocks Richard M. Peery, "Enterprising Entrepreneur Seawright Dies at 96," Plain Dealer, April 17, 2003.

SOURCES

BOOKS

Asbury, Herbert. *Sucker's Progress*. New York, Dodd, Mead and Co., 1938.

Bellamy II, John Stark. *The Kill in the Attic*. Gray and Co., 2002.

Brown, Albert M. *The Camp Wise Story*. Cleveland, Jewish Community Federation of Cleveland, 1989.

English, T.J. *Havana Nocturne*. New York, MJF Books, 2013.

Ezell, John Samuel. *Fortune's Merry Wheel*. Cambridge, Harvard University Press, 1960.

Heimel, Paul W. *Eliot Ness*. Nashville, Cumberland House, 2000.

Illman, Harry R. *Unholy Toledo*. San Francisco, Polemic Press, 1985.

Long, James E. and Siebenschuh, William. *Always On My Own*. Cleveland, Red Giant Books, 2015.

May, Allan R. *Crimetown U.S.A.* Cleveland, ConAllan Press, 2013.

McHugh, Roy, et al. *Pittsburgh Characters*. Greensburg, PA, Iconoclast Press, 1991.

Messick, Hank and Goldblatt, Burt. *The Mobs and the Mafia*. New York, Crowell, 1972.

Messick, Hank. *The Silent Syndicate*. New York, Macmillan, 1967.

Moldea, Dan. *The Hoffa Wars*. New York, Paddington Press, 1978.

Neff, James. Mobbed Up. New York, Atlantic Monthly Press, 1989.

Newfield, Jack. *Only in America*. New York, William Morrow and Co., 1995.

Newton, Michael. *Mr. Mob*. Jefferson, N.C., McFarland and Co., 2007.

Polster, Gary Edward. *Inside Looking Out: the Cleveland Jewish Orphan Asylum*. Kent, OH, Kent State University Press, 1990.

Monastra, Frank. *Brancato: Mafia Street Boss*. Mesa, AZ, Brighton Publishing, 2014.

Mosbrook, Joe. *Cleveland Jazz History (2nd Ed.)* Cleveland, Northeast Ohio Jazz

Society, 2003.

Porrello, Rick. *The Rise and Fall of the Cleveland Mafia*. New York, Barricade Books, 1995.

Porrello, Rick. *To Kill the Irishman*. Cleveland, Next Hat Press, 1998.

Porrello, Rick. *Superthief*. Cleveland, Next Hat Press, 2006.

Rubinstein, Judah with Avner, Jane A. *Merging Traditions*. Kent, OH, Kent State University Press, 2004.

Schatzberg, Rufus and Kelly, Robert J. *African-American Organized Crime* New York, Garland, 1996.

Tidyman, John H. *Gimme Rewrite Sweetheart*. Cleveland, Gray and Co., 2009.

Van Tassel, David D. and Grabowski, John J., eds. *Encyclopedia of Cleveland History*. Bloomington, Indiana University Press, 1996.

Veeck, Bill and Linn, Ed. *Veeck as in Wreck*. Chicago, The University of Chicago Press, 1962.

Waldron, Lamar and Hartmann, Thom. *Ultimate Sacrifice*. London, Constable & Robinson, Ltd., 2005.

Watzman, Sanford. *All the Way to Y2K*. Silver Spring, MD, 2000.

Wertheim, Sally and Bennett, Alan D., eds. and Rubinstein, Judah. Remembering: *Cleveland's Jewish Voices*. Kent, OH, Kent State University Press, 2011.

White, Shane and Garton, Stephen and Robertson, Stephen and White, Graham *Playing the Numbers*. Cambridge and London, Harvard University Press, 2010.

MAGAZINE ARTICLES

Evans, Christopher, *Mobster Mash,* Plain Dealer Magazine, Feb. 3, 1991.

Grzegorek, Vince, *The Last Ride of a Cleveland Hells Angel Informant*. Cleveland Magazine, Oct., 2013.

Roberts, Michael D., *Why They Blew Shondor Birns Away*. Cleveland Magazine, July, 1975.

Roberts, Michael D., *Public Enemy Shondor Birns*. Cleveland Magazine, Nov. , 1990

Roebuck, Julian B. *The Negro Numbers Man as a Criminal Type*. Journal of Criminal Law and Criminology, Volume 54, Spring, 1963.

Sheridan, Terence, *High Life*. Cleveland Magazine, Aug., 1988.

Sheridan, Terence, *The Fall of Shondor Birns and the Rise of Danny Greene* Exit Magazine, July 16, 1975.

Whelen, Edward P., *The Bombing Business*. Cleveland Magazine, April, 1977.

Whelen, Edward P., *The Life and Hard Times of Cleveland's Mafia*. Cleveland Magazine, Aug., 1978.

Wilder, Jesse Bryant, *The Last Untouchable*. Northern Ohio Live, March, 1993.

NEWSPAPERS

Call and Post
Cleveland News
Cleveland Press
Haboker Daily Newspaper
Lima News
New York Times
Ottawa Citizen
Plain Dealer
Toledo Blade
Washington Post

ONLINE ARTICLES

Bernfeld, Guy. "Bearer Bonds: From Popular to Prohibited." Investopedia, accessed Feb. 10, 2018. http://www.investopedia.com

Dubelko, Jim. "The Cleveland Union Stockyards." https:ClevelandHistorical. org. Accessed Jan. 30, 2019.

Locklear, Patti K. "[Dr. Bill] Corbett Presents History of Oklahoma WW II Prison Camps." Accessed Feb. 10, 2018,Woodward News. http://www.woodward-news.net.

"Why Prohibition." Temperance and Prohibition. Accessed Feb. 10, 2018. https://prohibition.osu.edu/why-prohibition.

Virtual Jewish World: Cleveland. Accessed Feb. 10, 2018. http://www.jewish-virtuallibrary.org/cleveland-ohio-virtual-jewish-history-tour.

Yronwode, Catherine. "Policy Blues." Blues Lyrics and Hoodoo. http://www.

luckymojo.com/bluespolicyblake.html. Accessed Jan. 30, 2019.

OTHER ONLINE SOURCES

FamilySearch
https://www.familysearch.org

The Mary Ferrell Foundation
https://www.maryferrell.org

FEDERAL GOVERNMENT DOCUMENTS

US Department of Justice; Federal Bureau of Investigation.

Investigation of Dominick Edward Bartone
Investigation of Alex Shondor Birns including "Joint investigation by FBI and
    other law enforcement agencies in the Cleveland area in connection with Alex
    Shondor Birns being involved in the murder of Mervin Lee Gold."
Investigation of Robert Freeman Boggess
Investigation of Mervin Lee Gold
Investigation of James Riddle Hoffa
Investigation of Joseph Raymond Merola
Investigation of William Alexander Morgan
Investigation of George Wesley Rothrock

US Department of Justice; Immigration and Naturalization Service. File of
Alex Shondor Birns in connection with deportation proceedings, Cleveland file
7-198012. Obtained through US National Archives and Records Administration.

United States Senate:

Special committee to investigate organized crime in interstate commerce, 1951.
(Kefauver Hearings).

Permanent Subcommittee on Investigations. April, 1988. Statement of Angelo
A. Lonardo.

LOCAL GOVERNMENT DOCUMENTS

Cleveland, Ohio Police Department:

Homicide investigation of Alex Shondor Birns, date of incident March 29, 1975.

Homicide Investigation of George W. Rothrock, date of incident Nov. 2, 1981.

OTHER GOVERNMENT SOURCES

Statement of burglar Charlie Broeckel to law enforcement officers, Jan., 1974. (Limited access provided to author by an anonymous source.)

Statement of gambling racketeer Martin DiFabio to law enforcement officers, date unknown. (Limited access provided to author.)

PERSONAL INTERVIEWS AND PERSONAL COLLECTIONS

Dozens of personal interviews over a ten year period.
Doris O'Donnell papers in author's collection.

INDEX

Hoge,
Frank 32, 53, 68-69, 107
Sherry (nee Coffey)* 295
Willie 68-69, 77, 107
Hope, Bob 70
Hot Springs, Arkansas 40
Hritz, Paul 233-236
Hudson, Del 226-227, 234, 271

Internal Revenue Service (IRS) 83-86, 95, 123, 125, 127, 129, 133, 140, 150, 196, 198, 203-204, 222, 246
International Longshoremen's Union 120, 199-200
Israel 15, 139, 162, 166, 177, 186, 247
Assuta Hospital 133
Kiryat Gat 137
Law of Return 132-133
Ministry of Internal Affairs 133
Ministry of Trade 137
Supreme Court 135, 137
Tel Aviv 132-134, 138-139

Jackson, Willie "Buckeye" 89-91, 113, 292
Jaffe, Harry 260
Jarus, Mary Jane "Janie" 211, 225, 228-229, 231, 236-237, 243, 256-259, 273, 275
Jazz 21, 24, 119, 199,
Jewel, Elsworth* 286
Jewish Boys (The) 43, 117, 141
Jewish Community Center (Cleveland) 19
Jewish Orphanage Asylum (Cleveland) 19
Johnson, Joan 40-41
Johnson, John "Hot Stuff" 32
Jones, Jonah 119
Jones, Rufus "the Emperor" 30, 32, 38, 102

Kahan, William H. 126-127, 135-136, 177
Kahn, Ali (aka William Barnes) 220, 245, 270

US Marshals Service 186, 254
US Naval Reserve 55
US Navy 23, 55-56, 60-61, 64, 67, 121
US Senate 83, 95, 107
US Small Business Administration 126-127, 134-135
US State Department 128

Valachi, Joseph 95
Van Tasko, John* 283
Veeck, Bill 71
Viccarone, Richard* 315
Virden, Samuel E.* 287
Visconti, Frank 130-131
Vondracek, John 163-164

Wagner, Richard B. 85-86, 173
Washington, D.C. 55, 60-61, 89, 166, 172, 182, 240, 247
Weinzimmer, Harry "Pony Boy" 32
Weiss, Sara – See Birns, Sadie
Wexler, Morris "Mushy" 20, 67-68, 119
Whelan, Edward "Ned" 251-252
Whitcomb, William 218, 221, 269
White, George 38
Williams, Oscar 42, 56, 68
Willis, James 118, 147-149, 155, 169, 171, 173, 177-179, 191, 195, 205-207, 212, 214, 227, 237, 239, 247, 253, 266, 278
Willowick Country Club 39, 42
World War I 18, 23, 64
World War II 58, 60, 62, 70, 73

Zagaria, Carmen 254
Zeid, Abraham "Abe" (aka Al Ross, Abe Seid) 38, 206
Zimmerman, George 135, 146, 177, 195
Zimmerman, James "Jimmy Z" 119, 228

ABOUT THE AUTHOR

Author, drummer, and former police chief Rick Porrello has a knack for writing books that attract interest from filmmakers. Hollywood snapped up *To Kill the Irishman—the War that Crippled the Mafia* before it was even published, and turned it into the movie *Kill the Irishman*, starring Ray Stevenson, Vincent D'Onofrio, Christopher Walken, and Val Kilmer. A motion picture based on *Superthief—A Master Burglar, the Mafia, and the Biggest Bank Burglary in U.S. History* is in development. Both books have also generated documentaries.

Rick's first career was as a jazz drummer. At the age of 18, he got his first big break when he started touring internationally with Sammy Davis, Jr. Despite a skyrocketing music career, Rick decided to trade his sticks for a badge, which had been his dream since childhood. What followed was a 33-year career as a police officer in Greater Cleveland, with the last ten of those years as chief of police.

As an organized crime historian, Rick Porrello's perspective is an intriguing one. He began writing his first book during family research into the murders of his grandfather and three uncles, all of whom, he learned, were mob leaders killed in Prohibition-era violence. *The Rise and Fall of the Cleveland Mafia* quickly became a regional favorite and has endured as a backlist title.

When he isn't hammering out his next book, co-authoring a screenplay, serving as a consulting or executive producer, or drumming with a number of bands, Porrello gives presentations on his books and on his writing and publishing journey.

www.rickporrello.com ♦ facebook.com/AuthorRickPorrello

CPSIA information can be obtained
at www.ICGtesting.com
Printed in the USA
BVHW042156131219
566655BV00017B/609/P

9 780966 250848